Neel Kamal Puri was born in Ludhiana, Punjab. She now lives in Chandigarh, where she taught English literature and media studies for over three decades at the Post Graduate Government College for Girls.

The Punjab *Stories*

~Two Novellas~

The Patiala Quartet

Remember *to* Forget

Neel Kamal Puri

SPEAKING TIGER

SPEAKING TIGER BOOKS
125A, Ground Floor, Shahpur Jat
New Delhi – 110049

This edition first published by Speaking Tiger 2024

ISBN: 978-93-5447-947-2

10 9 8 7 6 5 4 3 2 1

Dedication for The Patiala Quartet

To my brother Raji,
for our friendship, that grew as we did.

Dedication for Remember to Forget

To my sister Dodi,
for the many heart-to-hearts.

It is difficult to return home:
Who will know us now?
Death has signed our foreheads
Friends have trodden our faces
A stranger glances back in the mirror—
In his eyes there is the dim light
Of a house in ruins…

—Surjit Patar, 'Returning Home'
(translated by Nirupama Dutt)

Slowly the world tilts over on one side,
diurnally, forgetting all its deaths,
its birthdays, anniversaries, where a war
flowered like a boil, or when…

—Dom Moraes, 'The Way It Was'

Contents

The Patiala Quartet

1

But I Don't Live Here...

It was not an easy world to live in, particularly if you belonged.

As an outsider you could move on: a posting here, then on to yet another town. For Patiala was a town like any other in Punjab, with mushrooming supermarkets and beauty parlours and food joints; boys on bikes, hanging out where all the girls would be, and now, increasingly, the girls too, hanging out with the expectation of being found. You could simply pass by, spurning the old-world ambience and the sense of has-been royalty that settled on everything like winter fog. You could zip past the sprawling, majestic houses with their arched doorways and long cool verandas, sheltering behind the groves, and miss them altogether. You could absorb the town entirely through the Quickie Chicken Soup Corner or the General Merchant Store at Baees Number Phatak, the railway crossing, with its display of stacked socks, underwear, banians and pointed bras.

But if you belonged to the place, the past had a presence that was impossible to ignore. The Patiala Royal House, with its coat of arms which went back to the eighteenth century, was a 'real' working palace with a current king and queen, and it continued to tantalize the local imagination long after the royal houses had been subsumed into the Indian state. Like all other royal houses, this one too had its history of annexing territory and providing protection, of excesses and magnanimities, of stories that continued to be worth the telling, and others that needed to remain skeletons in the regal cupboard. And Patiala had never quite got over being the prima donna of states during the Raj, with its polo team that boasted the highest handicap in the world and a flamboyant Maharaja who so overawed the British that they usually let him have his way.

Social gatherings in Patiala featured heads discreetly veiled in sheer chiffon, the subtle glint of family jewels, tall, imposing men in long black achkans and conversation in soft, sibilant Punjabi. However, the men had very English names. There were the Jims and Larrys and Georges and Sams, all born with very Punjabi Sikh names carrying the customary 'Singh' as the suffix, but their easy-on-the-tongue British names were what they were known by. And they all had wealth enough to continue playing tennis, calling out 'Ball boy!' with the well-preserved hauteur of a British sahib and partying away the night. Their days were not tainted by the urgency of the early-morning rush to work. Nor was the style of their evenings cramped by a lack of funds.

Their progeny were equally easy-going. They had even acquired a defining nomenclature. 'Kakas', they were called, which would merely have meant 'young lads' in the original. But in this context the term resonated with the overtones of 'rich young lads hanging out in open jeeps at the Baees

Number Phatak, then zipping around town with a brutal foot on the accelerator'.

Even if you weren't to the manner born, you could fake it by digging into the royal closet of secret liaisons. Or you could hark back to a history where so many queens had fought for their king, and families had branched out in such profusion that almost anyone could trace his or her royal lineage down a complex route of marriages and kinship.

Monty could not. And perhaps that was where his troubles began. It is quite another matter that he did not want to belong, though his mother did. Her father, like his father before him, had been appointed administrative head of a village and was, therefore, an emissary of the Maharaja's court. Now, a generation later, this legacy meant little in monetary terms. But it did mean that Monty had to be a part of the 'royal' set whose members could focus on a partridge shoot to the exclusion of all else.

Monty's father was from a different world altogether. He ran a construction business in Delhi and made money, at a time when neither was the done thing. In the fifties, trade was an absolute no-no, and the businessman was a scumbag who waited long hours at the bureaucrat's door to get a licence or a permit to build. For true-blue respectability, money was just supposed to be there in the family coffers. You did not earn it.

'He looks like a peon,' Monty's grandfather, educated at Chiefs' College, Lahore, had told his daughter in his immaculate English. 'And imagine having *Mehta* for a surname!' He had been horrified at the thought of her marrying somebody who had no greening Punjabi acre to his name. 'What are you going to live on?' he had asked. And with a final damning statement, dismissed the entire bank balance of the young man in question: 'He earns nothing at all. A businessman is rich one day and poor the next.'

'He earns more than enough,' his daughter had retorted, the sparkle in her eyes reflecting the magic moments of clandestine drives in her lover's car and visits to opulent hotels whenever she was in Delhi.

'One bad deal and he may be left with no money,' her father had countered. Of course, after this ominous prediction, which she would recall many times afterwards, Monty's mother had been left with no choice.

'I will marry no one but him.'

Her father had given in to her finally, because he was a typical Punjabi mix of an open mind and stubborn conservatism. His decisions were always a surprise, emerging from either of the two extremes of his temperament. So, he let her become Mrs Mehta, although the name never quite tasted right on his tongue. The life she had chosen for herself would be very different from the one she had known since childhood, and he resigned himself to seeing her back in Patiala before long.

In sharp contrast, Monty's maasi, his mother's sister, had done the right thing and got married to someone who was very much of the regal conglomerate. He had money, he had land, he did nothing at all, and he beat his wife every night. But he did not marry again, unlike many other gentlemen of consequence, and that left Monty's maasi with a lot to be grateful for. It was all a part of this whole business of belonging. In Patiala, you could count on your fingers those who did not matter. However, as a statistical observation, this applied only to families of repute. The rest were only the hoi polloi and did not matter in the headcount.

So, Monty's maasi had married right. His mother had married all wrong. Though she was no revolutionary. Perhaps, her opting out of the charmed circle stemmed from her inability, or to put it in its right perspective, her disinclination to run an immaculate, patrician house. Monty's home always seemed to have a mind of its own. Objects went their own way and surfaced at will. There were no defined spaces for the various activities that are usually carried out within an average household, except, of course, for the bathroom.

It was a huge house—a material part of the ancestral inheritance. The rooms were many. And there must have been a design to it when it was conceived. But by the time Monty began going to school, their home had become a bewildering but workable chaos. They had stopped using the front half of the house. It was only the bedroom at the back that remained in use. Here, a pair of single beds sat at arm's length from each other, and Godrej almirahs hinted at other possessions. Across the courtyard was the kitchen, the location of which might have worked better in a feudal set-up. Translated into modern terms, it merely meant that you might, occasionally, need an umbrella to fetch a glass of water. However, given its current mistress's attitude to domesticity, the kitchen was in its rightful place as an unnecessary appendage. Monty's mother had often thought how simple life would have been if human beings had also grazed on grass to sustain themselves instead of going through the rigours of chopping onions and garlic into fine slivers for a meal. The spirit of an open house would, then, have been complete, since any new entrant could simply join the others on all fours and make the most of the patch of wild grass at the back. Of course, a knife and a serviette would be provided for that touch of finesse. This *was* an open house, though, for the door was never locked. The practice was to push a moorah against the closed bedroom door, securing it against the odd stray cat that might wander in. In any case, the creature was likely to prefer the kitchen.

Yet, this is, perhaps, a hop, skip and jump in time, encapsulating years in moments, since it had taken all of Monty's childhood for the household to move from the drawing room in the front to the bedroom at the back. The sofa set was still there, out in the front, but whoever came to visit went purposefully from the front gate to the bedroom door. And the moorah told them whether the family was in or not. Family, by this time, meant Monty's mother and his sister. From the recounted version of his family's history, Monty knew that at one time they had lived in Delhi, and were like any other family. His father had gone out to work and his mother had kept house. But all that was so long ago, it seemed never to have been. His father had long since been seized by wanderlust. His construction business had eventually hit one of those prolonged slumps characteristic of the line, and his business partner having defrauded him, he had become yet another Punjabi businessman selling auto spare parts, travelling to Kolhapur, to Thanjavur, and then back again, before setting off for Bhagalpur and Dibrugarh. It was then that they had decided to move to the family house in Patiala, which had been waiting stolidly for them for years.

'This is what my father had predicted way back then. I wish I had listened to him,' Monty's mother would say to his father. Naturally, that was not likely to go down well with Mr Mehta who now had to deal not only with a failing business, but a disgruntled wife as well. And each time she lamented over her failure to heed her father's words it marked the opening to a fight.

'So, why didn't you marry one of those rich landowners? If you had, I would have been a happier man today.'

'Where does the question of marriage come into it? All I'm trying to say is that you should have kept an eye on that man. He was siphoning money out of the business, but you never notice such things.'

'Well, if I *didn't* notice, I *didn't* notice!' he would announce.

Following an assertion of this nature, the quarrel would move into the realm of the illogical.

'What do you mean you didn't notice?' she would ask, not making any more of a point than he had.

'I'm telling you that this is the way I am,' he would declare. 'If you didn't like it, you should have married somebody your father approved of.'

'That is not what I meant,' his wife would say, trying to placate him now. And she did not really mean what she had said, because the reference to her own father was only meant to highlight the old man's wisdom rather than express regret at having married Mr Mehta. But since there was an obscurity to her intent and her words lent themselves to the obvious interpretation, Mr Mehta bristled each time she opened an argument with a reference to her father and his perceptions.

All the same, the move to Patiala might have been a welcome change if they had known what to do with the disparate influences that swept into their life. They had walked into the house with their sofa set, made cosy with multi-coloured cushions in keeping with the trend of the times. Quite like the different coloured teacups and saucers that made up a fashionable tea service in those days. It was a mix and match dictated by fashion rather than a scarcity induced by the '65 war, which had resulted in a rationing of sugar and all other essentials. Prime Minister Shastri had even appealed to the citizens to fast one day in a week but Monty and his family had to eat to keep up with the exertions of shifting house! Their sofa had not looked quite so lost then, in its new home, in the company of the huge gramophone player. There were other little knick-knacks around—the prints on the walls, the radiant sunflowers and the smiling *Mona Lisa*. The rainbow tea set had, of course, long since been reduced to a single yellow cup and a single blue saucer, each having lost its respective partner.

After the move, Monty had gone to school in Patiala. Just another little boy with dimpled cheeks, a heavy schoolbag and a home to come back to. But the constant fuss over his dimples had also nurtured in him that little-boy dislike of all that was 'cute' and 'girlie'. On Parents' Day, when Sister was preparing to put make up on his face before sending him onstage for a group dance, his male ego had been outraged. The Sister had chased him around the school compound with a cherry pink lipstick ready and unsheathed, her veil streaming behind her. He had made it onstage without a dab of cherry pink on his lips, feeling much more of a man than the other lipsticked little boys lined up behind him forming neat pairs with the parallel line-up of little girls.

The growing up involved at that stage of life was easy to accomplish because all you had to do was emulate the adults. Choices still had to be made, of course, of the wearing-lipstick and not-wearing-lipstick kind, and these had a do-or-die dimension to them. But life provided a ready reckoner. His father, he knew, did not wear lipstick and that had decided it for him.

A slightly older Monty was excited about moving to the haven of an all-boys' school and then, a few years later, that unerring volte-face—the excitement of the school going co-educational. But it also meant the arrival of his sister, Minnie, at the same school. That was a bit of a damper because it involved a precarious balancing act between eyeing the girls and keeping an eye on his sister. If he hated the crude male remarks aimed at her, there wasn't much he could do about it. He was slight of build and did not use his fists, although that was the prevailing dispute-resolution mechanism among young boys. Monty would, in any case, have to content himself with being just about five feet five inches tall even as an adult because his father too was a short man.

For the moment, however, it was quite enough to be cycling to school with the other boys, adding to their rowdy presence in the classroom, riling the teacher, playing a bit role as the arm-twisting policeman in the stage production of *Oliver Twist* and even pretending to be sporty. For sports was the big thing. You just had to be a part of it. Or you might as well grow feathers on your head and crow. The favourite cheer for the school hero on the sports field was 'Bhai Dataar, show them stars'. It was a different situation for the girls in the sports arena. For, ever since the school had introduced the concept of co-education, only around thirty of them had ventured to step into it. A nodding acquaintance with breaststroke in the swimming pool could mean a position on the victory stand for the 100 metres freestyle for girls.

In fact, once they learnt to brazen it out in this very male world, they really could set the rules. All the while that

Monty was busy being protective about his sister, she had pretty much learnt to stand with her hands on her hips and yell back at the anonymous voices passing obscene remarks from behind dark wire meshes.

On her way to the hostel mess for lunch, Minnie would station herself squarely in the middle of the volleyball court, right behind the boys' hostel, when the first catcall was hurled at her. 'You just come right out of there, Sam (a.k.a. Samarpal Singh)! I recognize your voice!' she would shout to the disembodied voice, whose owner imagined that he was safely camouflaged. A surprised Sam would exclaim to his classmates, 'Yaar, what's gone wrong with the girls in our school?' But he would never have the courage to shout back another obscenity. Minnie would repeat the challenge: 'You come right out and say what you have to say, instead of hiding in there!' Absolute silence at Sam's end. Soon, Sam had given up on his undercover activities.

Minnie had learnt that the best way to confound the opponent was to confront him. But the learning process had not been easy. It had meant a struggle to overcome her reluctance at braving the school corridor alone, the target of several pairs of ogling male eyes. Minnie had always fought the temptation of requesting another female schoolmate to accompany her down the seemingly endless stretch where monsters lurked. And at the end of it all, she was far more prepared to face the world than Monty was or would ever be. A trial by fire, but at least it had worked.

It helped to have learnt her lessons early. Monty's lessons came much too late. By then, the odds were stacked against him. But how was he to know that as he lugged his schoolbag around? There were no road signs to tell him of the disaster lying ahead. So, he just carried on doing the things that everyone else was doing. He made fun of the chemistry teacher who came to class wearing his NCC shorts, referred to the two spindly girls in his class as 'knife' and 'fork', while the third one (and there were only three) was IG because she had Indira Gandhi's long nose. He indulged in the usual friendly back-slapping and learnt the right vocabulary, with 'Oye!'—the popular form of address—thrown in for good measure. Yet, this was not really his world.

'Coming for a movie?' the boys would initially ask him, with a jeep, its engine revving, waiting outside the school's boundary wall.

But after Monty's first few startled responses—'Now?', 'Not now', 'No'—they stopped inviting him altogether.

'Oye, what sort of a chap are you? Bit of a scaredy cat, aren't you?'

'Just don't want to see a movie,' Monty would respond.

And the incredulous boys in the jeep decided to leave him alone.

Monty was an aberration. He enjoyed mathematics. And that in itself made him something of an oddity. He did not belong, and try as he might the only friends he ever made were the older girls who were his sister's friends.

The one male friend Monty did have was Michael, but that had more to do with the fact that Michael was his first cousin, his maasi's son. It was a friendship born of holidays spent in the same maternal village, when the difference in their personalities had not become obvious, when they could play cops and robbers together without most things becoming a subject for philosophical debate in Monty's mind. They would run wild, bathe in the tube well and gawk at the cows and buffaloes as they chewed through mounds of hay. But there too Monty could sit and gaze for long stretches of time. In fact, he could do just that all day. Perched on one of those beds woven with rough-hewn jute, which could be rather unkind to little boys in shorts, he would watch with unblinking fascination as the cow heaved itself into a standing position and proceeded to fan itself with its own tail. When Michael arrived to haul him into the next adventure, he would get off the bed reluctantly, the criss-cross pattern of the jute still imprinted on the back of his thighs.

2

Round the Bend

Michael was, of course, a man of action. He was 'Michael on the Cycle' at this stage, but later on in life, he would graduate to being 'Mike on the Bike'. Even on the bicycle, he managed to speed around as though he were trying to shake off a swarm of bees. And zip around as he might, they were always there, just behind him. That was probably the reason he could never really stop. He pushed himself nervously to go on. It was on one of these fly-high trips that he made friends with a bunch of kakas.

'Oye, what bike is that?' they yelled out to him, as he went past them once, and then again.

'Just an ordinary geared thing my father bought for me,' he replied with obviously feigned nonchalance.

'Can I take it for a spin?' one of them asked. And then each took a ride on it, patting the saddle in appreciation afterwards.

'Runs well,' each one told him. 'But Patiala just does not have the roads for a beauty like this one. Maybe, we can all go on a cycling trip in winter.'

Michael valued their acceptance of him because he really did want to be one of them. He was a thin, gawky boy and could not have bullied his way into their midst. His bright yellow bicycle with its turned-down handle was the ticket, and he made sure of keeping it with him at all times, just in case he needed to whip it out at the first sign of being denied entry. Boys on bikes were the only kind of friends he would ever really have.

Michael acquired a peculiar gait which, everyone presumed, was because he was most often seen on wheels than on foot. His mind was always driving his body into a pump-at-the-wheels motion, even when he was not astride his bicycle. He would bunch his shoulders forward in an attempt to grasp the non-existent turned-down handle, while his feet tapped out an awkward pedalling rhythm on the ground—a thump downwards, followed by an exaggerated lift-off. Of course, he could never really get anywhere walking that way. And one could well have applied that to his whole life.

Like his thick-tyred bicycle wheel, which turned on its axis, he was quite content to do the gehri—a derivative of a Punjabi word that indicates a round trip ending at the starting point. His was really a small world, meeting up at both ends. He spent every evening of his young life going round the block in top gear. The only time he did apply the brakes was on those horrible nights when his father beat up his mother. The wind in his sails would suddenly drop and he would bunch his shoulders still further together. During these times, he did feel that he should be doing something about it. Yet, the moment always escaped him, because his preoccupation with speed carried him just a fraction beyond it. He could only survey the aftermath, the damage.

When he woke up in the morning after nights like this, his mother was never there to serve him breakfast. She would just melt into the night and mysteriously appear at his maasi's house the next day. And that was where he would head at top speed. She would be there, his mother, talking to his maasi in whispers. They would shush each other into silence when they saw him.

And he would say accusingly, 'You didn't give me any breakfast.'

His mother would look stricken and immediately want to make amends: 'You want to eat an alu parantha, beta? A scrambled egg?'

Violence in the house necessitated some sort of an escape, howsoever brief. Myriad vistas opened up for Michael. There, engrossed in a book would be Monty, whom he could draw outdoors with a masterfully executed 'wheelie', a mid-flight lift of the front wheel of his cycle, achieved with a sudden, but calculated application of the brake. Or he could simply gawk at the rows of books on the shelf with a sense of wonder. He could even play with the mongrel, which invariably strayed into the backyard of the house. Besides, he could gorge on the alu parantha with the generous dollop of butter melting on it. And so each such moment passed, till his father, popularly known as Lalli, did it—yet again.

He did not quite know how to react to his father. It was from him that he had acquired his penchant for speed. All his own feats on wheels usually paled into insignificance when his father scoffed, 'Oh, that? It's nothing. I could change into a different set of clothes while riding my bike.' And though that might sound like a lot of hot air to most other people, Michael was quite willing to believe it because it set him a standard to aspire to. It was this same father, though, who beat his mother. Ought he to just reject him as the measure of all things, the boy wondered, or should he interpret the violence as only one more aspect to the life of adults? People in town took Lalli with a pinch of salt, of course. There were far too many stories about him and the authorship of most of these could be traced back to the man himself. The favourite one was about Lalli, the bandit. The story went that young Lalli had once held up a train with the right honourable purpose of looting it. Unfortunately for Lalli, this particular train had already been robbed once. Therefore, the sum total of the plunder came to a mere seventy-five paise—an amount that could, in those days, buy the most expensive fabric for a shirt and pay for the most exclusive tailoring available. Yet, those seventy-five paise constituted the only money he had ever really earned, if it could be called that. The rest of his money—and there were vast amounts of it—had simply been inherited, one half of the family legacy going to his brother. If there were any sisters, they had gone out of the reckoning long ago and had just dropped off the family tree. Even if they existed, no one knew about them. The two brothers got it all. Of course, the legacy had taken a long time to come to them. Their Old Man Sekhon refused to die. He played lawn tennis every day, setting out for the courts in the still-scorching, early-evening summer sun or the warm afterglow of winter afternoons. He played tennis on tough, unwrinkled legs. His white beard seemed to be the only hostage to time. That being the manifest, upfront indicator of age, many were fooled into believing that Old Man Sekhon was not likely to live long. But all those pretty, young things who took their chances and decided to start living with him from time to time, in the hope that he would die one day and leave them all his wealth, never really got there. He simply outlived their aspirations. Each of them got tired of watching out for that elusive end, fearful of fading into once-upon-a-time beauties with no options left.

Lalli resented each one of these women who came into his father's life though he should have had nothing to complain about. His father had set him up in a huge house and ensured an endless supply of money. But he would drop in on his father at odd times just to catch him in the act.

'Came by to see if you are all right,' he would say, since any expression of disapproval might have choked off the money supply.

'Of course I am all right,' his surprised father would snap back. 'What did you think had happened?'

When Old Man Sekhon did finally die many years later, all the gold-diggers had dropped out of the race, leaving Lalli and his brother as the sole inheritors of his assets. The only other beneficiary was Ruby, the last of the old man's series of companions.

Lalli, the more flamboyant of the two brothers, had always made extravagant use of the family money. But his splurges in the marketplace had very little to do with any domestic need. His purchases usually ran into a series. If he started buying cameras, for instance, he kept on acquiring one camera after another. Or it could be key chains. Having bought one, he would bring in a whole assortment over the next couple of months. Their house was bursting at the seams. Every table surface in sight was choked with bone china and cut glass because nothing came in ones or twos. As a result, dusting and cleaning the house every morning was a slow, laborious process. The two servants would bring out the cleaning rags from the storeroom, lift every vase, table lamp and figurine, wipe it clean and carefully put it back in its place. Michael's mother would go into the kitchen and make breakfast, while the servants applied themselves wholly to hunting down the dust.

It was in the midst of this plenty that Michael grew up. But unlike his father, he was content to purchase in singles. So, the yellow bicycle remained, till his legs grew much too long to push at the pedals. The brief interlude between the cycle and his black Yezdi motorcycle was the most uncomfortable period in his life. He felt a hole in his being and did not quite know what to plug it with. He tried to focus his energies on eating, but soon figured out that the hole was not really in his stomach. When the bike arrived, it was 'watch-out-here-I-come!' once again. People in town learnt to recognize the revving sound and scurried out of the way. They glued themselves to the pavement till the bike had gone past. But in spite of the near-clear roads, Mike managed to pepper his life with a number of accidents. No one knew whether this was a way of staying away from college and from the bees that very nearly got him, or merely his family history catching up with him. He really should have been his father's clone. That might have made things easier.

3

In the Hideout

Michael's sister, Karuna, was his mother's clone, however. Or so they thought, till she surprised them in the years to come. Karuna's favourite haunt as a child was the well of darkness under the staircase, which swept upwards to the master bedroom and a study where Lalli occasionally sat doing absolutely nothing. And going all the way up along with the banister was a row of marble statues in different stances of movement. Her hideout was, in any case, the only place uncluttered by the overflow from the rest of the house. Moreover, it was not in the direct path of the deluge of fancy table lamps, ornate timepieces, black-under-the-ears silverware and rubbed-to-a-glossy-smoothness wooden carvings that hurtled down the stairs when her father went into his frequent paroxysms of rage. She hid there when the going got tough in the world around her. Whether it was the Diwali crackers or her father exploding on her mother, it was always comforting to be hiding in there. And the adults, stretched to their full heights, failed to notice the hideout.

She watched helpless feet on the run, pattering down the hallway and enraged feet stomping after them. She watched faltering feet, thwarted in flight. She watched the large strides of the giant in her storybook, strides that could cover the hallway in one long leap. There never was any point in trying to run. But occasionally, the fleeing feet did manage to make a quick getaway, out through the front door. What happened beyond the door she never really knew because she waited for the angry feet to cease their crazed pacing and move out of the hallway into the bedroom, before she emerged from hiding. At other times, exhausted by the perennial back and forth, and oppressed by the air thick with tension, she dozed off right there. She would wait for an unnoticed moment, when all eyes were looking the other way, to come out, because she wanted this to be her own dark secret. The hideout remained a corner of comfort, and Karuna was happy to retreat into it at the slightest hint of a storm.

Karuna had not, of course, been so named because of her habit of cowering under the staircase. That came much later, anyway. Pity—for that was what the word karuna meant—had not been the defining characteristic of this lustily yelling baby girl. But a consultation with the Sikh holy book had indicated that 'k' would be an auspicious letter for this particular child. The first letter of her name had been chosen strictly in accordance with the dictates of the Sikh religion. The whole family had gathered in the prayer room. Three granthis who recited hymns to music had been summoned along with a priest. They had arrived, in their blue turbans and flowing beards. The servants in Lalli's household had followed the granthis, carrying their instruments for them. With great reverence, the tabla and harmonium had been lifted out of their cloth wrapping and placed in front of the granthis. The priest had stationed himself behind the holy book. The ritual had then proceeded following a well-defined sequence. The priest had opened the holy book randomly. The first letter of the first word of a hymn printed on the page to the right was the one chosen for this newborn. So, 'k' it was. The priest had gone on to read the entire hymn which would be the message for the day, as well as for the baby, born into turbulence.

The holy book had not mentioned turbulence, though. But it was easy to predict that this young lady in pink booties was in for a ride over rough seas. There was a father who controlled all the strings—to the purse, to the course of life—strings that he manipulated from his place up in his study, from where he could catch all the sounds from the well of the hallway, if he left the door open. There was a mother who had schooled herself into passivity and there was a brother who was just a blur as he whizzed past on his bicycle. So, early on, she learnt to be silent. As a child, she was neither seen nor heard, except occasionally. Her response to most mundane everyday questions was a nod of the head, a wave of the hand, an act of dumb charades.

Yet, the silence had not crept into her heart. Her greeting to any loving adult she trusted was effusive enough. She would come speeding towards that person and the momentum of her charge would carry her straight up his torso. She would make a grab for the adult's neck, from where she hung, confident that his arms would immediately encircle her to provide a perch. And further communication would involve vigorous nods on her part or a negative shaking of pigtails. But it was nods, more often than not, since learning to agree was among her first lessons. And so she grew to be a pleasant young lady of a shy disposition. Her existence in the house did not set off any storms. She walked in quietly after school, climbed the stairs to her room and neatly folded away her uniform. In her wake came no brooding remnants of an argument with a friend nor indignation at an unwarranted reprimand, nor even the grubbiness that mysteriously clings to every returning-home-from-school child. The only lapse in the overall neatness was a single, unruly twirl of hair. It was not the same one every day, however, since the rebellious strand, standing on end, was the result of a tweak she would give her hair to loosen a nagging twinge somewhere.

At school, the same one where Monty had led the nun a merry dance round the cemented courtyard dotted with swings and slides and see-saws, she was no different from many of the other girls who sat with earnest expressions behind their classroom desks. And since she did seem to be one of them, she had many friends too. Karuna had stayed on here, even after her cousins moved to the other school. Her father would never have allowed the strings to slacken enough for her to go to an all-boys-just-turned-also-girls' school. Though the swings were a little askew and you could hurt your knees, if not split your skull on the concrete ground, were you to fall down, there were other things a concerned father had to consider, apart from cracked skulls and grazed knees. This school was fine. Here, the boys had to transfer to another institution after completing junior school and that put cracked skulls and grazed knees in the right perspective of being the safer option. Lalli would make a biweekly visit to her school and have a chat with her class teacher.

'Is Karuna behaving herself?' he would ask.

'Yes, yes,' the teacher would answer impatiently. It was a question she was asked every week and she was a little tired of responding to it.

'Do let me know if you catch her at anything,' Lalli would say with a significant look.

'Yes, of course.' She always hoped that the promise of ready compliance would shorten the parent-teacher meeting but Lalli usually hung around expecting to sniff out the sordid.

Karuna hated these fatherly trips and when she saw him from a distance she would put on an act of extreme indifference, as if she did not know him at all.

Other than this biweekly embarrassment, Karuna enjoyed school immensely. She stretched her limbs to thaw them from the cramp into which they would be frozen after being holed up in the well of darkness, felt the swing rise high, leaving far behind the roofline of the school building and soaring way up into the sky. Her gaze skimmed the treetops from up there, untroubled by any fear at the sight of a fast-receding earth. She would have been happy if life had been an eternal ride on a swing. She had worked out that she could propel herself forward and up with a quick bend of the knees and a jerk at the rope. Higher and higher, till she was parallel to the sky, a bird in flight, but belly up. Her friends awaited their turn, down below.

Yet, she missed her cousins, since they all made up a foursome, growing up together. However, it was Minnie she missed most, Minnie who had a wildness of spirit that made life much more exciting. For, by herself, Karuna could only be boringly obedient. Her hands clasped defensively before her and her feet pushed into rubber-soled, crossed-in-the-front slippers, she could just be a miniature of her mother. But with Minnie around, Karuna became rebellious. Which is why everyone in the family tried to ensure that they were kept at arm's length from each other. Different schools, different friends, different birthday parties. So when Croaky came into her life, the shock far exceeded any anger they might have felt. The adults just went through the entire episode with their mouths hanging open in disbelief.

4

Mopping Up the Echoes

The only one not surprised was Minnie. She and Karuna had stolen mangoes from the grove in the care of the city club contractor and had shot off like bullets when the chowkidar showed up with his little stick. They had traded clothes to wear to the movies, and, in spite of being slotted as bad-girl and good-girl, placed at either extremity of the spectrum of morality, always ogled at the boys together. Yet, there was a cynicism to Minnie that would not allow her to succumb to the head-over-heels routine. She did not need any dark holes to hide in. She would just pull down her shutters, right in the midst of a severe scolding, and wait for all the bow-wow to be over. But she could also pull down those shutters in polite drawing rooms, where people made nice-weather conversation. The drawing room in her own home had long since ceased to exist, anyway. She did not miss it.

She had moved from the dormitory-bedroom in the back of their house to one of the other rooms, which had been lying vacant. The room carried echoes of the numerous arguments in the family, of her periodic rebellions, comfortable chats with her father and the happy laughter shared with her brother. All these and more were memories the echoes had nurtured for a while, bouncing them around and keeping them in play till the walls began to peel, the whitewash falling away to expose the grey cement underneath. The echoes had gradually weakened to a whisper, faded and died. The dust had then taken over and when Minnie moved into the room, she had just let the dust be. Separated from her mother and her brother by the length of a long corridor and a series of unused rooms with no particular function, she got on with her own life. Her friends would visit her, knocking on the windowpane to gain access to her one-room quarters. And, perhaps, that corridor was the distance between sinking and survival since there was an insanity to the rest of the house, which was bound to get to her sooner or later. She placed her bed in one corner, pulled in two single-seaters from a pile of abandoned furniture, installed her two-in-one music system, lined up her books and set up house. And from her vantage point, she watched her mother accumulate a bundle of contrary expectations with regard to her brother. From Minnie herself, the expectations were singularly linear. Just a nice, sweet girl, they hoped she would be, particularly, with dimples that were deeper than Monty's and more in line with the requirements of her gender. But, with her characteristic wilful streak, she simply tossed aside the 'nice girl' epithet and carried on from there. She was not a 'nice girl'. (When she made a break first for Delhi, and then across the proverbial seven seas, no longer inclined to share in the misery of their collective fate back in her home town, some even called her a bitch.) Minnie never learnt a stitch of embroidery. She neither made the mandatory ship-in-sail wall hanging nor did she ever bake nice cakes.

While everyone else was busy sorting her out, Minnie knew just what it was she was going to do and set about it with the application of a chess player, each move a well-designed precursor to the next. In school, she would get these anonymous love letters and the occasional braveheart who would appear before her, mumbling his love in clumsy schoolboy vocabulary.

'I like you,' a classmate standing on one awkward leg would say.

'I think you're nice too, but really, I'm not interested in anyone at all,' she would gently tell him.

'But if you like me, why can't we go for a movie sometime?' he would ask.

'I really don't want to get into any of that,' she would explain. 'I don't like boys,' she would add, hoping that this statement would act as the clincher.

But the youth would usually demonstrate a surprising perseverance. 'Please,' he would say, 'we can just be friends.' A firm 'no' from her would bring the subject to a temporary close, only to be reopened at another time, for in schoolboy parlance, it would be a matter of 'let me maro another try'. Cheering classmates would egg him on, watching from a distance, as he made his second attempt.

Inevitably, there he would be again, the following day, blocking Minnie's path. She would stop and talk to him, yet again, because there was a kindness to her which made her want to put him at ease. But that is, probably, what gave her a reputation for keeping boys dangling on the hook. So, she remained a mystery to some and a bitch to others. They talked about her long after she had finished school and moved to Delhi for further studies.

It was left to Karuna to provide the family its first scandal. Poor, mousy Karuna, who was not really made for the role.

5

Hot on Her Heels

The Karuna-Croaky story does not unfold like one of those great, undying love legends of Punjab. There are no soaring emotions, no one-eyed or one-legged, leering villain. It does not even sound like a teenage love story. Karuna was no heroine and Croaky no hero.

Poor Croaky had, in any case, started with the handicap of his nickname. His name was Gurjit Singh, but that had nothing to do with the nickname everyone knew him by. His voice had broken well before anyone else's and had stayed that way till well after all the others were done with their teenage flings. His singular broken-sitar-string voice may just have been the only voice he had ever had. But since no one had even noticed him or heard him before he entered his teens and started tossing lewd remarks at girls down school corridors, it was generally assumed that his voice was only on its way to becoming manly.

He had once hidden behind a pillar in the school corridor and yelled out after the chubby girl who had just joined: 'She has a natural quilt cover. Why does she need to wear a school blazer?' His rough tenor had given her such a fright that she had immediately complained to the authorities. Of course, there was no mistaking the voice when she described it to them. 'It sounded like this,' the plump girl had begun, red in the face, noisily clearing her throat to mimic it in the principal's presence. Croaky's signature voice had given him away. He had been pulled up for his rowdy behaviour and was even asked to do some front rolls in the stadium as a deterrent. Subsequently, he took to standing around with the leather belt from his school uniform, threatening to lash the plaintiff each time she went by, though he did not carry out his threat.

His voice never did go on to become manly. And it was with this very voice, which seemed to come off a sandpaper one minute and whistle down a pipe the next, that he called out his 'I love you-s' to Karuna, as he followed her all the way from her home to her college and back. However, Karuna was accompanied at all times by a man on a bicycle, one Pyarelal, ordered by her father never to lose sight of 'the girl'. But that was only a minor irritation, which Croaky overcame by manoeuvring all his overtures in the thickest of traffic, for that was the time the escort on the bicycle was least likely to notice what was going on. Having deposited his self-assumed charge safely at the college gate, Croaky would make his way to his own college, just a street away. And he would be back again at her college gate in the afternoon.

In the early hours of the morning he would be waiting round the corner, his bicycle shining and ready for the chase through the city gardens and past the statue of a woman drying herself after a bath. Over the years, this marble woman with her bath towel had had to be enclosed in a fence to protect her from the obscene pencil scribbles across her breasts, and from the young boys who showed a propensity to get themselves photographed standing beside her, their arms around her middle, their hands fondling her breasts, as she bent over to wipe herself. The poor woman could now proceed with her toilet in some privacy. If, however, she had ever taken time off her preoccupation with bathing, she might have seen this young woman cycling past every day, followed at a steady pace by a young man, also on a bicycle.

They would make their way through the winding bazaars, still in the process of yawning themselves awake. The young boy working at the corner dhaba would already be up, cleaning the tables with a filthy rag. The stationery shop next door would still be tightly shuttered, though it did brisk business during the day, sitting, as it did, plumb on the route to college. The sari shop came next. It was famous because of the salesman who would deftly pleat each sari and hold it in an elegantly feminine drape against his own body. The customer would have to ignore the bearded face and masculine torso rising out of the skirt of the sari and decide on a purchase. The sales gimmick evoked hysterical giggles, but it did bring in curious customers. At that hour of the morning, when Karuna, followed by Croaky, cycled past, this shop too would be closed, awaiting the arrival of its star salesman. The waste-water drain winding through it all would occasionally offer stiff competition to the rank smell of the dhaba boy's rag when the wind blew that way.

The bazaar was closely packed with tiny shops, which would flourish for years before the expansive department stores swallowed up many of them. From their perches behind the counters, the shopkeepers in these cheek-by-jowl stores had a ringside view of the road and many of them spent their leisure time watching the Croaky-Karuna saga unfold before their eyes.

Karuna and Croaky's return journey down this route, through streets now wide awake and crowded, was a far livelier affair. An occasional extra pedal and he would be abreast of her to repeat his message with the monotony of a spring-loaded wall clock. Out he would pop, say his 'I love you', and fall back into position, just one wheel-revolution behind. He even managed to tell her of his plans to join the Civil Service, which he hoped would go down well with her family.

The stationery man would tell his assistant, 'Look at that fellow! He is saying something to her, but she does not seem to mind.' This being the lunch hour business was, in any case, lean. The shopkeepers would lay bets on the likelihood of their getting married.

'These things never work out,' the much-married and cynical among them would say. The stakes went up when they discovered that this was Lalli's daughter they were talking about.

'I'll give you a thousand rupees if he actually marries her,' the stationery man would say to the owner of the grocery shop. In fact, the general sentiment among the shopkeepers was that Croaky would not marry Karuna.

But Karuna would go on to turn all these confident predictions on their head. And she would do it at a tea shop further along the road, only a few shops down from where the men sat betting on her future.

Croaky had set his heart on becoming part of 'the family'—the royal family—and the only way he could do it was through marriage. And yet, this marriage—a certainty in his own mind—was only going to take him into the remote fringes of royalty. However, in the true spirit of the compromiser, he had told himself that it was better that, than nothing at all.

His own family was a bunch of nonentities and Croaky lived in constant fear of being just that all his life. His father made money by foul means which, of course, was the only way it could be done. But these were the days before scams became part of everyday vocabulary. So, it meant inching forward laboriously, rather than gathering a windfall in one fell swoop. As a middle-rung functionary in a government office, he made his money by promising to push a file at a price or award a contract to the most obliging bidder.

The climb up the social ladder was an equally painstaking affair. Croaky's mother, a woman of generous dimensions, would drag his father into a rickshaw and they would spend their evenings visiting the city's glitterati—the deputy commissioner, the income tax commissioner, the superintendent of police and the chief engineer. They did not seem to care that their advent at the driveways of those huge government bungalows usually occasioned the inmates to curl up into balls of despair. Subsequent visits would set things right, they reasoned. In any case, it gave them the licence to say, 'The DC? We know him very well.'

Croaky grew up quite his mother's son. The pair would hoist themselves on to the only vehicle in the family, a 100cc motorcycle, and continue with the cultivation crusade. If the cycle rickshaw seemed inadequate when Croaky's mum happened to be the passenger, the motorcycle simply disappeared under the two of them. To the world at large, it was just two people fitted with castors who roared into driveways and smiled pleasantly in palatial drawing rooms, while their castors stayed behind, hoisted on a stand under the generously spreading branches of mango trees. And the small talk in those drawing rooms was so rewarding because the mother-son duo was privy to minutiae, among a million others, like the deputy commissioner preferring coffee to tea or Mrs DC having a penchant for English Twining tea. Croaky's mother was quite content with the course their life was taking.

But Croaky was much too thorough to be limping along on a single-pronged strategy. Of course, he saw himself as DC material and, towards that end, had chosen his subjects in college, history being the favoured option just then. That, in fact, was the subject he was pursuing for his postgraduate degree. But life had to be worked forward on many fronts. And as the second line of aggression, he had chosen to chase Karuna with a sense of application that was quite lacking in his other enterprise. Although he spent his nights working at his books for the civil services exam—with his mother serving him endless cups of tea and watching in admiration his nocturnal rendezvous with the table lamp—he began to realize that his talent lay in the manipulation of people rather than in absorbing the contents of books.

Even as he pored over his textbooks on modern Indian history, his mind was forever clambering up the social ladder. Sometimes, he would savour the imaginary climb, rung by rung—the pleasure of drawing up a glittering guest list, followed by the breathtaking moment when his wedding invitation would be received in the palace and finally, the regal lifestyle, with his nose acquiring that progressive tilt skywards. On other occasions, he would quickly clamber all the way up to the top, basking in the rarefied atmosphere of one of those large bungalows—this time his own—where obsequious people waited on him and the castors were no longer parked outside to remind him of the journey back. He did not, of course, heed Punjabi folklore which sang of Ramta, the mythical rural peasant who was surrounded by a bevy of white women in nebulous dreams, only to find his dog, Jackie, licking him into wakefulness.

Karuna was taking her own time, though. Needless to say, it never crossed Croaky's mind that she might be engaged in her own set of calculations: First, she knew that Lalli was never going to be able to stay on course to find her a husband. He might be able to spare a month for the venture, like he did when he purchased the key chains. But at the end of it, he would simply move on to other things. Second, she herself was not likely to meet many men in her life as long as she remained in her father's house. To these two absolutes she added another half, attributed to the fact that Croaky claimed to love her. Half because it was difficult to tell whether she actually did regard his 'I love you-s' as positive inducement. Love was, after all, the iffy factor in this particular love story.

Karuna allowed the wooing to run its full course, except for the brief interlude during which her father had negotiated a marriage proposal for her. The not so-young man in question had ballooning cheeks that merged with the contours of his chin. About the blubber lips, she learnt only later. They had gone to Delhi to meet him. He had sought permission to take her out in his car with the bucket seats and had even delivered a tentative goodnight kiss when he brought her back home.

The next day, before any decisions could be arrived at, he had again turned up, in his father's old, beat-up Fiat this time. He had driven her to a vantage point near the airport, where the flashing lights of aircrafts landing and taking off provided a romantic background, not to mention the privacy of completely desolate surroundings.

'I come here often,' he had said, lying through his teeth, merely to preserve the delicacy of the moment. The last time he had come here had been with a girlfriend from college. 'It makes me feel very nice,' he had continued in the same spirit of romance.

'Yes, it is very nice,' Karuna had agreed politely. She could not think of anything smarter to say.

'I wish we could have some music, but this old car is not really geared up for any such gadgetry,' he had said. Failing to add that in the toss-up between the bucket seats in his car and the old sagging seats of this one, the latter had won because it facilitated sitting close together. 'Anyway, what kind of music do you like listening to?' he had asked.

'Old films songs,' she had replied shyly.

'Yes, it would be wonderful to listen to old love songs with you sitting by my side,' Blubber Lips had gushed, certain now that he had just the right opening to move in.

They had sat there a while in silence, the prospect of an exciting engagement with exotic worlds beyond sparking the atmosphere with electricity, providing Blubber Lips with just the right steal-a-kiss opportunity. And that really is how he became Blubber Lips. She had felt revulsion heave within her and wanted to get away from those lips, but they had just locked on, spreading like clinging algae across her mouth. 'Don't,' she had wanted to say, but could only manage an 'Umm'. Maybe that had sent across all the wrong signals. Blubber Lips had thought she was enjoying it. So he had 'Ummed' even louder in response.

Blubber Lips was well on his way to becoming a stationary

sack of potatoes. He had just seemed to collapse all over her, ably abetted by the sagging car seat, even as she tried to prop him up against the torn backs of those sinking seats or set him up on his own backbone. And though it was almost as if she were handling a corpse—his lurch in her direction being pretty much that of a deadweight—there had been an odd movement in his trousers. In fact, she had gathered that he wanted her to pet his bumpy crotch and she had snatched herself back from it, as though singed. However, her eyes couldn't help straying to that sudden protuberance. That had sent yet another erroneous message to the owner of those blubber lips and now that bumpy crotch.

'Feel it…' said this hoarse voice from the darkness in the car and Karuna had to put her hands behind her back in an obvious gesture of distaste. But nothing had been obvious to Blubber Lips.

'Let's go back,' Karuna had suggested.

'No, no,' Blubber Lips had protested, his voice still more hoarse with desire unfulfilled.

She was entirely confused by this encounter, unsure as to whether it was her own naiveté that was to blame for its outcome or Blubber Lips's hands-on strategy. He had wanted to marry her, having, of course, noticed nothing amiss in Karuna's response to his amorous kisses and eager crotch. She had chosen not to go back to the hotel where her parents were staying, preferring to be dropped off at her cousin Minnie's one-room set-up over a garage, which she was temporarily sharing with a now-absent roommate. Blubber Lips had followed her upstairs. He had wedged his foot in the doorway and pleaded for that one last kiss, while Minnie and she had leaned on the door with their full weight from the inside. But he was a big man and had bargained from his position of superior physical strength.

'Please let me kiss you goodnight!' he had pleaded through the crack in the door, dealing with what he imagined was the coyness of an about-to-be bride. 'After all, we're to be married soon.'

'I don't want to marry you,' Karuna had declared.

'You needn't be so shy with me,' he had responded with the self-assurance of the chosen suitor.

'Go away. I don't want to kiss you.'

'Just come out once, please! Then, I will wait patiently till we are married,' he had cajoled, dense till the last.

Finally, Karuna had been compelled to go out and endure that kiss. Perhaps he had seen it as a parting well handled, for his parents were confidently ringing up, the next day, to finalize the negotiations. Luckily, her father had tired of the whole thing by then and was not particularly upset at Karuna's disinclination to marry the man. It hadn't stopped him from trying the usual ploy, though.

'You marry this boy or I will shoot myself!' he had threatened. 'What is wrong with the boy, anyway?' In matrimonial parlance, a bridegroom-to-be always remained a 'boy', irrespective of his age.

'He looks so old. He looks older than you,' Karuna had retorted, hoping that the reference to her father's youthfulness would soften him up. It did.

Karuna turned down the marriage proposal. But she was devoured with guilt as a consequence. It was as though she were waiting to be consumed by it. She felt guilty about the frequent battering her mother was subjected to, about Croaky cycling away behind her, about her brother not being able to clear his final exams. She had even felt guilty about the desperately keen man standing outside the door with his foot wedged in the doorway. But then she had always carried this guilt with her. It was something she had learnt at her mother's knee. When she was still toddling around, she remembered her mother getting up with a start to perform a forgotten household chore, almost as though she were trying to make up for some huge lapse on her part. And Karuna also learnt to be apologetic. But, somehow, she was not sorry about her refusal to marry Blubber Lips.

It was Minnie who had counselled her. Marriage, she had informed Karuna, was not all about driving around in swanky cars. 'After all, you will also be going to bed with him every night,' she had said. 'I know of someone who would hide under her bed every night because she was revolted by her husband. But he would drag her out and rape her.' And Minnie had gone on to explain that the woman went crazy because she could not handle the onslaught of sex. 'But none of this would be apparent on those pleasant social evenings when they waved goodbye to their hosts as they drove home in his fancy car.'

Karuna had felt instant empathy for the woman, especially after her own struggle on the breezy edge of the earth from where aeroplanes blazed into the night. 'I know exactly how she must have felt,' she had murmured.

Karuna's decision, however, did not please her mother who had hoped to see her daughter move out of Patiala, knowing that the town oozed a machismo which, she felt, Karuna would find difficult to endure. She had often been bruised by it. There were nights when Lalli would tug at his pyjamas and expect her to be ready and waiting, with her salwar neatly folded on a chair beside her. If she was not, the line between the sexual and the violent would be a very fine one indeed. It was easier to neatly fold her salwar, close her eyes and wait till it was all over. It never took long and that was why it seemed the better option.

Of course, to have a man brutalizing her body with the unconcern of someone pumping air into a bicycle tyre was an unfamiliar experience. So was the violence. The reason was that she had grown up in a house full of women—her mother and her sister. After her father's death, her mother had managed their agricultural land and all the male workers she employed. So this marital capping of the night with abuses and punches was a novel experience. But after that first time, it had acquired the familiarity of habit. Now, it was very nearly routine, pretty much like the hot-water sit-ins she had to do for the piles problem that was beginning to bother her. And while the bruises still hurt, inside, she remained unmoved. So, she put up with the battering, after which she stood outside her own front door in the middle of the night, and roused a rickshaw puller, curled up in deep slumber on the seat of his vehicle. He, in his turn, knew where to go. There was only one destination: her sister's house.

As such, she had hoped that Karuna would marry somebody from far away. And the man had owned a nice car, which augured well. 'Baby, I know he was not a hero,' she had argued with her daughter, 'but who is? Look at your father. I knew that I had to get married, after all. So, we were married and have been, all these years.'

It was not the best example to cite. It was certainly not the kind that would encourage emulation. And she had received a predictable response. 'But he is so mean to you. You don't want me to be running away from the house every night, do you?' Karuna had countered. This was the first time that she had put into words the scenes she had witnessed as a child from the safety of her den under the stairs, and overheard, loud and clear, from the seclusion of her bedroom when she was older. What could her mother have said to that?

6

Love in the Time of Hate

Karuna came back, relieved, almost looking forward to seeing Croaky on his bicycle. The fact that he was neither handsome nor rich had never bothered her to begin with. For though she often looked and behaved like her mother, she had, unlike her mother, no girlie daydreams. There was no knight in shining armour riding a horse in the landscape of her mind. In any case, it would take a really vivid imagination to see Croaky as the man on the horse. But, at least, he was deeply in love with her and that was something.

So, she let him follow her. And finally, she began to wait for him to catch up at the roundabout, before she made her way through the crowded bazaar. She had learnt to shake off Pyarelal. Racing at top speed, with the escort breathlessly following, she would suddenly jam on her brakes. But Pyarelal would already have propelled his bicycle to a particular acceleration to keep abreast of her and the momentum would take him inexorably forward and ahead of her. It was possible that Karuna had learnt this little trick of suddenly breaking speed from her brother and his wheelies.

On other occasions, she would go into a soulful phase of slow cycling, then, suddenly, race away. That would afford her some respite, before Pyarelal caught up with her. The former strategy, however, always worked better.

Karuna was growing up at a time when students cycled to school and college and she would have been deeply embarrassed to arrive in a car. The number on her car's licence plate would have been added to the arsenal in the boys' armoury. She would have found it scrawled all over the blackboard or called out after her, as she walked down the corridor. In fact, the few times she was driven to college, it was as though the car's licence plate were pinned to her dress and the boys were reading off it as she went by.

'Oye! There goes PUP 4224. Ask her to give us a ride sometime in that nice blue car,' somebody would call out, making it sound as though riding a car was the single most titillating thing to do, as though she had arrived in college wearing hot pants. And there would be no point in turning around to identify the source of the remark because a few steps on, there would be somebody else making the same suggestion in an equally leery voice. 'Hi, sexy PUP!' would be the next come-on, followed by the come-hither sounds one usually reserved for luring a shy puppy: 'Come here, here, here!' Next would ensue an orchestra of encouraging whistles.

An escort cycling with her was not a particularly pleasant option either. She did not enjoy being crowded on to the edge of the road with Pyarelal installed like a shield between her and the rest of the traffic. She would keep shaking him off and he would often lose sight of her. It was in these brief intervals that Croaky would make his overtures. Poor Pyarelal never suspected a thing, of course. He was so busy keeping up with Karuna. And what could he really complain about when he got home? There was no moral turpitude in cycling at various speeds, was there?

The deliberation of her actions was not lost on Croaky. He did not fail to notice, moreover, that the change had really come about following her absence from college for a few days. This was the second time that she had failed to show up on the road to college, and unlike the first time, when Croaky's love life had been brought to a standstill, things looked definitely more promising this time round.

The first time she had absented herself from college was on the occasion a call had gone out to organize a chakka jam or pahiya jam, a student protest that involved preventing buses from being run by the state. Jam the wheel, was the message. The students, egged on by an outfit called the Naujawan Bharat Sabha, were protesting a hike in fares. There was also an Anti Bus Fare Action Committee. Buses were the most common mode of public transport for students coming in from outlying villages. They would arrive in buses loaded all the way to the roof.

The protest had been spearheaded by the Left parties, who saw themselves as being uncompromisingly secular, and the Akalis, a political party, which had fashioned itself as the only representative of the Sikhs. The Akalis had a camp office in a gurudwara. Their entire political campaign against the bus fare hike emanated from the Sikh temple, a situation that could not have been very appealing to the Left parties. Strategic action proceeded unhindered, nonetheless. It was a strange political combination of the Left and the Right that had even formed a government at one time. Now in the

Opposition, they had come together, once again, to bring down the Congress government.

Croaky, however, had other things on his mind than heeding the call of Naujawan Bharat Sabha. In any case, he was not going to have anything to do with something that called itself a 'sabha'. Just not English enough. This fetish for things English would turn out to be a lifelong preoccupation with Croaky. In later years, after he had become the sahib he had always aspired to be and before he got hauled up for serious official lapses, he had raised an authoritative finger and declared that he wanted only an 'English cook'. Of course, he was referring to the nationality of the food and not the cook. 'He should know how to bake and steam and grill,' he had demanded, 'because I like to have English food once a day. And not one of those, please, who pick up a bit of Chinese cuisine and pass themselves off as English cooks.' That was the nature of his specific requirement. The student politics on the college campus had a distinctly Punjabi flavour which did not, obviously, suit his palate. Croaky was not interested in bus fares either. He was planning his life so he would never have to board a bus. How very infra dig to have to catch a bus to work and back!

However, the atmosphere was rife with political activity, in spite of the ignominy associated with a name like Naujawan Bharat Sabha. As part of the protest, the students hijacked a bus and brought it to the campus where it became the focus of a great deal of excited revelry. The bus stayed on campus overnight and the protest kept snowballing. Some of these committed types were arrested after picketing the Vidhan Sabha in Chandigarh. That really put a spoke in Croaky's wheel because the colleges were likely to remain closed for quite some time. He had also heard of some police firing in Bhatinda, which was a three-hour drive from Patiala. The account of what had happened was full of strewn notebooks, textbooks, identity cards, turbans and a single casualty.

A procession was to wind its way to the district courts in Patiala to protest the firing. The point, Croaky noted with interest, was that it would have to go past Karuna's house. Perhaps, this was his opportunity of keeping alive the flame of love? Lurking on the peripheries of the procession, he stationed himself outside Karuna's house, once the vanguard arrived there. He had all of twenty minutes, till the last of them, including the stragglers, got past. He had yelled and yelled and yelled, hoping that his distinctive voice would draw her out, but she never did hear. There were some in the procession who noticed his tangential activity and he very nearly got beaten up for it. Some of them surrounded him.

'Come and look at this guy!' one invited.

'Did you notice what he was doing?' a second asked.

'Bloody Romeo!' exclaimed a third.

'Oye, Oye!' said the fourth, the undefined word, in this instance, heavy with a threat unarticulated.

Croaky knew that a beating at the hands of irate students would break a few of his bones at the very least. His heart thudded. His head did a little spin. But he was aware that when angry wasps came buzzing your way, you merely cowered and held your breath—a practical strategy that Mike had never discovered as he tried to outrace his own set of bees. So, Croaky braced himself and shut his eyes, hoping that the moment would pass. And it did. Someone in the crowd urged the aggressors not to digress from the real focus of the protest. So they went back and joined the procession.

Through all the fuss, the house remained silent and immune to the swirling students on the road. The frog in Croaky's voice croaked even louder, but she did not hear him. The slogan-shouting procession took the protesters to their goal with a partial roll-back in the bus fare hike and the restoration of travel concessions. As for Croaky's insidious attempt at rejuvenating his love on the sidelines of the protest, it had failed miserably. He worried that this period of absence might undo all his previous efforts and that he would have to start all over again.

It was a strange time for love. It was a good time to hate, though. The climate was ripe. In Kapuri, a village barely twenty kilometres from Patiala, yet another political combination was now protesting the construction of a link canal, which would carry river water from Punjab to its neighbouring state. And further north-west, motorcyclists, with their identities camouflaged by mufflers, had waylaid a bus, lined up its passengers and shot them dead because they belonged to a particular community. Yes, this was a good time to hate. You could hate on the basis of state, community, religion and sect, individually or collectively.

Croaky, however, was not trying to break the circle of violence with his persistent 'I love you-s'. He was no maverick. On the contrary, he was a man with a steadfast belief in battered old cliches who thought women meant 'yes' when they said 'no' and that absence made the heart grow fonder. Therefore, it wasn't surprising when, after Karuna's second prolonged disappearance, he told himself that she had returned looking much more amenable to his overtures, which she had. This was his moment of triumph. One last burst of effort and he would be there, he knew it. It was the most exciting moment he would know in his whole life. He had never worked so hard at anything and never would. Therefore, this would be the only time he would taste success after a struggle. That was why he decided to prolong the moment. He carried on cycling at that same mild distance and let the days run on for a while.

College would soon be over, though. Croaky decided it had to be now—and consistent with his total lack of originality—or never.

'Will you marry me?' he ventured, one day, in the interval provided by the speed-up and jam-brake routine. There was no other moment he could have got close enough to her to articulate it. Though the phrase, in keeping with his character, lacked novelty, it was the oldest and most tried-and-tested turn of phrase in such matters. He would, of course, have liked to have said it with the flourish a romance deserved—maybe flowers, a ring and a beautifully worded two-liner. But balancing a bicycle between an oncoming tractor trolley and a persistently hot-on-his-heels rickshaw waiting to get past him, the will-you-marry-me from one bicycle to another was the best he could manage. It was done in front of the sari shop, the display of bridal saris in the window serving, perhaps, as a catalyst for the event. The salesman was, at that very moment, folding a bridal sari and tucking it back into its cardboard box, after having preened around in it for the young bride-to-be sitting before him. He glanced at the road and thought, 'There they go,' little realizing that the question had already been popped.

'Yes,' Karuna replied, 'but I will have to talk to my parents.'

She began by telling her mother about the boy who followed her every day and had asked her to marry him. That was easy.

'He says he is preparing for the civil services exams,' she told her mother.

Since taking the exam for the coveted service was almost a profession by itself for many young people, his proposal could not be dismissed out of hand. And when Karuna's mother put it to Lalli in one of his good moments—after his second drink and before the third—he was quite pleased at the prospect of being able to boast of a bureaucrat in the making in his own house.

Consultations began in the Lalli household. The lowly status of the boy's father militated against the alliance, but the likelihood of the boy himself becoming a civil servant provided the bait. One aunt wondered why Karuna wanted to get married at all. Aunt Veer (if you could roll the 'r' to give it a French flavour, so much the better), who connected their family to royalty down yet another route, had remained single and she wondered what the fuss was all about. She had actually been christened Veerpal, so as to beckon into this world a brother, a male heir for the family. The boy did arrive, but disappeared in his youth no one knew where. Veer had been pleasant-looking in her youth, with all that it took for marriage proposals to come in. She also had money. But she did not want to marry. Her family had gone through the entire gamut of persuasion—reasoning, pleading, cajoling and threatening. They had tried to paint a picture for her of impending loneliness. They had tried to convince her about how miserable they themselves would be. They had tried to tell her how wonderful it would be to have little children running around the house. For quite some time, she managed to steer through these negotiations. But finally, they declared they would either shoot themselves or her. Poor Veer. What could she do but agree to meet the 'boy'—lots of land and property; and tall, fair and handsome in the bargain? In Punjab, being fair was a prerequisite, a basic qualification to be considered eligible at all. So, at the age of thirty, she was to meet the fair-complexioned son of a rich landowner who had spent a good bit of his life shooting at people and getting shot at himself.

But before the meeting was arranged, Veer paid a visit to her dentist and got herself fitted with shining braces that flashed menacingly each time she smiled.

'I want my teeth perfectly aligned,' she had said to the dentist.

He could see that her teeth were pretty well aligned anyway, but he understood the whimsicality of the rich. 'We'll give you the smoothest curve ever, a Mona Lisa smile,' the glib professional had promised.

The blobs of silver sat squarely on each of her upper front teeth. Unlike most other wired-up people, she would part and stretch her lips to make sure the silver network in her mouth was visible. That should do it, she thought, but a peek at the mirror made her a little doubtful. A really determined man with an imagination might just be able to picture her with the braces off and realize that she was fairly presentable to look at. Her bank balance would do the rest. What else could she do to be left alone? A tattoo across the face? But all she wanted was temporary disfigurement. Orange hair, she thought. That might be just the thing. Her light brown hair would lend itself easily to 'taking' any startling colour. She would, of course have to limit her expression of weirdness to a single colour, because the fad of streaking hair hadn't caught on in those days and certainly not in the beauty parlours in Patiala. So, she visited one.

'Flaming orange?' said the beautician. This was a rather unusual request. All the women who came to her for mehndi treatments to camouflage the grey strands in their hair, fretted over the possibility of their head looking bright orange in the sun. That was a shade worse than white. And here was someone actually opting for orange! She thought she owed Veer a word of advice.

'Indian skins don't really go with orange hair. Why not go in for a head massage and a shampoo instead?' she suggested, reluctant to lose a potential customer.

But Veer was adamant on orange hair. 'As orange as possible,' she insisted. 'Maybe, you could also make it a bit frizzy?'

'You know, this is a strange request,' the nervous beautician confessed. 'I don't actually stock an orange hair dye. But I'll try to get the effect you want.'

'Don't worry. Just go ahead and play with colour,' Veer encouraged her, settling back into the chair with a satisfied sigh.

Weird, thought the parlour lady, as she wielded her paintbrush.

'I am to be married,' Veer volunteered.

Weird, thought the parlour lady, yet again, but went on to say, 'Is that why you're colouring your hair? I'm sure you would have looked just as nice with your natural colour.'

'I would like to shock them,' Veer explained.

But that only mystified the parlour lady more.

Veer stepped out of the parlour, ready to meet the 'boy'. The meeting was a fiasco, of course. Her own family—her mother and her uncles; her father had died a long time ago—

was upset. The prospective bridegroom and his family were horrified. The 'girl' is quite insane, they said. Word got around very quickly. And then, who would marry poor Veer? The lady in question loved her spinster existence, of course. She did what she pleased, slept when she pleased and got up when she pleased. That was nineteen years ago.

She had been through her moments of wanting to get out of this place. She had worked with a travel agency in Delhi until it folded up, and had come right back to Patiala, telling herself that she needed a break. But in reality, she was quite happy to be back. The pace here suited her. Initially, she told herself that this was merely an interlude between one job and the next. She slowly realized, however, that she was not even thinking of moving out. She settled down in her home with her mother. Life seemed so perfect. She was quite happy to let the tide of time wash over her lazily.

She was not worried about becoming a stereotype—the spinster aunt. In fact, she loved it. She got herself a dog, which she adored and went only where the dog was sure to go. She became 'the spinster obsessed with her dog', but she couldn't care less. An occasional cricket match between the Royal Eleven and a visiting team from abroad would provide her the kind of outing she enjoyed—garden umbrellas, sun hats, cold beer sipped out of sparkling glasses and a periodic peek at the match through half-shut eyes. The event would be quite enough to sustain her for the next couple of days. And the good thing about her insular world was that you only met the same people again and again. So, after a while, you could even give up the effort of dressing well or wearing those agonizing contact lenses. It was all so comfortable. Rather like slipping into well-worn bedroom slippers.

It was inevitable that Veer would be entirely unmoved by the excitement of a marriage. Heaving herself out of her languor, she decided to have a chat with Karuna.

'Don't do it,' she advised her, sitting in her ample garden chair under a large mango tree, her dog comfortably curled up in another chair. 'Just don't.'

But Karuna did not have Aunt Veer's advantages. No inheritance. The house wouldn't be hers, the mango trees wouldn't be hers, the garden chairs wouldn't be hers and as for the dog, she did not want a dog. She could not for the life of her understand why Aunt Veer doted on this stupid-looking animal—white, furry eyes shut most of the time, barking when it should not and not barking when Aunt Veer's house was broken into. It just sat there, curled up at the foot of the bed, in the direct path of the cold blast of air from the AC, while Aunt Veer flailed her arms at the neighbours and mouthed abuses, standing in her huge garden. No one heard her, of course, because the vast expanses of land around her house absorbed the noise. However, the intruder fled, daunted perhaps by the sheer volume of sound she generated. Aunt Veer herself told Karuna of the studied silence maintained by the dog. 'Poor thing! It was so afraid,' she had murmured in sympathy, patting the ball of fluff. No, Karuna did not want a dog.

But she did have to get married. She tried explaining this to Aunt Veer. 'You know I will count for nothing when Father makes his will,' she told her aunt. 'He will leave everything to my brother. What am I supposed to live on, if I don't get married?' If this sounds as though she were complaining about the fact that she had a father and a brother, it needs to be clarified that it was not how she felt. She loved her brother. And her father was, after all, her father. But she was also aware that she had to work out things within the given framework.

'You know,' she continued, 'I have a choice between marrying him or marrying someone my father finds for me. That man in Delhi was horrible. You know, he took me to a deserted part of the city and was all over me. I hated him!' She proceeded to tell her aunt all about Blubber Lips.

That nearly got her aunt going, all over again. 'I always knew that marriage is not a good idea at all. Why do you want to go in for it?'

The previous argument had to be repeated, with Aunt Veer and Karuna returning to their respective opening dialogues.

'Don't,' said Aunt Veer again.

'If I don't, what will I live on?' Karuna countered and, as a second line of argument, added, 'I don't really have the guts to visit the dentist or have my hair dyed orange, the way you did.'

That pleased Aunt Veer. 'Fine, she said, 'but at the first sign of trouble, make a run for it. I will back you up.'

'I will,' Karuna assured her, unaware of how prophetic her words would be.

For now, preparations for the wedding went into overdrive. Clothes were bought. Guest lists were drawn up. Food. Liquor. What, how much, when? However, these were only rhetorical questions since liquor would, necessarily, have to be available in abundance and at all times. Otherwise, the celebrations would be deemed to have been a failure. In fact, an uncle or two losing it and keeling over, topped up with liquor, was a prerequisite and would constitute a part of the lore that any wedding, a wedding of consequence, that is, should spawn.

The story of the uncle's big fall would then be recounted in the context of the generosity with which liquor had sparkled out of Scotch bottles carrying distinguished labels. There were issues other than liquor, which also had to be taken care of. The colour of the wedding card: Red and gold. The wording: 'To meet and bless the newly-weds.' Was that good enough or should the message be more poetic? It could even be pious, with a few lines quoted from the religious texts. Two thousand cards, the printer was told.

In the meantime, Croaky, having finished his post-graduation, had paid his way into the state civil service. His father had to go and meet a tout who named a price over which they had haggled.

'I cannot pay so much,' Croaky's father had told the man. 'I am just a poor government servant. Where would I have that kind of money? Can't you bring it down a little?'

But the tout was adamant. 'These are fixed rates and those people don't negotiate,' he had retorted briskly, obviously trying to imply that those who took the money were some undefined people out there and he was not one of them. 'Besides, there are so many people who have to be paid off. The money you give will just about cover costs.'

Ultimately Croaky's father, poor government official that he was, had managed to find the money and Croaky became a state civil servant, well on his way to the huge bungalow he had dreamed of. That changed his bargaining position in life. He could now look at love and marriage from his elevated perch.

That was when trouble started brewing. It waited for the flurry of excitement generated by a marriage in the house to reach fever pitch before manifesting itself.

7

Counting Teeth

Michael was quite lost in the midst of all the wedding preparations for Karuna. He would wander around the house, trying to look as though he were a part of the proceedings, but there was a vacant stare in his eyes. People in the house and family were quite used to the sense of purposelessness in Michael's movements. He was not taken very seriously because he was this funny guy, slightly dim-witted, whom you could joke about, as though he were not there and he would not mind. He would show up in doorways, watch his father having it out with the food contractor and back off, only to show up in his parents' bedroom, where a number of relatives were just sitting around. And he would hurry out of there as well.

The only time he came into his own was on his bike, which he could no longer ride.

Michael had been truly happy only in the company of the group of boys who shared his passion for movement and who were involved in a sport that seemed to be tailor-made for him. It was called Moto Cross. It required you to ride a bike down a dirt track with a number of obstacles thrown in your path. The track wound round in concentric circles (no wonder Michael felt at home here; from going around in circles on his cycle as a child to doing the same on the bike as an adult offered him a kind of comforting continuity) and a committed audience could cluster around the outermost circle, watching the race through the haze of dust raised by the motorbikes in action. The sport had already found its own set of fans. They came every Sunday morning, well scrubbed, presumably after a leisurely bath on a non-working day. They did not mind the cloud of dust that engulfed them, their eyelashes a light fawn at the end of each such session. There were always a large number of girls in this dust-coated audience, lending Mike's manner a flamboyance that had been foreign to him before.

Michael had somehow grown up with the belief that women loved motorbikes. He had meant them no disrespect of course. But he had been under the impression that all you did was gesture with your thumb, pointing to somewhere in the region behind your back, and say, 'Hop on.' And that was it. It never quite worked that way for Michael. No one was willing to risk a ride with him—unless of course there was no other option available—because with his penchant for movement he had also developed one for accidents. However, the lack of a pillion rider was forgotten in the excitement of making new friends. He had driven all the way to Chandigarh to meet them—Chopsy, Gutsy, Hardy, and so many others. Given that all the names ended in a 'y', by some unspoken covenant of the biking brotherhood, it wasn't surprising that over time he too graduated to 'Mikey'.

Early on Sunday mornings, he would ride his bike to Chandigarh and reach Hardy's house with just enough time in hand to wash his face and be ready for the track. The rest of the morning was spent on the track—revving the bike to take a leap over a ditch, zooming up an incline and flying through the air, leaving the dip in the ground far behind, and manoeuvring a U-turn, using one leg as a swivel.

After a morning of sport, the group would usually drive into the hills that rose up to the north of Chandigarh. A number of girls had become regulars too. They did not come to ride bikes, but to applaud the participants in the sport before joining them on the uphill drive. The availability of another pillion seat was welcome. Mike, of course, always catered to the odd woman out. So, for many Sundays running, he had a different hop-on each time.

There was this girl who had just finished school and had to avert her face every time a car approached or overtook them, which was pretty much most of the way. She was convinced that her parents were always right round the corner.

'God! A white car. Can you read the number? I'll duck behind you. Just make sure you get the number,' said the girl, her voice muffled behind his jacket.

'CHK 5270,' read Michael, having to slow down considerably to concentrate on the number plate.

An agitated voice from his pillion would pay no heed to his words, but mutter with a desperate urgency, 'For heaven's sake, don't slow down! They'll see me!'

'But how else am I to read the number? Dat is the only way I can read when I'm riding a bike.' The quirk in the way Michael pronounced 'that' would go unnoticed.

In the meantime, the car would have wound its way down and out of sight.

'So, what was the number?'

'CHK 5270,' Michael repeated, affording momentary relief to his rider. But not for long, since there were always plenty of white cars winding down the slopes. White seemed to be the most popular colour among the car-buying populace, and Michael was rattling off car numbers all through this pleasure trip.

Another pillion rider was forever warning him about an approaching vehicle, as though he were riding his bike with his head screwed on backwards.

'Watch out, watch out!' she would yell. 'It's coming straight at us!' The first time she did it, a startled Michael had very nearly lost his balance. But soon, he learnt to anticipate it and even managed to find a few comforting words to say to the girl.

'Don't worry. I'm a very careful driver,' he reassured her, and was indeed careful not to tell her of his record as far as accidents were concerned.

However, the girl lived in perpetual fear of being mowed down by a larger vehicle and no amount of reassurance could tone down the volume of her periodic maydays.

Of course, it took all sorts to make a world. So, there was yet another girl, forever egging him on to speed up. All of them were nearly always keen on catching up with the others. 'There goes Hardy!' they would say. Mike felt a twinge of envy within. For most of them, Hardy was the chosen one, but not all of them got to sit on his bike. It was some of these deprived, lovelorn creatures that Mike often carted around. But he would have been quite happy circling on his own in a never-ending spiral. That he had a pillion rider, albeit a reluctant one, was one of life's unexpected rewards.

The first ever Moto Cross competition organized in the

northwestern region was to be held on the first of February. That was what these bikers were gearing up for. 'Don't go,' said his mother, when the day arrived. She knew of this 'chakka jam' thing which had been brewing right through January. 'Don't go,' she said to Michael, as he spruced up his bike in the cold, early-morning darkness of February. After all, a wheel was a wheel, she thought. Those who were holding up buses could be just as opposed to the movement of all vehicular traffic. Which was not quite how Michael looked at the whole affair. As far as he was concerned, wheels were meant to turn and nothing else made sense. What was all the fuss about? And so he left. And she sat and waited for the bad news.

Michael rode out of Patiala and did not encounter a single obstruction on the way. Not even a cow. It was much too early in the morning. Too early even for the protesters. It was an uneventful ride to Chandigarh, except for the morning gradually breaking all around him and the sun promising to be there for the Moto Cross. At the venue, there were lots of people, lots of girls, lots of banners and lots of bikes. A cloud of dust rose as the twenty-eight bikers that had come all the way from Calcutta and Jaipur, hit the sandy track. And the dust just hung there, hitching itself on to the excitement in the air and swinging from it. Spirals of dust tiptoed on air, weaving through the crowds before settling down on the eating stalls at the far end. Columns of dust chased the bikes, even across the most intimidating obstacles. Actually, it was the dust that seemed to be having all the fun. It teased its way through shut eyelids, edging around branded sunglasses, surged down open mouths and inched its way down shirt-fronts. By the time the event ended, no one was arguing with it any more, but letting it have its way with a resigned acceptance.

But Mike was having fun too. He was not really bothered about winning. His was an exhilaration born of the sensation of movement. A 'Yahoo!' sensation that made him want to fling his arms up in the air. But he hung on to his handlebars and beat down the dust track. He was among the eight who made it to the semi-final round. Hardy had had to retire because of a mechanical fault and Cooky had simply lost his zing. 'Come on!' shouted the girls in the audience, the ones who had been Mike's hop-ons from time to time. And the voices tugged at his accelerator bar. It swung into full throttle of its own volition and there, in that semi-final round, he landed in a heap, the bike piled on top of him and a cloud of dust performing a little war dance around this awkward mess. Of course, he had fallen many times before, but never in front of an audience that had been egging him on. The 'come-ons!' that had already been launched out of cheering throats, stood suspended for a moment on the swirling dust, before falling to the ground with the dead weight of stones. He lay there under the bike. And as the gasp of the audience pierced through the envelope of dust, an eerie silence hung in the air. No, he was not dead. He sat up while the bike still lay on his leg. The pain slowly climbed up to his brain and he screamed. Hands picked him up. Other hands dusted him down. Still others brought in a stretcher. He had broken his leg. He was hoisted on to the stretcher and carried off the dust track.

His mother knew. She had, in fact, been prepared for just this. Of course, she had imagined marauding hordes of students stopping his bike to jam the wheel. She had also imagined him breaking a bone as he tried to get away. When the phone rang, she simply knew. He had broken a bone. And though her prescience about the matter offered her no satisfaction, perhaps, it did make it somewhat easier when the phone finally rang. She did not have to yell a shocked 'What!' into the phone. She did not even need to sit down and absorb the information nor cry just a wee bit. She could launch into action right away. She and Lalli set out for Chandigarh. But by that time, the jam-the-wheel protest was at its peak. Halfway to Chandigarh, they came up against squatting protesters who had blocked the road. They sat there, many rows deep, making sure that even the dusty edges of the road were not left unguarded. Lalli had to reverse the car and turn off the highway. He took a road to a village and from there, on to yet another link road to the next village. Thus they went from village to village, keeping to the route that led in the general direction of Chandigarh. These narrow roads wound their way through rich green wheat crop. The wheat fields sometimes closed in on the intruding road from either side; at others, they allowed it a fair passage, as though doing it a huge favour. The road was battling a lot of unprecedented traffic because there were many others, like Lalli, who had taken the same detour. And each time they met an oncoming vehicle, there was a lot of reversing and nudging and edging past—and abusing, of course—that had to be done. Progress was slow, but they did get to Chandigarh, eventually. By late evening, when the blockades had been lifted, they brought back a plastered and bandaged Michael, hopping around on his crutches.

The restless sound of his crutches thumping all over the house made everyone feel guilty about their own able pair of legs. Karuna and her mother tiptoed around, hoping he would not notice. There was not much else they could do.

Michael, on the other hand, did absolutely nothing at all. He read no books. He had no friends. He just wandered around on his crutches, wishing they would turn into wheels. And then the family knew just what they could do. They brought him a wheelchair, although with a bit of trepidation. He might well turn the wheelchair into some sort of a racing automobile. And that was just what he did. They managed to stop him just short of the porch steps, after he had propelled himself into a momentum with a shove against the front door. 'Just checking to see how fast this thing can go,' he said sheepishly. Yet another time, they had to pull him back, seconds before his outstretched, plastered leg rammed into the wall. It was a difficult time for everyone, but Michael, at least, was not moping. He had found himself a new toy and that obscured his memory of the Moto Cross and his collapse into a heap before a cheering audience.

He began to count his days off on a calendar, like a prisoner in a cell cancelling out strokes on the wall. Six weeks to go, and an hour later, he would tell himself, 'Less by another hour.' And then the countdown shifted from the calendar and the strokes on the wall to Jeet Maasi's teeth. It happened the day she decided to stop by on her way back from the dentist. Monty's mother was having the usual kind of trouble with her teeth. Nothing that others did not have. Routine stuff—a toothache, a cavity, a filling. But she came back from their neighbourhood dentist feeling totally distraught. Rocking her swollen cheek in her cupped hand, she declared that she was going to have all her teeth pulled out and make short work of all the anticipated trips to the dentist over the next twenty years.

'I will simply get myself fitted with dentures,' she announced to all the raised eyebrows around her. To start with, everyone thought she was merely tripping with the pain and getting back at it in the hope that her vengefulness would lessen the intensity. 'Here, take that! Dentures it will be, and then what will you do?' she was, perhaps, saying to the pain.

However, it did begin to seem as if she were serious. And then came the exclamations: 'All your teeth! No! Jeeti, you can't do that!' Mike's mother tried to enumerate the disadvantages of having dentures. She tried to remind her of all the sugar cane at their mother's farm and how natural teeth could tear through sugar cane on a sunny winter morning. She tried to evoke the aroma of roasting corn on a hot summer evening and attempted to describe how keenly the teeth longed to dig into it. But Jeet Maasi was adamant.

'Sometimes it is a cavity and a filling and when I have barely finished dealing with that, I have to rush back to the dentist for a root canal. I don't need any of it!' cried Jeet Maasi, baring her teeth angrily.

So, she waited for the swelling to subside, then went to the dentist with the request that he pull out all her teeth. The dentist, in the tradition of the professional who had set Aunt Veer's smile into a Mona Lisa number, was not going to let this business opportunity go by. The first tooth was pulled out. It was a harrowing experience for the dentist. His balls were squeezed and not just in a manner of speaking. The first time he introduced his instruments into Jeet Maasi's mouth, she had involuntarily swung her arm out, palm upwards, and made a grab for the doctor's balls. The attack was so sudden and unexpected that he had bellowed in pain as she hung on. His assistant's eyes above the mask had widened with shock.

'Please don't do that,' the dentist had pleaded.

'Do what?' the innocent Jeet Maasi had asked.

It would have been a bit indelicate to spell out to her what she had done. The dentist realized, however, that he would just have to protect his own interests. So, during the next consultation, he had positioned himself some distance away and leaned forward with the probe and the mirror. But Jeet Maasi had long arms and she nearly made a successful grab, yet again. However, the dentist had managed to intercept her hand before it got into locking position. This sequence of events having been repeated a few times over, the dentist had stationed his wide-eyed assistant right next to him and asked her to hold Jeet Maasi's hand very firmly. The first extraction had then got under way.

Jeet Maasi had bought a brick of ice cream and had stopped by at her sister's house. She was triumphant at having successfully pulled off her coup.

'Even the dentist told me that this was one way of dealing with dental problems,' she had declared, quoting, perhaps, what must have been the man's diplomatically non-committal response to her chosen course of action.

She wondered, of course, why no one else had ever hit upon this idea before. That the idea was a sound one was never in doubt, but people lacked the courage to handle novelty. Here she was, with her brick of vanilla ice cream that would feel so good as it swirled in her mouth. She declared that the next sitting with the dentist would follow in a few days. But first, the raw wound left by the previous extraction would have to heal.

She came by, every other day, following a visit to the dentist. She had not quite realized just how long the whole process would take, that it was not going to be a conclusive sock in the jaw which would knock down a whole bunch of teeth at one go. She had not anticipated that the extraction of each tooth would mean days of healing before moving on to the next, that every time she came back minus yet another tooth, her chewing capacity would be that much more diminished. And how long could one survive on the excitement of ice cream? Her meals became unvarying goo—bread soaked in milk. She slopped through her fit-for-doggy meals and began to wonder if this was such a good idea, after all. She had also not visualized the finale—a mouth sans any teeth at all and how the gums needed time to settle down before dentures could be fitted.

Anyway, the felling of her teeth provided Michael with a much more entertaining calendar. 'Jeet Maasi has had three teeth pulled out. It means dat I have another four weeks to go.' He would look forward to her visit. Not because of the ice cream—he hated ice cream—but because it would mean yet another eliminating stroke across his mental calendar. Gradually, he took to doodling on his plaster. 'One molar, right side, upper jaw,' he wrote, just above the knee. And three days later, it was, 'Two molars, right side, lower jaw,' and the list travelled a little way up, then down and wound its way around the plaster with corresponding dates. The calendar should really have begun with incisors and canines because that was where the trouble had started in Jeet Maasi's mouth. Her two front incisors had been dangling loosely in her mouth, ready to topple, and those were the first ones to have been knocked out by the dentist. But by the time Michael began regarding her teeth as his own reference point, the dentist was already dealing with the molar that had given Jeet Maasi a swollen cheek. There were, however, many premolars and molars to run through. Twenty, to be precise. And Jeet Maasi had to visit the clinic every alternate day. The dentist, for his part, alternated the jaws from which he extracted teeth, focusing on a tooth in the left upper jaw one day and the corresponding tooth in the lower jaw after the rest days in between. The same procedure would then be repeated on the right side.

'The day you get your last molar extracted, I will be going to the hospital to have my plaster snipped. But, maybe, I will bring back the plaster with me, because you and I can always look at it and tell just when a particular tooth was taken out.'

'It's a big joke for you, no doubt, but I'm already quite fed up of going to that dentist,' a peeved Jeet Maasi muttered.

'Oh no, I'm not joking at all. It will be nice when it's all over for both of us.'

He would then spend the morning being nice to her, since that was what she needed right then. The rest of the household moved around doing this and that, but the two of them just sat there, he with his outstretched plastered leg and she with her swollen cheek. They would talk about things. Her teeth were not her only problem. And Mike would listen to her with the patience of a stoic.

'Monty is always buried in his books. It is not healthy for a growing boy. He never plays games, never has any fun and hardly ever talks to me,' she complained.

She felt Mike understood, but that was really because he did not argue with her the way her own children did. He did not argue because he never had an opinion contrary to the one being expressed. She saw him riding around on his bike, very much the man about town and that met with her approval. She did not understand why her children could not belong here, why Monty could not be a swaggering male among the men. He was studying engineering, but did that really have to make him a bookworm? She had completely given up on her daughter, so Monty remained her only hope. Mike would hear her out and sprinkle the conversation with an 'Everything will be all right in the end'.

By the time Jeet Maasi had run through thirty of her thirty-two teeth, Mike was very nearly on his feet again. The quirk in his gait had become very pronounced, but what was more painful was the fact that he did not know how to recapture a lost momentum. Somehow, something in the moment he went down in a heap at the Moto Cross had changed his life. Of course, at the time he did not notice the momentousness of the occasion. He was not given to too much thinking. But it had been one of those decisive moments that change personal history. It was a moment that slowed him down forever. Having been thwarted mid-stride, he did not know whether to continue to stick his best foot forward or just mark time. Those bike buddies must be meeting every Sunday on the dust track and then in the hills. He thought of them often and wondered if he would ever be able to burst in upon the scene one Sunday morning, just like that, even after his leg had completely healed. 'Hello, I'm back. What's happening? May I join in?' Maybe not. He had a horror of imposing himself, which was why he stuck to the time-tested relationships he was already familiar with.

8

Death Toll

Michael spent a good part of the next couple of years at his maternal grandmother's farm on the outskirts of Patiala. This wiry old woman bounding around like a spring released from its catch, seemed much more in control of her life than either his mother or his maasi. In better days, when she could still come into town, Michael would be the one taking her around on his motorcycle to the bank, the post office and, sometimes, to the dentist. Her teeth were her own. Her black hair was streaked with only the occasional strand of white and she was willing to take the risk of sitting on his bike. Though she was not one of those old people given to bouts of nostalgia, she always told her grandchildren, 'You all keep falling ill because none of you eat the way we used to when we were children. I used to have desi ghee in my daal, in my saag, on my roti and in all the sweets that were prepared in the house. When my mother made kheer, we would help ourselves to a bowlful each time we went by. And when she made a huge platter of besan barfi, it never lasted beyond a couple of hours.'

'But Nani, there are so many calories in that stuff,' they would tell her.

'That is the trouble with you,' she would scoff, 'you are always counting calories.'

Whether it was the famed Punjabi desi ghee or just a genetic quirk, the fact remained that she was one member of the family in fighting-fit shape and entirely capable of managing the thirty-acre farm left to her by her husband.

Her father-in-law, Michael's great-grandfather, was a Sardar, a landowner who had been granted ownership rights over the land in the early twentieth century. The land settlements that had taken place in the Patiala state followed the British pattern. Sardar Sahib had, therefore, been appointed a biswedar in 1920, an appointment that was the outcome of his kinship with the ruling elite. Sardar Sahib and others like him were part of the biswedari system under which they were entitled to receive rent from those who were already cultivating the land as well as a share of the produce. They could also claim perks from the tillers, which would, in today's corporate language, be covered, perhaps, under the headings, 'household expenses' and 'entertainment allowance'. Sardar Sahib had a son, Chhote Sardar Sahib or Junior Sardar Sahib, Michael's maternal grandfather, and in true dynastic tradition the biswedari passed on to him.

However, Chhote Sardar Sahib had to deal with the protests of farmers who had been denied ownership rights to the land. He had to occasionally hire goons to beat up the tenant farmers and make sure that they paid him rent. He did manage to retain most of his land and, in fact, add to it in the initial days of youthful energy. But subsequently, living had turned out to be an expensive business. He was an immaculate Englishman who had let his daughter marry the man she wanted, much as he disapproved of her choice. He was also of 'royal' birth and that entailed certain obligations towards his own lifestyle, which he fulfilled with the greatest meticulousness, splurging in a way that only the rich and the royal can. Thirty acres was all that had been left of the land.

On those thirty acres, Michael took his turn on the tractor with Balwinder, spending a part of the day following Balwinder around on his grandmother's land and the rest of the time at the tractor's driving wheel, with Balwinder being jolted along, as he sat atop the mudguard of the spinning wheel, his vision a blur with the juddering movement. Balwinder worked on his grandmother's land, just as his father had worked before him for his great-grandfather. And as Michael saw it, this was how it had always been and this was how it would always be, and it was probably this changelessness which lent a certain mythical quality to Balwinder's stories, in which his grandfather, Gulab Singh, an active participant in a peasant agitation, had tried to wrest ownership of the land he was ploughing.

Gulab Singh had not been alone in this. Two hundred villages in the surrounding area had gathered under one banner, as the wheat ripened, to carve out their own little place in the sun. In the first decade of the twentieth century, regular land settlements had taken place under the direction of the British settlement officer. The tillers of the land had come forward with documents in support of their ownership claims. But the biswedars were an influential lobby and when the land records were drawn up they ensured that they were listed as the owners. The battle raged on.

The slogans of the day were 'land to the tiller' and 'no rent'. Chanting them to the beat of a drum, the agitating tenants would march into the fields. Gulab Singh had joined the Riasti Praja Mandal and travelled all the way to Lahore to participate in the first conference held on the fringes of a session of the Indian National Congress at Bradlaugh Hall. His moment of glory had, however, come ten years later, at the sixth session of the All India States People's Conference, held in Ludhiana. He had been able to garland Pandit Jawaharlal Nehru who had come to preside over the conference. For Gulab Singh, the moment had marked a convergence between the struggle for freedom from the British and their own ongoing battle with the biswedars. 'We will be free,' he had thought, as he lovingly garlanded the national leader, imagining a land that was free of the white sahibs and the home-grown landowners.

But he had to come down to ground reality very quickly. He was severely beaten up by the goons hired by the biswedars. As protest movements go, this was a glorious moment of unflinching confrontation with the enemy. But equally it was a moment of failure. Gulab Singh lost the ownership of his fields, though he would be counted as one of those who had gone down fighting. He was evicted from the land and his stock of wheat, piled high and waiting for purchase, was taken away by the landowner's goons. That was how he had come to be working on the land of the elder Sardar Sahib and subsequently that of Chhote Sahib. And history would merely repeat itself over the coming generations.

For Michael, the marvel of this story from the past simply lay in the fact that things had been different at one time. That Balwinder might really have been his neighbour on the adjacent plot of land. He could never understand change anyway; he was in awe of it. And he liked Balwinder, for whom these accounts involving his own ancestors were just narratives, folk tales he had grown up on, entertaining stories from his mother's repertoire. They were not meant to fire his blood.

Balwinder, who lived in the outhouse with his mother, had tried to go to school years ago, but had learnt nothing, not the stuff that books taught, anyway. He knew all about sowing and reaping, but his books were full of things that were alien to him. He had, however, learnt to mimic the cadences of fluently spoken English. From a distance, he could sound like the expat, a drawl filling the gaps between words and sentences. But up close, the steady flow turned out to be gibberish. Even so, an unaware listener was likely to question his own powers of comprehension, so authentic were the sounds that Balwinder produced. In fact, the few classes he had managed to get through had been on the strength of the American drawl translated into a scrawl on paper with a sprinkling of letters from the alphabet. A harassed examiner going through a huge pile of answer scripts might see it merely as yet another one of many scribbled in appalling handwriting, and assign it a pass mark as a safe option. Balwinder could have got past many more classes than he did with his 'American' scrawl, but he chose to opt out. He kept up his non-resident Indian act, however, which tickled Michael no end and led to frequent requests from the latter for yet another performance.

'Yaar, once again,' Michael would beseech him in English, since that was part of the trigger that got Balwinder going.

'End of day, it important not to buy the wonderful. Gee he keep on talking about but it could have been done have done. It awesome and a crazy. I be darnned if he go...' So on it would flow, for another ten sentences, with aspirated 'c's and 'p's, the 'a's delivered with the lower lip dropping and the 'r's rolled.

'But you must go on,' Michael would prompt at the end of Balwinder's breathless delivery.

'It must go on, has to,' Balwinder would say, picking up from Michael, as if this were the continuation of a conversation. 'Happy to go. It not difficult but go Neuork and business there. You must come and join the busy time. Kistmis time wonderful.' 'Kistmis' was, of course, Christmas, 'Neuork' was New York, thrown in to authenticate his brand of Americanisms and the 'b' of 'business' would, of course, be a 'bh'.

'You have business there?' Michael would ask.

'Yes of course. I have the business and the many dollars. You see they surprise of my friend go to alaay. And then the highway. It come and go to the awesome. Some place it the new and join the wonderful khofee.' Balwinder would suddenly stop, refusing to do any more, claiming to have twisted his tongue in the attempt.

Michael would hold his belly and laugh, his head falling backwards. The two would spend many happy moments together, an odd couple, having come together from opposite sides of the fence.

And more recently they were sometimes joined by Raminder who was on a brief visit to his native village. He was an expat Punjabi in jeans, sporting a single earring, and was part of the workforce that puts up sets for Hollywood films.

'Have you seen *Annie?*' he would ask Michael and even Balwinder.

Of course no one in the village had either seen 'Annie' or even heard of her.

'Who is Annie?' Michael had innocently asked.

'It's a great movie and we prepared the sets for it but you probably don't see too many of those movies here,' said the lofty Raminder—Ramy back home. He, however, was far too sleek for the other two who preferred each other's company to Ramy and his 'Annie'.

Balwinder seemed to have the same propensity as Michael for moving a little beyond the designated halt, when in motion. The police had once flagged him down on a village road when he was speeding along on his tractor trolley. But even as he attempted to jam on the brakes, his lumbering vehicle had rolled on a short distance ahead. Enraged policemen had pulled him down from his perch and given him a hiding. One of them had even yanked at his beard to deliver the ultimate insult. 'You will stop when we tell you to,' they commanded him, impervious to his explanation about the free roll of his wheels even after the brakes had been applied. However, a policeman with a loaded gun is hardly the appropriate adversary to pick for having an argument. Balwinder had been taken to the police station where he knew he would have to do a lot of explaining.

But Balkar Singh, the Station House Officer, had been in no mood to listen. Sitting behind his desk in full regalia, a pistol hitched to his side, he had looked formidable. Behind him, on the wall, was a portrait gallery of important national leaders staring into the promising distance ahead and as unaware of Balkar Singh as he was of them. A trio of chairs was ranged across his desk and a bench lined up against the wall. Even the furniture looked subservient, as though waiting for an audience with the great man. When Balwinder had been thrust inside the room, he knew that he would have to join the ranks of the three chairs and the servile wooden bench, blending with the furniture till the SHO decided to take notice of him. When Balkar Singh did finally raise his head from his important-looking papers and survey Balwinder, it was as though he were doing so from the perch of a pedestal. His questions were merely rhetorical and not meant to be answered, though Balwinder did make the initial mistake of trying to respond to the first one.

'I was only...' Balwinder had begun, when asked why he had not stopped.

Across the table, an authoritative-looking hand had gone up, motioning him to stop. 'You listen to me,' was the message it conveyed. And Balwinder watched, mesmerized, as the hand went on to express this and other such significant sentiments. The hand had a language of its own, as it thumped the table with each probing question put to Balwinder, threatened him with a raised finger, counted off the daring experiences its owner had braved, disdainfully waved aside despicable emotions such as fear, twirled its owner's moustache into a stiff, upright position and finally-curled around the gun in a bold display of power.

Having bombarded Balwinder with a series of questions, the SHO had gone on to tell him all about the hard work he had put in with the police department. When it came to storytelling, policemen, like soldiers who have just returned from the front, had a great deal to say in those days, for many of them had confronted these terrorists who claimed to be fighting for a separate state.

The Indian state had declared that the terrorists were coming from across the nation's borders. The terrorists claimed that they were Indian Punjabis fighting for independence in the same spirit in which their ancestors had fought the country's British colonial rulers. The people said that this was political misrule, that the government's own Frankensteins were merely coming back to haunt it. There was a great deal of debate over how it had all begun, but the cumulative effect was horrific. Beginning with the killings that had taken place soon after the picketing of the link canal, there was a steadily rising death toll every day. And the police was having a rough time. It was only a few years into this dance of death that the police began to retaliate and chalked up its own tally of exterminated terrorists.

'I have killed many of them in encounters,' Balkar Singh had proclaimed. Presumably, these narratives were meant to drive home to Balwinder the depths of his own insignificance. 'I have seen many like you,' the SHO had carried on, in case the point had been missed. Before coming to this little place, he had been posted in Tarn Taran where terrorists sprang up like mushrooms. He was not lying, though, when he said that he had killed many of them in armed encounters. He was merely showing off. He was, indeed, one of those involved in the police operations in areas that were regarded as the hotbeds of terrorism. He had begun by narrating the episode in which he had been at his heroic best. He, along with others, had laid siege to a house where terrorists were holed up. After many rounds of firing from both sides, they had stormed the place, arrested the insurgents and, to bring the situation to its logical culmination, shot them dead.

Since the finer details of the event would otherwise fade into oblivion, Balkar Singh had come back to the site the next day, along with some of his constables and a hired videographer. The poor videographer had been terrified. His normal professional brief did not extend beyond filming local weddings, where his favourite shot usually featured the bride looking into the mirror and pretending to adjust one of the heavy gold earrings she was wearing for the occasion. It was nice, tame work, at the end of which he got to eat a sumptuous meal before going home to edit the wedding film and insert romantic film-song audios as part of the atmospherics.

But Balkar Singh had wanted him to film the terrorist-police encounter, which the SHO would recreate for the benefit of the camera. And, of course, he himself had played the central role—the man heading the charge, fierce, undaunted. Some of his men had re-enacted the roles of the terrorists, while the rest were only required to be themselves. All of them had been very awkward each time the video man switched on his powerful flash. In the searching beam of its light, they had forgotten to swing their arms while walking and had stiffened their facial muscles into a mask. They had ended up looking quite ridiculous. But then acting was not the profession they had chosen to follow. Only Balkar Singh had made up for his lack of histrionic ability by his sheer enthusiasm for the filming enterprise. Balkar Singh had insisted on making this film footage each time he was involved in a terrorist encounter. While the policemen continued to be unresponsive actors, the videographer had soon got the hang of things, realizing that all he had to do was ensure centre stage for the SHO.

'I am going to show these films to my grandchildren,' Balkar Singh had told Balwinder. 'After all, they should know what their grandfather did,' he had continued, proudly thumping that portion of his chest where he assumed his heart to be.

So, he had these 'kiddie' films locked away in a steel

almirah at home. But everyone knew about them and he gradually acquired the reputation of being slightly kooky.

In any case, policemen were a much-disliked species and had acquired the nickname 'mama', inspired by the term referring to the wife's brother, the most disparaged relative in the staunchly patriarchal family tree. With this deep-seated antipathy in place, when it came to taking sides in the years that followed, people sometimes found themselves ranged on the side of violence and insurgency in their haste to distance themselves from the police. But Balwinder could never nurse a grudge, and recounted his brush with the 'mamas', spicing it up with his own brand of ready humour.

Laughter, however, was fast disappearing from the Punjab of the eighties. Balwinder's comic act was increasingly getting interspersed with horror stories. If not in the neighbouring village, then in the one next, killers would leave behind a pile of corpses before vanishing into the night. Balwinder brought back stories of how the migrant labour, coming in from Bihar and Uttar Pradesh to work on the fields, was the target of these attacks. Asleep in one room, they were easy prey. Killing them required neither skill nor planning. With such a profusion of targets, the score was always high. Balwinder said there was some talk of Khalistan, a nation of Sikhs carved out of India, its map extending all the way to the Indian capital.

Ramy too seemed to think that Khalistan was a good idea. He would hold forth on the virtue of a nation of Sikhs. And when during the census a number of schoolteachers had set up camp in the village school to take down the names of all those who qualified to be registered as voters, he had waylaid one of the teachers as she wandered down the corridor looking for the toilet.

'Looking for the loo?' he had asked in his most American English.

The startled teacher had been slightly overwhelmed at being confronted by an English-speaking, jeans-clad inhabitant in a village. The encounter had provided a welcome break from having to scrutinize forms all day. She had started work at eight in the morning and had been taking down names and addresses since then. The whole exercise was unbelievably monotonous. The same names. Most of those who came in for enrolment in the voters' lists were either Ramu or Raju. Sometimes, even the addresses did not vary. It would be House No. 64 for ten applicants on the trot because ten would be sharing a room to be able to save money and send it back to their families in Bihar and Uttar Pradesh.

'Loo?' she asked.

'Toilet,' he explained.

And that provided Ramy with an opening for a conversation.

'You must be wondering what I'm doing here. I belong to this village, though I live in America. I am here to find a bride,' he told her, skipping his usual introduction which required an acquaintance with Annie.

The young schoolteacher became a little coy, weighing the possibilities in the situation—an eligible bachelor settled abroad, in conversation with her. And things became still more confusing when he went on to say, 'I wanted to talk to you about something.'

She coloured a little, not quite sure what she should expect. 'Yes?' she said.

'Don't enrol these Biharis as voters,' said the young man who had come back home after ten years. 'They don't belong here. Let them go back to their own state and vote.'

'But they have lived here most of their lives,' she protested.

'True. But once you register them as residents here, they will never go away. And they will end up spoiling the atmosphere here, if we allow them to stay too long.'

She wanted to point out to him the shifting ground from which he was making this statement, but she did not argue.

Anyway, only a few days after this conversation, Ramy left the deteriorating tranquillity of the village and went back to his chosen home.

Soon, there was a pile of bodies in this village too. It had its own death toll to report. The crop in the fields was a carpet of very deep green under the blazing sun, but a dark veil for the killers at night. They would hide amidst the tall sugar cane, then simply walk away to safety. The landscape became an increasingly tormented one. When dusk descended, it was time to go indoors, time to find other reserves of entertainment, which Michael did not have. So, the evening meant sitting around and listening for sounds. Michael found himself idle once again. Not with a plastered leg propped up on a stool, but frozen into stillness, the sensation of fear creeping up his limbs and enveloping him in a white sheet. He was not used to stillness.

The fear began to spread. It was not just the migrant labour any more. It could be anyone, and that brought fear right to the doorstep. Michael's grandmother would bolt and bar the doors and windows early in the evening. Echoes of evenings spent behind a wall of sandbags, while the bombers roared through the sky, came back to Michael. He had been a child then and the war with Pakistan had seemed like a strange intervention in his life. The siren that signalled danger had sounded and he had even thrown up when he tried to stuff a hanky into his mouth according to the precaution drill they were taught during the day. But there could be no precautions against this in-house war.

One day, Balwinder's mother turned up. The bolts had to be undone, the bar stretching across the door lifted out of the way. The door was opened just a crack, then thrown wide open to let in the tumult. She was hysterical, a wailing banshee, and incoherent. Something had happened to Balwinder.

In the golden-turning-into-brown evening, Balwinder had been walking back to the village with a friend. This was a land where, at one time, the only ominous things about darkness were the shapes conjured up from innocuous trees and bushes by the willing imagination of childhood. But this was no childhood. This was a world in which the shapes materialized into reality. And in this land terrorized by the night, dusk was the hour when everyone scurried home. Three men had stepped out from behind the bushes and lined up Balwinder and his friend along the broken path to the village. 'Are you Sikhs?' they had asked. This was all about the Khalistan business, thought Balwinder and nodded. Yes, they were. They were Sikhs, anyway, though of the 'convertible' kind, a term born, perhaps, of the great Punjabi love for the automobile. Both sported beards, but wore their hair in a close-cropped style. A turban would have established them as Sikhs, though it was meant to be tied over uncut hair wound into a knot on top of the head and held in place by a comb in conformity with the religion's five mandates. In fact, the very act of snipping hair was seen as a form of defilement. If Balwinder were to be judged by the three other mandates, which required a practising believer to carry a sword and wear a steel bangle and underpants of a particular length, he would fall short on many counts. The beard and the short hair lent Balwinder and his friend a certain ambiguity as far as their identity was concerned. But minus the turban, they could not have escaped this inquisition. 'Why have you cut your hair then? And why aren't you wearing a turban?' the muffled faces before them had asked. There could be no answer to that. The question had hung in the air between them, stalking them with watchful eyes. They dared not twitch even a muscle in response to the menacing inquiry about their lack of a turban, lest it be the wrong muscle, inadvertently conveying an answer that might prove inappropriate for the occasion. Time had held its breath too. The tension of the moment had been somewhat dissipated by the arrival of yet another unfortunate walking back to the village. He was stopped, lined up and questioned. Once again, the tension began to mount. The air was again dense with an unanswered question. The third man had no answer either. The 'convertible' Sikh was not an unusual presence in any village. In fact, many young men in the village chose to cut their hair short while sporting a beard. It was an optional Sikh identity.

When the fourth man without a turban appeared on the road, the moment had suddenly broken loose and exploded, leaving the protagonists with no time to think. The fourth man, on being stopped, had started shouting hysterically for help. The men with the guns were startled into a response. They shot down the man, cutting the hysterics short in mid-flight. Then they turned to the others and blindly shot at them too. Balwinder's companion was killed right there. The other was wounded in the hand. A fleeing Balwinder had caught a bullet in his spine. That was how his mother had found him.

The blood was very, very red. It was not a sight that Balwinder's mother should have been subjected to. But there are no options when a son has to be lifted off the sodden ground. She had arrived screaming for help at Michael's door. It was a long haul to the hospital in town and an even longer one through the rest of the days to come. There was no getting away from blood and pain. On the hospital bed next to Balwinder's was the victim of a bomb blast. Most of the man was in tatters. Piecing together life and limb was a painful process. The patient's old father stood by, while doctors worked on him. Michael had never been through anything like this before, this in-your-face encounter with life. He had no idea what it meant to be heroic. His own heroism had been fairly circumscribed, a spurious heroism of the kind that can take you over lumpy roads and dusty dirt tracks, but will stop short in the face of all else. The fear came flooding back into his veins, drowning him, as he bit into his fingernails, which also tasted of fear.

He watched Balwinder come out of it—a man in a wheelchair, his legs frozen into immobility forever. And now he would never grow his hair because the simple, everyday business of handling his daily routine had acquired colossal dimensions. Everything that represented the humdrum pattern of living, washing, eating, sleeping and moving about, everything had become a monumental chore. A knot in the hair and a turban would merely have been an added burden. Where was the time or the energy to introduce yet another dimension to the already laborious step-by-step countdown that began from the moment he woke up in the morning and ended when he went to bed at night? His mother was a whirl of frenetic activity as she attended to the fulfilment of his needs. Balwinder would only laugh, 'Turban? Fear? This is the same old village. Why should I bother?' He still told jokes about his attempts to learn English in the village school. But much had changed. He no longer launched into the spirited sound simulation of the Americanized Indian. Nor did Michael have it in him to ask. There were plenty of adjustments to be made. He could not ride on the spinning wheel of the tractor. He could not stride through the greening fields and another farmhand had to be trained to take up all that he had been doing.

Michael's view of the world around him too had transformed from one that had him alone sitting in a wheelchair, to a world of many wheelchairs with just as many people folded into them. It was a sea of people in wheelchairs, criss-crossing through hospital wards and out into the streets. Michael did not know how to deal with this altered perception. That was why when he returned in the midst of Karuna's wedding preparations he had that haunted look about him. It was a look that made everyone ask, 'What's the matter? Are you all right? Have you seen a ghost or something?'

'Beta, what's wrong? Tell me, what's wrong,' his mother urged him. But she wore such a preoccupied air that he was not likely to tell her anything, even if he had been so inclined. In any case, most things had to be withheld from parents.

So, Michael merely replied, 'Nothing. Why *don't* you just leave me alone?'

'But I am your mother,' she protested. That was the very reason he would not tell her anything. But his relatives would not stop asking him questions, over and over again. Even if he bumped into the same aunt thrice in one day, out she would come with her query each time. What could he tell them, all those aunts and uncles? What was there to say anyway? Michael had little command over the niceties of language that would have enabled him to describe the exact nuance of what he felt. Nor would the usual 'Oye' suffice.

9

A Wedding in the Family

Karuna's wedding day was drawing close and relatives had begun to arrive in expectation of a good time. There were droves of them swarming all over the house in high spirits. Behind every door, there were uncles and aunts unpacking suitcases, hanging up their best finery, brushing off a non-existent particle of dust from the expensive new fabric and gearing up for many evenings of revelry.

The men would be in achkans or three-piece suits and the women laden with family heirlooms, their lehngas weighed down with gold embroidery that had been carefully folded in tissue paper and preserved from the onslaught of time. The load of family jewels would stretch the women's earlobes into skin as fine as parchment. A jhoomar would adorn their hair, a tikka dangling on their foreheads, just below the parting in their hair, each piece studded with pearls and gems. Their grey hair and wrinkled skins offered a startling contrast to this overload of ornaments, but then, some things just had to be done in the interest of upholding tradition. However, as things turned out, they were not required to obey the call of tradition. In fact, it was brazen modernity that crossed their unsuspecting paths. Nothing—not the suitcases their minions had packed for them to bring here, nor the effusiveness of their manner, adapted to suit the mood of the festivities—nothing had prepared them for what did happen.

Karuna, however, was quite prepared. Or, at least, she must have been, considering the way she handled it. She had decided to marry Croaky...well Gurjit, to grant the enterprise the measure of respectability it deserved, and to go by what the wedding card said: Gurjit Singh. As love stories go, she knew that she had taken the best of a set of bad options. And so Karuna could be pardoned if she did not exactly come across as an excited bride-to-be. She contemplated the flurry around her as though it were being caused by something else. She did not see herself as the centre of all the attention. She had a way of slipping out of an inquiring circle of relatives while they continued a conversation, forgetting that they had started out with her as the object of their concern.

Her mother would be constantly hovering around her, wanting to know if she had bought chunnis to match the clothes the tailor had just brought in.

'Beta, have you given your dupattas to Hussein for dyeing?'

'Haanji,' she would answer in the affirmative, 'but I need to go and fetch them.'

'Michael is no longer riding his bike. Otherwise, he could have taken you there. Only a two-wheeler can comfortably reach Hussein's shop in the bazaar. Wonder what has happened to Michael, though. Anyway, I will ask your father to send somebody for the dupattas.'

'Haanji, but, maybe, I will take a rickshaw and go and fetch them myself after the tailor has left.' Hussein's shop in the narrowest of lanes could be spotted from a long distance away, what with its colourful profusion of dyed turbans strung up outside to dry, like the sails of ships at sea as they catch the wind and swell to a fullness ready to burst into movement. Hussein's feet had developed bunions and his ankles were swollen from having to stand for hours on end before a huge cauldron of boiling water, in which a stark white dupatta or turban gradually drank in the colour from the swirling dye and underwent a metamorphosis. All those hues he gave to the turbans and the dupattas—the red and blue and green and yellow and purple—had seeped into his hands, resulting in a colour mix that defied description. It was the colour of Holi revellers after they had finished celebrating the festival.

Karuna thought the trip to Hussein might be an effective way of leaving behind all those aunts and uncles. But first she had to attend to the tailor.

The old tailor would arrive on his bicycle. He was bent double with age and the hunched back that was almost like a haversack strapped onto his shoulders would have put many out of action. But not Santokh Singh. As far back as Karuna could remember he had always been as old as he seemed now. On the one occasion she had gone to his one-room hovel near the city's waste-water drain, she had been unable to accept the reality of the young Santokh Singh, smiling down from the photographs on the mouldy walls—a Santokh Singh with a black beard, equally black and bushy eyebrows and a ramrod-straight back. He had stitched clothes for two generations of maharanis from the royal house of Patiala, arranging the gentle swirls of the Patiala salwar, pleat by painstaking pleat. The Patiala salwar swallowed up yards and yards of cloth. It was these many yards of royal fabric that Santokh Singh had handled with the dexterity of a magician. The photographs on his walls told of better days, when Santokh Singh was the designated royal house tailor. He might have been a reasonably well-off man, if he had handled his life and finances with the same caution as he did the fine silks. But here he was, living in an area that was actually an encroachment on the city's sewerage, the clogging of which resulted in a periodic drowning of the city during the monsoons. However, there was nowhere else to go and when an inordinately heavy monsoon swept in, his house would be a virtual ocean. Pots and pans would start putting out to sea and the family would have to wade through the waters to rescue their belongings. The pictures hanging on the wall had survived most of these deluges, but for the damp that crawled up to them, tinting them a sepia brown. Santokh Singh, however, was a temperamental artist who drank himself silly every night. So what if he was stitching clothes and not applying brushstrokes on canvas? That was an incidental matter of detail.

As children, they would watch him get off his bicycle and marvel at the agility with which he managed it. They never really watched him mount it again because they never had the patience to wait for the protracted transaction between their mother and the tailor to be over. By the time she had taken the tailored garments from him, tried them on, suggested a few alterations, handed him some more material for new outfits to be made, decided on their necklines, hemlines and piping and gone indoors to fetch the money to pay him what she owed, some other source of excitement would have claimed their attention. How he managed to get on to his bicycle remained forever a mystery.

Then, as Karuna grew up, he took to stitching her clothes as well. The marvel of his mobility was not just a childish preoccupation with Karuna and her brother. Their interest merely heightened with age—his and theirs.

The tailor wore a pair of spectacles with thick lenses. He squinted through these at each new piece of fabric that was handed to him, caressing its texture as though acquainting himself with a new-found friend. But his calloused hands did not look as if they could be sensitive to any form of subtlety. He carried a half-bottle of liquor in the side pocket of his shirt, which seemed to have been designed just for the purpose. The kheesa was cut deeper than usual and fashioned from stronger fabric so that it could bear the weight of his half-bottle, his adia. And in spite of the fortification of his custom-made kheesa, his perpetual complaint was that his pocket had been picked. That, of course, was meant as some sort of a convoluted explanation for the half-bottle of booze peeping out of his pocket.

'I just bought this adia because I was terribly upset about losing so much money from my pocket. Perhaps, you could advance me some money towards my tailoring charges, now that I have lost everything,' he would suggest.

'Master ji, you will merely drink that up as well,' Karuna's mother would argue, knowing all the while that she would ultimately give him some money.

Master ji would touch each of his ears in turn, disclaiming any such vice. 'Na, na, Beeba!' he would protest.

But his seams never went wrong and he had sworn to Karuna's mother that he would not allow himself to die till he had finished stitching her daughter's wedding finery. 'I am not about to die,' he would promise, waving his hand in a gesture that dismissed the very thought of mortality.

'You had better not,' Karuna's mother warned him, mock-serious. 'Otherwise, we'll have to send Karuna off as a bride dressed in old rags.'

Though each time he came he looked more bent and drunken than on the previous occasion, his seams still traced an immaculately steady path. For a bride-to-be he always kept a lot of margin in the seams. This would irk most young girls who regarded their streamlined figures as impervious to change. And much to the disbelief of the prospective young bride, he would say, 'Girls always put on weight after they are married.' The finality of his pronouncement nipped all argument in the bud.

He had just brought in yet another consignment of perfectly stitched suits and handed them over to Karuna for trial.

In the midst of an engulfing cloud of veils and silks, Karuna deciphered a whispered message going around. Everyone seemed to know something that she did not. She was sensitive to the murmur of undertones. 'Shh…!' she heard, as she paused by a group of uncles and aunts. Each time she passed them, their warning hiss revealed the guilty shock of being taken unawares. But the aspirated 'Shh…' of her parents betrayed a hint of anxiety. Just as Karuna's habitual self-effacement would not allow her to see herself as the focus of happy attention, it would not have crossed her mind that she could be the cause of some worried, last-minute reorganization of plans. Finally, she decided to ask her mother what it was that everyone was whispering about.

'Is something wrong?' she asked.

Her mother's eyes cast about for help to answer this one

and seeing none available, she merely said, 'Don't worry. Your father and I will take care of everything.'

Her father, for his part, told her to keep out of things that were not her concern. But she was concerned. Then Michael told her that Gurjit alias Croaky had politely told her parents that though going to work on a two-wheeler was not a problem, a car was essential when he took his wife along on social rounds in the evening to visit friends. In fact, a longish list had followed his initial polite request. Written down in black and white, it might have unfurled like a roll of toilet paper.

'Don't you worry. Dad is figuring it out,' Michael reassured Karuna.

'Oh no! How can I not worry? First Mummy and now you are asking me not to worry. But this is terrible! I have to do something about it.'

'What could you possibly do? Now, don't you go and do anything silly! He is entitled to a dowry, anyway, now dat he is in the civil services. So stop brooding about it!'

'But imagine! He wants a car!' exclaimed the wondering Karuna.

Lalli had no objections to buying his future son-in-law a car and much else besides, as a wedding gift. But in those days, cars could not be picked off a department-store shelf like a bag of popcorn. That explained the conclaves of grey heads huddled together that Karuna had chanced upon. She stepped outdoors to ponder this development. Should she go and talk to Aunt Veer who had steered clear of the build-up to the festivities? But then, she knew that she would only be met with an 'I told you so', which would not really help. She could not wait for Minnie either, though her cousin was the one who had helped her hold the door shut against the masculine might of Blubber Lips. Immediate events called for a similarly spirited barricading.

Minnie was in Delhi, working on her postgraduate degree in English Literature. She was the only one who brought to Karuna whiffs of another world, a world that smelt of samosas and tea in overpopulated canteens bursting at the seams with excited voices driven by tutorial deadlines, a world of gossipy late nights and unbrushed teeth in early-morning classes. It was a world that Karuna was much too timorous to enter. She wished she had some of the aplomb that came so easily to Minnie. She wished, for instance, that she could burst through a door after opening it with a bold flourish instead of giving it a tentative prod to peep around its edge and take a surreptitious look at what she was about to encounter, before feeling her way in hesitantly. Minnie could swing through bank doors to find out what kind of loans were available to students for studies abroad or slam the door shut when she stormed out after an argument with her mother. Minnie could accost strangers with queries, while all Karuna could manage was to pigeon-toe her way up to the unknown before being struck dumb by its awesomeness.

That was why Minnie could not believe what she heard when her worried aunt finally got through to her on the hostel telephone after a finger-breaking routine on 'dial' and 'redial'. It was never easy to get through to a girls' hostel. There were those interminable, sitting-curled-up-in-the-chair telephone conversations happening most of the time, and the girl in the chair, feeding monosyllables into the mouthpiece for the next one hour, was usually oblivious to the waiting groups outside. Minnie had just come in after a long walk and had meant to sit down to study, since she was going to be spending the next few days in Patiala. Then, she had been told of this phone call waiting for her. She had been urged to hurry, because there were many others expecting phone calls with infinitely more promise than a conversation with an aunt from Patiala. She went downstairs, anticipating nothing more than a reminder to get back well in time for the wedding in the house.

What she had not expected was the frantic voice at the other end. Her aunt began by asking Minnie to come over immediately, which was quite along expected lines. But the fact was that she was now being asked to go for a wedding that was not going to happen.

'Can you come and talk to Karuna? We can't understand what's got into her head. And just when the invitation cards have already been dispatched and the house is full of people!' her hysterical aunt cried, as her eye fell on a bunch of aunts entering the room.

'But what's happened?' Minnie said, more to herself than to her aunt.

'You're the only one who can make her see sense,' her aunt continued. 'She listens to you. Everyone is so upset. Her father has not stopped raging since. Tell her that girls from good families don't do things like this.'

'Don't do what? What has she done?' Minnie still did not know what her aunt was talking about.

After more such confused exchanges, her aunt told Minnie that Karuna had rung up Croaky and asked to meet him. They had arranged to meet at an innocuous tea shop in the ad hoc little market that had sprung up near the roundabout with the fountain. The venue lay on the route that she and Croaky had taken to college every day. Of course, her aunt was not privy to all the details. Minnie extracted the ribcage of the story from her. The fleshed-out version she obtained from Karuna herself, when she reached Patiala on the first available bus.

And so, Minnie found that Karuna had called Croaky to this tea shop, where the light from zero-watt bulbs struggled against opaque paper lanterns. There did not seem to be any ostensible reason for having a dimly lit restaurant, since there never were any young couples sitting around in the unyielding darkness. The town was far too small to allow an anonymous rendezvous. Everyone knew everyone. So, all that this dimly lit place could boast of was boisterous students from the medical college close by, who came in for some respite from the rigours of study. They would probably have been much happier in a brightly lit-up, perky environment. But it never really struck them to offer their suggestions to the management which would have gladly obliged, since the students were their only clientele. Anyway, Karuna had chosen this place simply because it was the first name that came to mind. She was not looking to hold Croaky's hand. Nor had she selected this restaurant because she wanted to pass unnoticed. In fact, none of these calculations had anything to do with what was going on in her mind. She could only think of that long list, which if written down would unfurl like toilet paper.

She sat in the twilight gloom of the restaurant, unaware of the spectacle she might have created as a woman alone at a table in small-town Patiala, and waited for Croaky. She had no idea as to what she was going to say to him. Perhaps, she could ask him to roll up his list and use it to clean up. She was very angry. Perhaps, it was an anger she had accumulated over the years, kept in cold storage for just such an exigency. She knew she was not part of a love story. But she was not ready to see herself as the pitiable protagonist of gossip-tainted tales exchanged across the hedge on pleasant winter afternoons.

Croaky had no idea, of course, that he was about to unleash such a flash flood of fury. He swaggered in nonchalantly with the confidence of a man who had conquered the world or, at least, most of it. He had not understood the point of this meeting. But he was in an indulgent mood and had agreed to come to this rendezvous. In fact, his sensibilities were rather tickled by the furtiveness of the enterprise, though it was not a sentiment he would have liked to acknowledge. He was merely being magnanimous, he thought. He walked into the darkness of the interior and peered around, surveying the place with smug satisfaction, happy to find that there were plenty of people who would see him having coffee with his young bride and envy him his good fortune. He was quite sure that Karuna would already be there, waiting for him. And she was. He sauntered up to her, the twirl in his moustache perked up at just the right angle. She, of course, had decided to dispense with all courtesy, surging ahead on the intensity of her anger. So, she took him head-on, as he was grandly lowering himself into the chair opposite hers. Her question caught him just as his posterior was a few inches from touching base and he landed, finally, on the seat of the chair with a thud. The incipient doctors heard the thud and went back to their banter, but they were to hear more.

'Just because the invitation cards have already been distributed, you think you can do whatever you like.' This was delivered not as a question, but as a statement of fact. It was also articulated in a loud, accusing voice, which the aspiring doctors heard clearly enough. *'Don't think I can't cancel the wedding, even now,'* she continued. And this line, rendered at that particular pitch, became history in the family annals. It made everyone sit up and notice her. Minnie, aunts, uncles—everyone. In fact, the whole town. It was not as though these were the only two sentences uttered in the course of that rendezvous, but in all subsequent texts of that meeting it would be those first two lines, delivered at the peak of Karuna's fury, which would be gone over with a highlighter: 'And you know what she said…!'

The two of them then went on to have a smallish argument, Croaky still reeling with the surprise quotient of the attack. He mumbled some incoherence about custom and tradition and even tried to turn the thing around, so that the list would begin to sound like a big favour done to Karuna.

'After all, you are used to travelling in a car,' he reminded her.

'Buy one yourself,' she shot back. 'Don't you dare come up with any more fancy demands!'

'I will, I will,' he said, at a loss for any further elaboration. And as an afterthought, he added, 'I won't,' in response to the latter half of her statement. In any case, there was not very much he could say. The exchange went on in more muted tones.

'You expect my parents to give you money to marry me. Big favour you are doing me, haan?' said an unrelenting Karuna.

'Oh, no, I love you! That's why I'm marrying you,' said a nervous Croaky.

'I no longer believe in all this love business. How dare you do this to me and to my parents!' Her voice trembled with anger, as she tried to speak in undertones.

'Okay, okay,' Croaky said placatingly.

'No, it is not okay. In fact, I am going to call off this marriage,' said the raging Karuna.

'How can you do that? Everything is already fixed!' Croaky had been quite confident to start with, feeling that all he had to do was allow her to let off steam. It took him a while to realize that the reservoirs of her steam were seemingly inexhaustible. And then he began to plead.

'Please...please... I have followed you so faithfully on a bicycle all these years,' Croaky ventured, laying claim to the one steady input that he had given to this relationship. 'Please marry me! I love you!' A contrite Croaky was trying desperately to resurrect the magic of his initial courtship.

But Karuna was well versed in saying an unrelenting 'No'.

'You cannot actually do this, you know.'

'I can.'

And that is just what Karuna did. She went on to tell Croaky that the marriage actually stood cancelled. Then she stormed out of the restaurant, leaving a whole bunch of would-be doctors looking at her retreating back, not to mention the open-mouthed Croaky who just sat there awhile, wondering what to do next. He watched her for a bit from the glass front of the restaurant, before looking around to check if indeed there were as many people in the restaurant as he had thought there were when he had made his initial grand entry, wondering all the while how much of the exchange they had heard and what they made of it. After a decent interval that would allay any impression of him scurrying after her, he got up and swaggered out, trying to look every inch the man in control. The doctors had gone into a huddle over the incident they had just witnessed. 'Wow yaar! Some girl!' a few of them had exclaimed. Some of the others were not so sure.

A determined Karuna came home to break the news to her parents and, subsequently, to the concerned collection of uncles and aunts. All hell broke loose. Her mother thrashed about helplessly. Her father threatened dire consequences. 'I will shoot you till you are dead,' he roared, wagging his finger at her. He made a move to go and fetch his weapon but one of the uncles wrestled him down into a chair. Each time the uncle loosened his grip, Lalli would spring up yet again, shouting, 'Let me get to her, let me get my hands on her throat—till she is dead!' Michael just stood by, the eternal observer. Her uncles and aunts repacked their finery and slowly slinked away after they had made all the appropriate interjections and exclamations. But Karuna was quite sure that she was not going to marry Croaky. She had cowered under many an angry deluge, ducking into the darkness under the staircase. She knew that life did continue afterwards. She was not going to let the anger, now directed against her, lay down the rules of her existence.

And that was when her mother had rung up Minnie, although she had recognized a determination in her daughter's eyes and, therefore, did not really expect the aborted marriage plans to be revived. Even as she looked every inch the shattered mother of a girl gone haywire, in some deep vault within her that she herself had never opened, there was a standing ovation. However, just then, there was no time to explore any of it, because a marriage had to be formally undone, even before it actually took place. That was about as much hard work as the preparations for the wedding itself. And by the time Minnie arrived on the scene, things had settled down and were smoothly in rewind.

A wedding in reverse! As children, Minnie and Monty had often pleaded for 'Just one more time!' on a backward run of Lalli and Maasi's wedding reel. They had come upon this wonder quite by chance. Lalli had a couple of projectors, bought, of course, during his projector-buying phase in those days when films were rolls tightly wound around spools. You could hold them up against the light and identify people. The sealed mystery of the video cassette and the VCP was not around then. So, naturally, Lalli had stocked up on projectors and spools. They now sat accumulating dust in the storeroom. He had pulled them out at one family dinner and offered to show the children his wedding film, more out of a desire to find a legitimate reason to tinker with his gadgetry, than to play the favourite uncle. The projector was hoisted on to a long-legged table and some thick books had to be found to support the projecting eye at the correct angle, so that it focussed squarely on the wall. Maasi had some bound volumes of *Woman and Home,* recipes and knitting patterns that she had clipped and preserved for many years. And it was these that she now fished out from the store to provide a prop for the projector.

The wall, where the film was to be beamed, had Lalli's picture smiling down at everyone in his Freemason's regalia. That had to be taken down with the right amount of ceremony, dusted carefully, handled reverentially and gently placed against the cushions on the sofa, so that Lalli, the Freemason, could continue to benignly survey the occupants of the room. While Lalli, the Wonder Uncle, ran the spool in reverse to get it to the right tautness, there on the wall were the guests at his wedding, magically bringing food out of their mouths and putting it on the plate. Half-eaten chicken drumsticks became whole, viands on the plate multiplied instead of being depleted, waiters took food back from the plates of the guests and stashed it into the serving dishes. Minnie and her cousins had laughed hysterically. They watched the wedding ceremony where Maasi and Lalli went round the holy book in reverse gear. It had been so much more fun than the staid sight of rows of people either gorging themselves on chicken drumsticks, which constitute the staple of a rich Punjabi wedding, or just standing around, grinning foolishly into the camera.

'Just one more time,' the children had pleaded.

'You children like this?' asked the magnanimous Lalli. And he had obliged, running his wedding reel in reverse and quite enjoying the absurdity of it all.

Minnie was now a witness to a real-life wedding in reverse. The caterer had to be rung up and instructed not to prepare the wedding feast, the florist had to be told not to bring flowers and guests had to be informed that the event was not taking place, the implication being that they should not come. Of course, the bridegroom had already been told. What was left was only rearguard action. Karuna maintained both a ramrod-straight back and a stiffly starched façade through the entire proceedings. She was the one who made the telephone call to Croaky's parents, telling them that she would not marry their son. She did so quite unflinchingly and even went on to tell them why. Minnie was told that Croaky's father had taken the call and the volume of his anger at the other end had travelled down the telephone line and arrived almost undiminished at Karuna's end.

'I paid money to make him an officer. I educated him,' he shouted, implying that he needed to be compensated for lost dividends on an investment. 'I will see to you, shameless creature!' he exclaimed, angry thoughts in Punjabi crowding his brain, which he then proceeded to translate into verbal English.

Karuna merely said, 'I do not want to marry your son.' But her cool manner merely aggravated the fury at the other end of the line.

'All of you bitches, whores!' he cried, throwing the niceties of gender to the wind, for he was referring to Karuna's entire family.

Karuna remained silent, choosing not to respond. Then Croaky's father decided to drop his attempt at English sophistication and launched into abusive Punjabi. Everyone in the room heard him and winced but Karuna did not buckle. She simply held the steaming mouthpiece at a little distance from her ear. This was the new, seasoned Karuna, tempered by a life under the staircase, who had bounced out of hiding to become a toughie. Perhaps, she had surprised herself too.

Needless to say, the bridegroom-not-to-be was incensed. One is not really sure if it was his heart that was broken or his ego that lay in splinters, but he expressed his displeasure through the medium that had become a rage in those years. Like some weak-hearted men, he loved weapons and had been looking around to acquire one. It was easy in those days. He merely had to mention his fancy to one of his subordinates in the office. The man used to come in from an outlying village and had asked him in a whisper, 'Sir, would you like a small pistol? I have asked Sukha in my village. He knows a number of these fellows, terrorists, and they say it is no problem getting Sir a pistol. Only thing, Sir must never tell anyone whom Sir got it from.' Buying a pistol was, of course, a hush-hush affair, but the subordinate was always in conspiratorial mode, even when he was telling him of a routine file he had placed on his table. 'Sir, this is the housing file you had asked for yesterday. I have been able to find it.' He would bring his mouth close to his boss's ear and deliver the tidings, while the hot exhaust from his breath and the excited spray of saliva inflamed Croaky's ears. He would move his swivel chair out of range. But the man was naturally inclined to be secretive and would inch forward till he was within spitting distance once again. In this instance, however, it was only right that he speak to Croaky about the pistol in hushed undertones because this was going to be an illegal transaction. It was a different matter that Croaky subsequently chose to make a public display of his weapon.

A woman had delivered the pistol to him. When she arrived, he had nearly shooed her away, taking her to be yet another salesgirl with a door-to-door sales pitch, for which he had no patience. She was a young woman and carried a bundle of clothes slung over her shoulder. But even as he ordered her off his premises, she had determinedly squatted on his front veranda and untied the bundle she carried. She had offered to show him embroidered veils and cushion covers. The bright colours of phulkari embroidery had burst forth as soon as she untied the knot, but she had also managed to point to a pistol hidden among the veils. At first, he had frozen into stone, imagining that she had come to kill him. That would not have been unusual. The only novelty would have lain in the fact that it would be the first terrorist crime committed by a woman, since, so far, women had operated only as couriers. Poor Croaky had already been shot down by one woman at the threshold of marriage. His sensitive heart would not have been able to survive another female onslaught. He soon discovered, however, that she was here only to deliver a weapon to him and so he took heart once again. That, then, was how Croaky came to acquire a Star pistol assembled in Darra, Pakistan.

The sound of a pistol shot right outside Karuna's house brought them all rushing to the windows. And as they peered out, they saw Croaky standing at the gate, brandishing a pistol.

'Just send that bitch out! I will settle scores with her. Who does she think she is? A princess?' he shouted in that same hoarse voice. While the hoarse voice had given to the sentiment of love a certain fullness, it was entirely misplaced in the attempt to spew obscenities. He sounded like a nervous, ageing gangster trying to survive on his bygone bravado.

They had no idea what he intended to do next. But soon, Croaky had stalked off. While the violence swirling around him—the daily death toll that seemed to write newspaper headlines in blood, the threat that lurked just below the thin veneer of life—provided him with the lexicon of the gun, Croaky was still the mean but gutless bystander who only managed to throw his little stone from the anonymity of mob frenzy. He came to Karuna's gatepost for many evenings thereafter and fired that one signature shot. The whole family came to accept the sound as part of their everyday lives. Lalli would stretch in bed, waking up from an extended afternoon siesta and wait for his evening tea. He knew that the sound at the gate was a trigger for the servants to set the water to boil and prepare the tea tray. Sometimes he would languidly get out of the bed to catch a glimpse of Croaky's retreating back.

10

...And a Funeral

That was probably why no one heard the sound of yet another gunshot indoors. Or, heard it, perhaps, but did not find anything untoward about it. The sheer everydayness of its echo had diluted the horror. The daily newspapers that came hot off the stands were also steaming with the aftermath of the report of anonymous guns: '12 shot dead in Ludhiana', 'Bloody heap with chapattis in hand', '11 of a community killed in Punjab', '11 massacred in farmhouse', 'Women, children also killed', 'Red alert in Punjab'. A small square inch of space in their sensibilities was cultivated to deal precisely with all this. It also had to be quarantined, so that it wouldn't spill over and infect everything else. The rest of life could then proceed unhindered. But the sound had come to their doorstep and turned the corner into the bedroom. The carefully constructed compartments inside burst dams and in the vortex of this swirl of horror lay Michael, his hand, holding a gun, still draped across the dresser against which he had fallen. There was no explanatory note, but the evidence was overwhelming. It was a suicide and the mirror atop the dresser, tilted on its elaborately carved supports, was leaning over to catch a glimpse. It was an act played out with the mirror as the chosen audience.

The mirror had seen better days when Lalli was a young man and spent time preening before it or checking the fit of a new pair of trousers. It had also captured the image of Lalli accosting the young maid in the house and exhausting his sexual energies on her with considerable huffing and puffing. Lalli liked to see himself in the role of the indefatigable stud. His sex life had provided the mirror with a purpose.

Michael, on the other hand, normally kept his eyes tightly shut, even as he stood in front of the mirror to comb his hair. He would dig his finger into the jar of gel, gouge out a substantial quantity of the contents, smear it on to the hollow of his palm and rub it into his disobedient hair. He then combed it into a servitude which, however, conformed to no particular style. The mirror was, perhaps, justifiably indignant at the indifference to which Michael subjected it, thereby nullifying its existence.

However, this evening with Michael was scheduled to be different. He had looked into the mirror much oftener than he usually did. He had then pulled open the top drawer of the dresser and come up with a pistol. A small, unobtrusive, fit-in-the-palm thing that he held up to his temple. This time he had not closed his eyes and shut out his own reflection. The mirror, of course, felt the helplessness of the inanimate. Michael leaned forward to stare harder into his own eyes. Who knows what he thought as he aimed the pistol at his head? The reflected image certainly did not, as it stood encircled by the heavy rosewood frame. It merely did what the protagonist asked it to do. It very obediently lifted its hand, locked around the pistol, to its head. It would never have pulled the trigger of its own accord. Not while Michael looked at himself with such quizzical eyes. Not while the last rays of a pleasant winter sun peeped in at the windows. Michael had pulled the trigger and the image had to do likewise. The mirror had leaned forward to watch him fall. It was then too shaken to move back into its upright position.

His parents had looked out of the window casually when the shot rang out, expecting to see Croaky swaggering down the road. It was when they did not see him that their senses had sharpened, focusing on the direction from which the sound had come. Lalli had readied his weapon for a sure-fire confrontation with that damned Croaky who, he was certain, had entered the house. And with the shadows slowly lengthening, every corner seemed to spring a Croaky on him. With a stance that announced a readiness for battle, he moved through the house. Down the stairs, into the drawing room, the lobby, the family room. He burst into each room, certain of coming upon the rejected bridegroom each time. But the house seemed to have settled into its usual silence, as though the pistol shot had never been, as though the walls and drapes and sofas had swallowed up the sound without leaving a trace. His wife followed him at a distance, not comfortable about letting him stalk the intruder on his own.

It was in the bedroom, Michael's bedroom, that the nightmare seized them. It was a moment that scored grooves of sorrow in their veins and would do so forever afterwards. Of course, they rushed him to the hospital. The doctor felt his pulse and shook his head sadly. That was when the reality sank in. A hospital is not a place that allows mourners a unique status on account of their sorrow because everyone is weighed down by their own burden. Particularly at a time when terrorism-afflicted Punjab was wearily registering its seemingly countless dead every day.

So Mike's parents became just a pair among all those others in the hospital who were also grappling with death.

On the bed next to Mike's lay the corpse of a little girl, surrounded by a bunch of strangely silent people—elongated faces, gaping eyes, mouths caving inwards. 'He's gone, he's gone,' Mike's mother kept saying to these shadows, over and over again. The shadows did not respond. They only became longer.

The dead child was Paramjit's daughter. Of course, Mike's mother would not know him. Nor would Lalli. How could they? He belonged to the hooded world of those who struck terror by night. And it was here in the hospital that their disparate worlds had come together over death—a brief encounter, before they parted again to go their separate sorrowful ways.

The dead child's mother was Nirvair Kaur who had grown up in two tiny, mud-plastered rooms, hemmed in by a small courtyard, in a little village on the outskirts of Patiala. She had blossomed into a young woman just when the call for insurgency had sprouted a number of young men carrying guns. One of these young men was Paramjit Singh, designated area commander in the terrorist fighting force. He had knocked on Nirvair Kaur's door one foggy night.

Nirvair had been forced to accompany the midnight callers. Paramjit had married her and set her up in a house in the neighbouring village. He would come and go, his underworld activity making frequent demands on his time. But she had been widowed soon after the birth of her child. Paramjit had died in a gun battle with the police, the kind that SHO Balkar Singh recorded on video cassettes to be viewed by his grandchildren. She had then started living with Bishandi, yet another young man carrying a gun. But this time, both Bishandi and Nirvair had died. The police, however, had been spared this particular encounter, because Paramjit's terrorist outfit had been furious. Their morality had obviously been outraged by what they described as Nirvair's defection to Bishandi's bed. They said she was 'a slut, a whore, a prostitute, a woman of loose morals' who was 'only waiting for an opportunity to go to bed with another man'.

At the police station, the officer on duty had said much the same thing when Nirvair's parents had gone to make a complaint about her abduction after the midnight knock. The policeman stationed behind the desk, with his paunch wedged in firmly behind the table top, had said, 'All these women who go away with the terrorists are immoral. They marry one and after he dies, they marry another.' So, the parents had not gone back to the police station when they heard of her death. There did not seem to be any point. The now-dead baby girl was delivered back to the reluctant grandparents when the mother died. 'Better dead, perhaps,' thought the grandparents. They were not really grieving.

Obviously, Mike had also thought that it was better to be dead. But his mother wished she knew why. She was faced with a heap of regrets. Beginning with the present, they just burrowed backwards in time—to those years when Mike was a little boy and cycled over to his maasi's house after a night of violence that shook the walls of the house. The pile of regrets kept growing and his mother spent most of her time rummaging through it. She would pick one out and examine it carefully, then fling it back in with the rest.

It started out as a desperate hunt, a frenzied, nervous run through the entire lot, before gradually settling into a habit that aged along with her. Her conversations usually tapered off into a vague, empty stare. Most people began to avoid the 'mad aunt who was best left alone'. And she, in turn, did not even notice that she was being shunned. She shut herself into a room with the windows barred. During the day, the curtains were drawn close. At night, when they were moved aside, the windowpanes reflected the interior. There did not seem to be a world on the other side.

Everyone blamed it all on Karuna. Had she not put her brother through the humiliation of her stalled marriage, he might have lived. Delivering that brave one-liner—'Don't think I can't cancel the marriage even now'—and walking out of the marriage-to-be had been far easier than having to deal with what she was now up against. For she was left holding half a childhood—with the other half having been consigned to the flames of domestic violence—and now, an equally thwarted youth.

She did not think that Michael had been particularly upset about her aborted marriage. In fact, he had been quite encouraging. 'Dat was well done,' he had told her.

'But Ma and Dad are very upset about the whole thing.'

'Don't worry, they'll get over it and so will everyone else.'

And now, Michael was not there to make it any easier for her. Nor could he ensure her acquittal in the accusing eyes of the world. She grieved over her brother in the deepest recesses of her being. She felt that the burden of her guilt was too heavy to carry around, at least, in these surroundings.

It was Minnie who came to the rescue, once again. Karuna packed her bag to travel with Minnie to Delhi.

'Can I go with Minnie? I feel very depressed here. Everything reminds me of Michael,' she told her parents.

'Go, go!' her father replied with a distracted wave of his hand. He could not be bothered with her just now.

The trip to Delhi lifted her spirits a little and it established a pattern for her that would endure all her life. She knew now that getting away from it all helped. Suddenly, she could let her hair down. She went out dancing at one of those discotheques, where the larger-than-life faces of Madhubala and Nargis stared down at an enthusiastically gyrating crowd of people. She hung around in a world where most things were not taboo, where morality was a code of conduct you developed for yourself. She enjoyed the anonymity of being among unfamiliar people and streets. And when she went back to Patiala, secure in the knowledge that another world did exist out there, it made the claustrophobia of a small town closing in on her that much easier to bear.

Over the next two years, she went on these frequent get-away trips and during one of them she even lost her consecrated virginity. She had arched her body to welcome the sensation, which was hard to define. However, this event too was marked by a great deluge of blood. It sent the man in question into a flurry of mopping the floor of incriminating signs.

She had met him on the dance floor. He had whispered his name into her hair as they shuffled around on the floor. She could not remember his name now, but she did remember him coming up to her and saying, 'Would you like to dance?'

'Yes,' she had said, 'but I'm not really good at it.'

'Doesn't matter. It doesn't take much. All it needs is getting into the spirit of things.'

The rest of the conversation had been a washout, for it involved a great deal of shouting to be heard above the high-pitched volume of the music. The dance had started off vigorously enough, with the flashing lights dictating the pace, but as the evening progressed, there were those vaguely fluffy, nebulous romantic sentiments floating around. And some of these had come and settled on Karuna and her partner. The vigour of the dance gave way to close dancing and apart from his name, many sweet nothings were also whispered into her hair. Karuna finally found herself in her partner's apartment. That was where she had lost her virginity, but her hymen had heroically fought the intrusion. And all the while that she bled profusely, he mopped. She left a trail all the way from the bed to the bathroom and the water turned red as she washed herself. Despite the crimson trail she had left and the harshness of the judgement it could bring down on her, she had experienced a sense of cleansing that only Minnie could understand. It had put blood in an altogether different perspective for her. This was not life-threatening. In fact, there was almost something gleeful about the way her blood had gurgled its way down the drain. She had seen her brother in a pool of his own blood and that no longer need be the last memory of redness in her mind. But she could do nothing about the dreams at night, the ones that began in a familiar room, a house, a street and then, without warning, metamorphosed into strangely mutilated red shapes that threatened to swallow her.

11

Pin-drop Silence

Minnie too was looking for an exit. After Mike's suicide, Minnie could just see her mother jawing her way into her brother's life, thrusting upon him the contradictions of her own existence. And while the image of a toothless ogre might not sit very well on the now-middle-aged woman, Minnie's view of her, as she pushed her son relentlessly to fit in, became slanted at a particularly unflattering angle.

In some ways Monty's mother wanted him to be part of the idle rich, but then she also wanted him to be a professional with a career, unlike the kakas who lived off their bank balances. For his part, poor Monty was as much of a misfit in suits and ties at fancy parties as he was in the classroom, where his contemporaries could not understand his interest in books.

His mother approved when Monty hung around with that particular group of young boys in the city whose life revolved around an invitation to the royal palace for a dinner party. They spent the year getting three-piece suits stitched, then picked one out with great care: 'Uncle, do you think this blue tie will match?' For the occasion, they also wore an obsequious body language, their behinds protruding just a little bit to ensure a shuffling walk, which would go well with their desire to please. At these parties, they would wait reverentially in the wings until they were noticed. With a drink in hand they would stand around within hailing distance of groups that included the most important people in town, and were then very pleased when called upon perhaps by the income tax commissioner to refill his glass. They would be willing to fetch and carry anything, from whisky pegs to a plate of chicken tikka, or the cordless telephones which they would bring to the maharaja and then wait in the shadows to put the phone back on its cradle in the grand hall with its imposing staircase, after the call. During the finale, when they said their 'byes', they would bow their way out.

Minnie had lost all desire to visit the house in Patiala. In any case, Monty was not much company these days when she did go back as he had taken to reading philosophy and would talk only in abstractions. He would be carrying around Bertrand Russell's book everywhere he went and would quote him as having said that philosophy was a corrective to the errors of science and religion. Though it was easy to make excuses for not going back during the holidays, she wanted to go far away, so that excuses would not be needed to justify her inability to visit. She had no idea, of course, that she would be carrying her own share of guilt all the way to another land, stuffed into her baggage, layered into each piece of clothing that she so carefully put into her huge VIP wheeler. The mail that arrived for her at the hostel in stiff white envelopes was thick with forms from foreign universities. She pored over forms, wrote letters, paid huge sums of money and chased professors for recommendations.

The one with the rounded Gandhi spectacles and hair that inclined towards being longish wanted to hold her hand. Conversationally, of course.

'Bright students like you will go a long way. I can tell from your face that you have the right spark to make it,' he told her, along with much else that might have turned her head, had she been inclined that way.

But she was a diehard realist. Her response, therefore, would usually be a practical query: 'Would you like to write a testimonial yourself, or should I put down something and you can then look over it and change it according to your own opinion of me?'

That, however, proved to be a leading question, providing the professor with yet another opening gambit to hold forth on his fine perception of her and her unique capabilities.

'Yes, that would be fine. Your term papers have been very good. We can meet again next week,' he told her.

The recommendation would take a long time, since the wording had to be thrashed threadbare. He would insist on giving her a cup of tea and when the unwashed young boy from the canteen arrived with two glasses of steaming tea, comfortably nestled in a wire mesh, he would get up to switch off the fan. It was a ritual that had nothing to do with his sexual proclivities. He would get up unthinkingly, each time that the tea arrived, and go straight for the switchboard. The one triggered the other and Minnie had learnt to recognize the sequence. A few sips of tea and he would be up, once again, this time to switch on the fan. Perhaps, this was part of the careful cultivation of an eccentric image, which then allowed for aberrations and much else.

Holding her hand was also cloaked in the garb of a ritual. Minnie was, in any case, not the kind who would play the role of the distressed damsel at the first hint of danger. She was all for giving the world a chance before assuming that it was out to get her just because she was a woman. Maybe, he really was the absent-minded professor who did not know the difference between her hand and the inkstand on his table. Maybe, he only needed to fidget. Maybe, he had a baby-pink soul that was not even aware that he was fondling a student's hand. But the purity of his soul notwithstanding, her palm felt sweaty, smelly and uncomfortable, especially when the fan was switched off. She wished he would not be so particular about what he wrote in her testimonial. It was, at any rate, too hot to be looking about for 'ifs' and 'buts'. Ultimately, however, she would discover that signs are usually tell-tale. And sure enough, the professor's tail was beginning to show. He had patted the seat next to him on the sofa.

'Come and sit here,' he had invited, 'I have some articles you can look at.'

'Yes, sir,' she had said, noticing a table in front of him, laden with paper.

'I would like you to read through these and we can discuss them the next time you come.'

She had gone and sat down, all the while fighting down the feeling that there was a deliberate design to the setting of the table. Then almost in the manner of a slapstick comedy, he had slithered closer. He had put his hand on her knee and was in the process of sliding it upwards when she decided that this was molestation, no less.

'What are you doing?' she had said a trifle awkwardly, since it was taking her a while to change the cadence of her speech from reverence to outrage.

'What's wrong, beta?' the professor had inquired, his expression of innocence slowly coming unstuck with the redness that was fanning outwards from his cheeks.

'How dare you behave with me in this manner? You should be ashamed of yourself!' She had, by now, made the transition from the student-teacher relationship to the girl-roadside Romeo equation and was, therefore, not hesitant about raising her voice and spitting out the words with venom.

'But you misunderstand me,' the professor had protested somewhat pathetically. By that time, however, she had sprung up from her seat and stormed out of the room.

She had to then go looking for another professor who would give her a letter of recommendation without a wordy foreplay.

She also needed to take stock of her finances. She would have to pay a portion of her fee and a sum towards her survival. Her father would give her some money, she knew. He always managed to bring some out of nowhere. Her bank would extend her a loan, which she would have to start repaying once she was abroad. But that was not enough. And that is why she had applied for a job at the various colleges in Punjab's small towns, where she could accumulate her salary into a neat little nest egg at the bank. She was going to treat this period as two years of self-imposed exile from which she would emerge, ready for flight.

That was how she reached Kala Afghana, a village that was very nearly a town flush as it was with money from non-resident Indians. It was, perhaps, in the fitness of things that she had landed a job in a college at this place. The whole region was crawling with incipient illegal emigrants who would subvert laws and sail the seas. Her classroom too was full of these hopefuls. The journey for an illegal emigrant begins with a huge amount paid to a slippery travel agent who arranges for a fake passport and visa, and an initial flight out, a question mark hanging over the final destination. The first phase of the journey is usually completed successfully. It is only later that the young emigrant finds himself abandoned in an alien land—surviving on a diet of cooked wild grass in Moscow which, the emigrant tells himself, tastes like saag at home, a frozen ride across Canadian borders in a meat-transport truck, crucified like the other carcasses to escape detection, and, maybe, a jail term in Greece or, perhaps, death by drowning just off the Italian coast.

Some of the houses in the area were modern, brick constructions built out of money sent home by the sons who had managed to make it past the check-posts at the borders between countries. It was in one of these that Minnie had managed to get paying-guest accommodation. From her window, she could see yet another brick house with the overhead water tank in the shape of an aircraft. It was poised there against the skyline with 'Boeing 747' written right across the length of the body. With no pretensions of subtlety, this icon of the region's spirit stood proudly at a vantage point, while down below, an occasional girl in a miniskirt went by. 'Back home on a visit from England,' explained the awed locals.

It was easy living here, as long as she played by the rules. And that she could manage, since the situation was not weighed down by the burden of eternity. She only had to get through two years and, at twenty-one, that is not forever. So, she played herself down in her primly worn salwar-kameez and kept pretty much to herself, reading and listening to music in the privacy of her room. That did excite the imagination of her neighbours, but after a while, they had exhausted all possible speculations and left her alone. Infrequently, she climbed into the bus to Patiala and found that an entire three-seater had been vacated for her because she was a 'teacher', an identity that attracted little more than condescension from city slickers, but seemed to carry much weight here. She had never been particularly partial to urban sophistication, anyway, the social world of drawing-room etiquette being quite alien to her. So, this home-grown brand of veneration was refreshing.

It was only when Karuna arrived on a visit that there was turbulence once again. Not that Karuna was one of those 'fast girls', as popular parlance liked to describe it, with a promise of undefined possibilities. She was only someone looking for an exit.

Her father had made life unbearable. He would berate her at each meal as they sat at one end of a long dining table. She did not have permission to leave the house without him except for the occasional visit to Minnie's. The moped that he had bought for her was only an expression of his love for gadgetry rather than any desire to accord her some freedom. In fact, she had even seen him checking the milometer of her moped. The near-zero mileage on it had put a smile on his face for the next few days. Karuna breathed easy only when she came to see Minnie.

She had soon made friends with the NRI next door, 'back home on a visit'. Once again, this was no love story. It was an exigency. And since it was not a love story, it did not matter that the protagonists had their own peculiar shortcomings, which would have to be put up with. The NRI groom could have a ponytail and might not arrive on a stallion. The indigenous bride need not be a virgin.

'I never found anyone there. The Indian girls there look down on us first-generation settlers and we are not quite at ease with the foreigners,' he had told her. His marriage proposal to Karuna had been equally honest.

He had been born and brought up in this semi-town, but had grown up with a well-thought-out liberalism that had not quite fitted into its narrow confines. He loved watching his mother roll chapattis and learnt to make them too. There was something therapeutic about watching the ball of dough turn into a moon under his rolling pin. The dough would spin around under it, enlarging itself as it went. Not that rolling chapattis was the ultimate sign of his liberalism, but it did reflect his ability to swim against the tide of masculine disapproval. Unlike many other youngsters, he had gone abroad on a student visa and had, subsequently, worked his way into a permanent status there.

'Come and meet my family. My parents are very old. I am the youngest in the family. And I have a number of brothers and sisters. They are all here now because of me.'

'Yes, I know. There does seem to be quite a mela at your house. Before I got to know you, I often used to wonder how many people were jam-packed into that house. In my house back in Patiala, there are only my parents and me, but don't even ask to meet them. My father would probably shoot you.'

'I won't chance it,' he said. 'I hope I never meet him.'

'Now you know why I want to get out of there. But I am not a difficult person and I am sure we could get along,' said Karuna. It was honesty in return for honesty.

Furtive meetings were a little difficult in Kala Afghana and Minnie had to provide the venue, the alibi and the respectability. She even had to climb into her room through a window to uphold the respectability end of the enterprise. She had been strolling around in the lane outside her window while Karuna and Ponytail were in her room. Up and down she went, but when she turned from the 'up' end of her sojourn, she found Karuna hanging out of the window and trying to catch her attention.

'There's someone at the door,' she said. But it was her gesture of simulating a knock with her crooked index finger that conveyed the information, for Minnie was still some distance away. 'I only shouted "Coming". But that was a few minutes ago,' she told Minnie as the latter came up.

'Say "Coming", yet again, while I figure out how to get in,' said Minnie.

Karuna could not have opened the door to reveal Ponytail and herself alone in the room, for a village-turning-into-a-town does not allow for such indiscretions. So, Minnie had to clamber in after carefully setting aside the potted plant on her window sill, seriously compromising her own image as a shining example to students. Fortunately for her, no one spotted her in the act and both her reputation and her knees came through unscathed, in spite of the sharp edges of roughly hewn wood.

She had managed to open the door to the landlady who had handed her a letter and left immediately. Any more such heart-stopping moments and Minnie's credibility would have been in jeopardy. Fortunately, NRIs usually can't stay long. For Minnie, things settled back into their placid rhythm when Ponytail left to get back to work. Karuna returned to her unhappy world of a mother who would not notice her and a father who she wished would not notice her. After a lull, Lalli had intensified his vigil over her movements and he was not going to allow her the liberty of finding yet another suitable boy.

But Karuna wasn't the only one to have lost her liberty. Monty had surrendered his freedom to speak. In fact, there was an eerie silence that hovered over the whole town. Monty had become one with that silence. At the best of times, he had not been garrulous. But if a change was apparent in him now, it only meant that he had become entirely speechless. The unspeakable horror of an event in the town had left everyone shaken.

The university and the colleges were on strike, but there was no demand clamouring for fulfilment. It was a strike marking stunned sorrow. Quiet processions wove through the town, through the shuttered marketplace, down the Mall Road and in front of the government offices. A procession of grim faces, hollowed eyes, their emptiness reflecting the enormity of the crime that had been committed. Nineteen students had been gunned down by five weapon-wielding terrorists. They had driven up in a car, threatened their way past the guard into the campus in the early hours of the morning, and walked into the common room where a contingent of visiting students slept. The students had come all the way from the engineering college in Kanpur to participate in the youth festival. One student, the first to reach the site of the massacre, later said that he thought someone was bursting firecrackers, until he heard the cries for help. The warden of the hostel had slept on, thinking that boys would be boys and were bound to make a racket.

One of the injured boys had given an account of the incident to the police. 'There was a knock on our door at two a.m. and these men asked to come in, introducing themselves as policemen who were conducting a search. One of us then opened the door wide to them. They asked me to switch on the light, which I did. And then they began firing at us. It was all over in a minute. Then they moved into the next room. I have no recollection of how they got the other room opened up. When I sensed they had left, I just managed to crawl to the door and thumped on it for help.'

The men with guns were on the campus for a mere five minutes. They left behind dead bodies, bedsheets and quilts soaked in blood, boots, briefcases and bags lying scattered around in helpless disarray. And that brought all hope of festivity to an end. It was time for mourning.

It was in the midst of such speechless mourning that Minnie arrived, a little worn out by her role as the douser of all flames, the fire extinguisher forever. Her fire-fighting gear was, in any case, beginning to wear thin. She had earlier been summoned to make Karuna see sense. If they knew her for the subversive she was, they might never have asked her to intervene. She had, in fact, egged Karuna on in her resolve not to marry Croaky, stoking the fire instead of putting it out.

This time it was different, since she found herself ranged on the same side as the adults in the household. Monty had to be drawn back into the world of the living. This was her little brother. Identical dimples marked their cheeks. Yet, their smiles reflected their different ways of communing with the world—his morose, hers amused.

She tried very hard. 'What's wrong, Monty? Why don't you talk to us? Have we done something to upset you?' she asked him. Alternatively, she would say, 'Why don't you go and see what's happening in college?'

But he just chose to sit at home and mourn. He would not join those silent processions. He would not volunteer to sit at the control rooms set up to answer queries from worried parents. She tried to needle him into loud laments. But only an occasional monosyllable escaped his lips which could have been slotted into either of the primal categories of yes or no. Perhaps, he was still living in a bad dream, where danger lurked right there at his heel and much as he wanted to shout for help, no sound would issue forth from his throat. Monty sank further and further into the morass of wordless inactivity.

His silence was monumental. It fanned outwards, spreading out over the town like a thick layer of smog. It went from door to door, knocking at each one, peeping in at the windows, holding a finger to the lips to seal the words in. It seeped in through keyholes, when the door was not open. And while its ability to curl and float might make it seem light and airy, in reality it had a very heavy presence that lowered itself inexorably on to the heart of the town.

Minnie might have been able to slap her baby brother into howling if it had been only him. But this was acquiring the scale of an epidemic, expanding into epic dimensions. That year, there were no visible celebrations on New Year's Eve and this was so in all the homes. Of course, the Sekhon and the Mehta households, with their doors and windows bolted and barred, did not realize that other houses were similarly dark, that they were all actually obeying a writ. Those gun-wielding terrorists who came wearing masks and disappeared into the anonymity of the night had issued instructions that no one was to celebrate the onset of the New Year. It was not that they were expressing remorse or sympathy for the nineteen dead. It was not to be celebrated on pain of death because, well, they said so. It was part of a list of other writs, which forbade women to wear jeans or skirts, insisted that they cover their heads, that Sikh men keep flowing beards, and that no one dance, drink or eat meat. 'No egg, leg, peg,' said their order.

It was easy to comply with the order banning New Year celebrations, since any ostentatious show of jollity would have struck a jarring note in a town where so many young lives had been lost. Midnight of 31 December came and went and a silence enveloped the town. But the silence of the exterior did not necessarily mean that a similar wordlessness had engulfed the interiors. Somewhere, deep indoors, glasses were being clinked, but the windows had been blacked out to ensure that not a hint of revelry escaped into the night outside. Tell-tale sounds were similarly dealt with. Old towels were pushed into the chinks under doors and these stood guard against the stray note of music that might sneak out. Conversations were a muted whisper, hardly louder than the rustling of leaves and only a shade louder than the last words of the dying. But on the outside, all was quiet. No one could tell that somewhere in the cavernous insides of those houses, there were living people, eating and drinking and, occasionally, even laughing. Or, perhaps, crying. On the stroke of midnight too nothing happened. Monty stepped into the New Year wrapped in his cloak of silence. His last words before dipping into the sea of silence had been uttered when his mother asked him, before he left for college one day, what he would like for breakfast. He didn't want any, he had said, before adding, almost as an afterthought: 'I had enough last night.' His last one-liner achieved as much a cult status in family circles as Karuna's one-liner to Croaky. There was an attempt to locate the trigger to his silence in those words, but that was after he came back, effectively sealed inside his sound-proof existence. They could only scrutinize his last words. And going by those, he did seem to have had enough of whatever it was that he did not want any of. In fact, the whole town seemed to have had quite enough.

12

Grain by Laborious Grain

'Enough is enough!' thought Karuna, as she dodged, for the hundredth time, her father's threat to blow her brains out if she so much as ventured to put her little toe beyond the doorstep. Not an uncommon threat, since it had been used many a time by the chastising parent, but the thin line between voicing an idle threat and putting it into actual practice was easy to cross. More so when one takes into account the fact that Lalli had not put down his arms since the day he stalked the ghostly gun that had gone off in Michael's bedroom. It sat in his lap at all times, his finger curled around the trigger. And so, if the line did get crossed, there would not even be that half-minute for Karuna to make good her escape before threat translated into action. In this instance, there was every likelihood that the line would be crossed because Karuna was contemplating putting not only her little toe beyond the doorstep, but her entire life. Ponytail had promised to marry her and take her with him to a border town in Canada. On one of his trips back home, he brought along a British passport with her photograph on it, although the passport had been issued in a different name. In fact, Ponytail wanted to take Karuna with him, instead of waiting for the solemnization of their marriage and its certification and registration in court, followed by an application for migration. Ponytail's childhood friend, Harinder, had a British passport as well as a Canadian one. Having moved to Canada from London, she had long since stopped using the British passport, which featured her as a little girl. Ponytail had submitted this passport for renewal, along with a photograph of Karuna. A freaky oversight had resulted in an updated passport. And so, Harinder had grown up to become Karuna in Britain's official records. Luckily for her, Karuna had decided not to travel on the alias passport, for the gamble could have meant an ongoing skirmish with the law.

Later, when this fake passport was discovered in Karuna's room, an infuriated Lalli had been quite set on registering a complaint with the police. 'I'll show her who Harinder is!' he had stormed in a foaming-at-the-mouth frenzy. There was much else he had said, but most of it being no more than a string of abuses, the substance of it could still be extracted to mean 'I'll show her who Harinder is'. It was Minnie's mother who had saved the situation from becoming a hunt all-the-way-to-the-horizon, because Karuna was, by then, far away. Yet, the desire for vendetta had been known to drive many an irate Punjabi parent round the globe in pursuit of an errant girl.

Minnie's mother had to spend many hot afternoons cooling down her brother-in-law's frayed temper. She even had to discredit her niece, professing an antipathy towards her she did not really feel, to make her line of argument more convincing.

'Let her be,' she would tell Lalli with an exaggerated flavour of distaste in her tone. 'She has gone far away and you are better off without her. Let her go and stick her face into filth. At least, the stench will never get back to you.'

Lalli did see the point, but how was he to explain this to a town that was, perhaps, even now, shaking its head and saying, 'Poor fellow!' Besides, Lalli would not be man enough if he were to take the whole thing lying down.

'You remember Jassi's parents? They came all the way here looking for their daughter. They have been in Canada long enough, but there are certain things that must not change. I really think Dhaliwal did well in catching Jassi, even if it meant hiring detectives and coming all the way here to finish off the business.'

'He killed her!' She was horrified. She knew that Lalli would do the same, if he were to continue this line of thought. So, it was important to convince him that there were alternate ways of dealing with the whole affair. 'Why spend so much money and energy on her, now that she has gone away?' she said to him, playing down the effectiveness of this particular course of action, trying to take his mind off its neat conclusion.

'But that bitch! I have to show her what it means to trick me like this, the whore! And in any case, who is this bitch Harinder? I'll show her who Harinder is!' Lalli fumed.

'Why are you bothered about this Harinder? Let her be who she is,' said Minnie's mother. This was only in a manner of speaking, since Lalli did not have much choice but to let Harinder be who she was.

The attempts to soothe him suffered yet another setback, however, when he discovered Karuna's lost moped parked in the Anardana Bazaar repair shop. He had spent two days puzzling over this one. She could not have driven away on her moped to some unknown, distant destination. Whizzing down at an optimum speed of 35-40 kmph (Michael had laughed uproariously when he had taken the 'thing' for a trial run: 'Look at my hair fly! This thing really zips. It's doing a Grand Prix 35-40!'), it would not have carried her beyond the outskirts of town. And from the look of her cupboards, she had taken with her more than just a change of clothes. The moped had neither roof nor boot. So, how did she carry all her things? And then he discovered that she had actually driven out on it...well, sort of.

The mystery of her belongings, seen by her father as the one vital clue to her disappearance and whereabouts, constituted, in fact, the tale of Karuna's ingenuity. Bit by painstaking bit, she had transported her stuff out of the house. Like the bird in Grandmother's never-ending story for the never-satiated child, she had picked it up, grain by grain, from a granary bursting at the seams and stored it away for later use. 'The bird came into the granary, picked up one grain and flew out...and came again, the next day, picked up yet another grain and left, and then, on yet another day...' droned the story, while the exasperated listener wanted things to move on rapidly from there. But there was a whole granary to go through before the story could progress to the next sequence of events. The impatient listener was already asleep. And just like the bird, Karuna took forever, or at least very nearly forever, which lulled her father into a certain complacency about her.

The ritual involved a careful scrutiny of her belongings at night. Having set aside the cargo to be transported the next day, she would go to sleep. Given her father's threat to blow her brains out, she knew that she could go out only after he did and that she had to be back before him. She would lie low in the morning till he had left the house to pick up his mail from the post office and stop by for a coffee somewhere and a beer at the club. He loved to sit there talking politics to other non-doers like himself. Campaigning was on for the parliamentary elections and ever since the Patiala royal house had become involved in politics, Lalli had begun to see himself as an authority on the subject. It was very comfortable to be sitting languidly in one of the lounge chairs at the club, holding forth on the kind of political initiative that the royal family should take. He could stare ahead at the vast stretch of green that was the cricket field and conjure up his next idea from the verdant blaze. His favourite openings were: 'I was telling Maharaj Sahib the other day...' and 'If you ask me...' The trouble was that no one was asking him. Nor did he have a clue as to how the system worked. But that did not deter him from putting forth his studied opinion.

'Major Sahib,' he would say, addressing the occupant of the other chair, 'the trouble with these fellows is that they are not confronting the situation. Next, we will have bandits contesting elections. Bar boy, one beer please! I was telling Maharaj Sahib the other day that he must put up his candidature. After all, if we don't oppose them, they will naturally win.'

'They' was a reference to terrorists, or 'terrys' as they were called by the nervous bureaucracy, whom most places in Punjab threw up as candidates. In Patiala, a member of the Khalistan Liberation Organization was standing for elections following a career in violence. None of the established political parties were contesting because everyone was afraid of raising 'terry' hackles. It had been an elect-me-or-else campaign with slogans that warned, 'If we win we plunder; if we lose we thunder.' And with this threat of violence in the air, an equally nervous populace was likely to vote in favour of the 'terrys', hoping, perhaps, that the bully would abide by the rules if he were made the class monitor.

'I agree,' said the voice from the chair.

'The fellow who is contesting elections this time has so many criminal cases against him. If you ask me, he should not be allowed to ask for a vote.'

'Quite true,' said the voice from the chair.

'I told Maharaj Sahib that I would offer him all the support he wanted. He would be a sure-shot winner from here.'

Lalli never went on to specify the kind of support he was willing to extend. It would, probably, be along the lines of holding up a frothy glass of beer in the day and a chilled whisky at night to propose a toast. 'Cheers to the victory, which will be ours!' would be the only slogan he was likely to raise. And since elections are not won on the strength of a drunken toast, it was just as well that no one was relying on him for support. However, his propensity for political analysis was proving to be very useful to Karuna, since it left her with ample time to fetch and carry and get on with her plan of action.

She would be out of the house on her father's heels, an extra shirt on her back, a weighed-down handbag slung over her shoulder, and a carry-bag gingerly balanced on the moped held in place between her knees. The old servant understood her need to get out and saw nothing subversive in her daily visits to her aunt. He would have looked the other way even if she had hauled a suitcase out of the place. She did not, however, want to leave him vulnerable to an accusation of complicity. A quick dash to Minnie's house with her moped pushed to full throttle. And there, she would offload her cargo.

One corner of the abandoned drawing room had been designated as the dumping ground. An old suitcase, pending the arrival of a new one, had been placed there, its surfaces worn out to reveal its cardboard innards. The sofa pulled up in front kept it out of sight. So it was into this chewed-to-the-bone cardboard box that Karuna would empty the contents of her bags. This took only a few minutes and her aunt, resting on her bed with her feet propped up on a pillow, would never even notice. As she lay there, her mind played indolently with its own thoughts or rested thoughtlessly on a pillow, in counterpoise to her feet. It would never push itself to the point of wondering why Karuna had to rush off in an oblique direction every time she entered the house. Her aunt was not given to undue exertion, physical or mental. But she also never mentioned these visits to her brother-in-law who, she knew, was a man with a temper.

Thus it was that each time Karuna left home, she carried some of her clothes and her belongings on her person and in her handbag because she could not be seen leaving the house with anything more than was strictly necessary for the occasion. It was in her handbag and, perhaps, a carry-bag or two that she had to accommodate all she wanted to take with her.

The choice was so difficult. What she left behind today would be gone from her life forever. There would be no coming back. This was the moment when she had to draw upon the essence of her life. Did it consist of her favourite clothes and shoes? And what about her collection of glass bangles? Were the 3-D birthday cards collected over the years a must?

In her writing case was a shopping list she had drawn up when she first learnt to formulate letters and string them into words. Her mother had preserved it, perhaps because each item on that list had been intended for her. 'Scint for sweet mumy, shoos for mumy,' Karuna had written with the creative orthography of an eight-year-old. Karuna's mother had pulled out this well-preserved shopping agenda from the deep recesses of her cupboard and had shown it to Karuna when she was older. Karuna had kept it with her ever since. And although her mother was now left only with a list of regrets, Karuna could, perhaps, continue thinking of her as the perfumed, elegantly shod mother. So, this shopping list had gone into her bag. There was also the birthday card Michael had made for her at an age when birthdays evoked enthusiasm. The cover featured a sketch of Michael, looking suspiciously like a cartoon character, and his dog which obeyed all the 'Sit!' and 'Stand!' orders. When asked to speak, the pooch promptly came out with an untutored 'Happy birthday, Karuna!' while Michael lay in a swoon, knocked out cold by his pet's overpowering genius. This too she had to take along with her.

There was also the 'official note' on a leaf from a notebook, where the drunkenly meandering handwriting of a nine-year-old trespassed with a blithe irreverence the red and blue lines meant to contain and define the letters. The note, a pot-pourri of the grandeur of a bygone monarchy and the bits of a political system that had penetrated through to a child's sensibility, was dated on the top right-hand corner and went thus:

Mr Lalli writes to Master Michael—Mr Michael Pal Singh my son should be king of Patiala. When Mr Michael got the letter he went to the Minister and showed the letter. Then the Minister said to his men to make a palace for me. Then Mr Michael wrote the letter to Mr Laljit Singh his father. Then when the palace was made many policemen stood at the door of the house. Then he phoned to his father should come to his palace and lived. Then they lived happily in his palace. Love Mike (Mr Michael Pal Singh).

Karuna carefully folded Michael's 'official note' into her bag, although she would, of course, have to leave behind this mythical palace with its errant promise of a happily ever after.

The pile in Minnie's drawing room grew prodigiously and it soon became obvious that a dispassionate observer would have to be requisitioned to throw out all that was less than necessary. In fact, at one point Minnie had to step in to say, 'Why do you need to take these old slippers?' But those were the slippers she and Michael had used as ammunition to bring lizards down from their elevated vertical perches on the wall and nudge them along in the right direction to precipitate their exit from the house. It was a bloodless coup, centred on a strategic throw of the slipper, which had to travel a considerable distance to reach its target in this house with a very high ceiling. Michael and Karuna would then collapse in a heap of light-headed, giddy laughter. But then, in the interests of travelling light in life, Karuna had to learn that memories could be carried inside the head instead of burdening a bag with old, worn-out slippers.

For the time being, however, the act of selecting, carrying and dumping kept Karuna going till the rest of the details had been worked out. Not a morning would go by without her depositing some part of her cupboard into the cardboard box. It would register another day gone and another day less. Like Michael's rendezvous with time through a series of tooth extractions, Karuna had established her own rhythm. She became increasingly innovative as the days went by. It was a challenge. She had to fit her wardrobe on her back and her life into a handbag.

Of course, there was also the new wheeled bag, which had been purchased surreptitiously when almost all the things Karuna would take with her had been transferred to Minnie's drawing room. The bag left Patiala much before Karuna herself did. It had never had the good fortune of being the centrepiece in a room where packing for a journey was in progress. It had never hogged the limelight, the way most other acknowledged travelling bags do. It had slinked its way into the house only in the last stages before departure. Then too, it had been forced to cower behind a sofa till it left the house, awkwardly shuffled out, once again, in the dead of the night. It had never sat on a bed with its cover thrown back, occupying twice its designated space like a particularly heavy tome that is proud of its contents, while visitors, who had come to say goodbye and who were ranged around the room on different perches—their eyes on the bag, as the would-be traveller puzzled over the intricacies of packing—periodically tossed in helpful suggestions about travel: 'Don't take so many shirts, you won't be needing them' or 'Carry only one pullover, but it should be the warmest you have'. So, this particular bag might well have been in a greater hurry than Karuna to leave town and its life of ignominy. One of Ponytail's friends had picked up the bag from Minnie who had come to Patiala only to hand over the bag from her ghost drawing room to a ghost-black car that was barely distinguishable from the surrounding darkness. Ponytail's entire network of friends in the country had been requisitioned for the smooth operation of the elopement. The bag would travel to Delhi, where one friend would pass it on to another who would then deposit it in a friend's house that was closest to the airport. There it would wait for Karuna and Ponytail.

After many months of these trips to and fro, Karuna got a call from Minnie, asking her to be ready for a wedding at the local Arya Samaj temple. The ceremony at the temple would then be the showcase for an application to the civil courts for a registration of the marriage, accompanied by photographs of the ceremony.

Karuna already had her bridal wear in readiness for a wedding that had never taken place. She had worn these only in the trial room and knew for a fact that they did fit her. The tailor had died somewhere between her not-happening and happening marriages. He had promised to stitch clothes for her trousseau and he had kept his promise. However, stitched as they were for a more conventional marriage, the wedding clothes were far too elaborate for one of the runaway variety, where the whole idea is to pass completely unnoticed. It is difficult to be anonymous when the tinsel on the veil, the shirt, the salwar, catches the sun and reflects it back in a high beam, blinding the onlooker. She could not have walked out of the house in these clothes. Information on the spectacle of his daughter stepping out in bridal glitter was bound to reach her father very quickly.

So, she did the one thing she had specialized in over the past few months of fetching and carrying. She wore her wedding finery and pulled on her plainest suit over it. With her veil neatly tucked into her bag, she was ready to rush to her own wedding. Once there, she only needed to unpeel her top layer to be transformed into the bride. With fingers crossed against any abortive contingency, she waited for her father to leave the house. And he did. She too went out as she did on any other day, except that she felt against her skin the soft rustle of silk and the pinpricks of the elaborate embroidery in gold that adorned her dress.

In case these loveless liaisons establish Karuna as a woman without a heart, it might also be recorded that as she started up her moped she felt against her chest the hammering of her heart which, in fact, was a greater giveaway than the occasional peek of the bright shirt from under the drab camouflage. So it was that laden with a noisily beating heart and two layers of clothing on a hot June day, she came up against a police cordon. They just waved her away.

'Go home,' they told her. 'Don't you know what has happened?'

But she did not. Nor did she have time to find out, for she now had to take a detour, while the sweat trickled down her back in rivulets. A bomb had exploded outside a school building. People had quickly gathered around to help the wounded. Two young men had started up a scooter to carry an injured child to the hospital. As they drove through Sheranwala Gate, there was a second explosion, for a bomb had also been planted in the scooter. The splintered pieces of flesh had scattered all over the marketplace and some of them had even reached the compound of the State Electricity Board Office on Mall Road. The police had quickly cordoned off the area.

Even as Karuna made her way across the other side of town, forensic experts were combing the place for signature clues on the blast. Ambulances were carrying the wounded to hospital. It was not the best time to be getting married, but people had learnt to carry on with their lives.

The wedding at the temple was witnessed by a small group of people. They bunched together every time a photograph had to be clicked, just so that the portfolio on the event would not look desolate. Aunt Veer was there in each of these snapshots, looking smug and providing it the much-needed respectability. The irony was not lost on anyone, particularly, Aunt Veer herself, who was entirely satisfied (and actually quite gleeful in the privacy of her bedroom) to be lending to the event the one quality known to have flown right out of her window when she came back with her orange hair and silver braces. It was in her house that Karuna had halted to remove her extra layer of clothing and put on a layer of make-up. It was she who had driven her to the temple in spite of the suddenness of the role that was being thrust upon her.

'A runaway marriage! This sounds like fun,' said Aunt Veer who had studiously avoided the fanfare of Karuna's aborted marriage, but was game for this furtive enterprise. 'But are you sure you will be happy? What is he like?' she asked Karuna.

'He is nice. I feel very comfortable when I'm with him.'

'What is his family like?' she asked.

'They live in Kala Afghana and are quite happy about the marriage. So, that does make things a lot easier. I think I quite like them.'

'You're sure he doesn't have a bride stashed away somewhere in Canada?' asked Aunt Veer suspiciously. She had heard of many an NRI bridegroom making marriage a business enterprise, contracting a series of marriages like branch offices to the business, collecting dowry on each of these occasions or, subsequently, picking up insurance money on every bumped-off bride. 'Hope he's going to treat you well,' was all she said, though.

'I'll take my chance,' said the matter-of-fact bride, as she gathered her glittering veil around her. She seemed to have reconciled herself to weddings that were either aborted or needed to be performed clandestinely.

In the course of the ceremony, Aunt Veer had filled in for Karuna's parents. They had even gone to her house, subsequently, for a little bit of celebration. Aunt Veer's dog had made the most of it. It had licked its chops over huge slices of cake and mournfully waited for the next item on the menu, a stance that compelled everyone to take pity and drop some more goodies on the floor under the table. And, occasionally, it danced around to draw attention to its hungry palate. Everyone else was too nervous to eat, overcome by the enormity of an event that had been organized without parental approval and at the definite risk, moreover, of parental gunfire.

After the flurry of the hastily conducted marriage, Ponytail initiated proceedings to get the marriage registered in a court and arrange for Karuna's emigration through whatever fast-moving channels he could tap.

On the appointed day, Karuna left on her moped. Later on, when the old servant was questioned, he looked genuinely puzzled as he reported a complete lack of any spectacle through a usually quiet morning and described her commonplace departure. Lalli had no idea where to begin looking for her.

The moped had thrown him off the scent and given her that head start to be able to reach Delhi and board a flight. It had been a master stroke to sail out on her moped, arrive in Anardana Bazaar and hand in her vehicle for a servicing which was very much due. This was standard practice since she had often left her moped sitting in the shop for days at a stretch. She asked the proprietor to ensure that the spark plug got a thorough cleaning. 'Will be back in a day or two,' she told him cheerily. By the time Lalli traced the moped, two days had gone by. It was a very nervous proprietor who had met him. No one would have wanted to deal with Lalli, a difficult customer at the best of times, but particularly volatile in this situation. 'I have absolutely no idea,' the proprietor kept saying, lest he be drawn into the controversy about her disappearance.

Thus Karuna left—without shedding a tear. Why would she cry, anyway? She was leaving behind a dead brother, a brain-dead mother and a trigger-happy father. The uncertainty of her future might yet be worth a few tears, but not the heartlessness of her past. The formalities at the marriage-registration office delayed their departure till late in the evening. When they did finally drive out, the premature darkness of a winter evening had already lent an air of mystery to the surroundings. The police check-posts were in position. Those were bad days. At least, that was what a police inspector manning one of those posts said to them. Of course, he looked distinctly cheerful, so they were not quite sure what he meant when he described the days as being bad. Were they bad because there were gun-wielding terrorists holding the state to ransom or was he referring to a moral degradation of the youth? At the end of their own interrogation, they were inclined to believe that he was concerned about the latter, but, given that youth will be youth, he might as well make some money out of it. The armed criminal was anyway too dangerous to confront. That was why he had flagged down the couple's car.

Their fugitive hearts had stopped beating when he stopped them. All along, they had been looking over their shoulders to check if they were being pursued. They had blundered into the police post ahead with their eyes glued to their tail. It was when they sensed trouble breathing down their necks that they spun around. They saw a posse of policemen at a series of randomly placed barricades. One of them asked Ponytail to step out and accompany him further down the road, while the other poised himself with pen and paper at Karuna's window.

'Your name?' he asked, then pointed to Ponytail in the distance. 'Who is he?'

'My husband,' said Karuna, tasting the strangeness of the word in her mouth.

And so, the policeman traced his whole family tree—the number of brothers and sisters, their names, their marital and professional status.

Luckily for the couple, the focus was on Ponytail's family. Had Lalli figured in this question-answer session, there would have been far too many known quantities to allow for an anonymous exit. But the interrogators were more interested in Ponytail's ponytail and his NRI status. Therefore, Karuna had to know all about his family to establish her credibility as his wife. A similar line of questioning for Ponytail to corroborate Karuna's information, a quick exchange of notes between the two uniformed men and they had established that they were married and not just two youngsters on an illicit night out.

That was when Ponytail had asked them why they were being subjected to this inquisition and the polite man in uniform had informed them of the bad days. 'These are bad days. One can't be too careful,' was his morose, doomsday pronouncement. Down this very road, only hours ago, a car had speeded right past the check-post. From a distance, the policemen on duty had noticed barrels of AK-47s sticking out of three of the car windows. This was the car that had moved up abreast of the official vehicle of the excise and taxation commissioner, as he drove into the Baradari Gardens, the green heart of the city, where a number of important offices lay nestled between giant trees, and the marble bathing beauty with her towel was forever drying herself in the privacy of her enclosure. The killers did not even have to bother to step out of their vehicle. They shot down the commissioner through the windows of their car. Even if the police had tried to flag down the car when it was entering the city, the result would not have been very different. The car would still have sped past any attempts to stop it, but a couple of policemen would have been dead. The police had, therefore, given heroism a miss.

However, in this instance of a young couple headed out of town, they decided to exercise their policing duties, only to step back in deference to matrimony, which simply implied that they would not be able to blackmail the young couple. (The men did not know that the very fact that this couple was married could have been useful and lucrative information fetching them good money.) So, it would be best to let the two go through in a fanfare of civility. And that is how Karuna had left the city, politely bowed out by the city police.

Her father could only tear his hair out, his impotent rage directed alternately at the missing moped, the phoney passport and the decamping daughter. His mind made some convoluted connection between Karuna's departure and every misfortune that now came his way. It could be a lack of parking space at the increasingly populous, trendy market on the Baees Number Phatak, or a neighbour failing to greet him—just about anything would do. Of his inability to find parking space right here in his own town, he would say, 'This market is practically out of bounds now because there is nowhere to stop the car.' Then, working himself up to a sudden burst of anger, he would follow it up with, 'I'll make sure this whole damn town is out of bounds for Karuna.' Or 'Look at what she has done to us! Even the neighbours no longer acknowledge us. They must have seen her driving away on that moped of hers. I should never have bought it for her.' At all such moments, his tirade usually wound its way to the story of the missing moped. 'She left the moped as a gift for the man at the workshop!' he would rant. His anger then took an entirely predictable course, dwelling on patently unoriginal observations about how she thought money grew on trees. From there he would move to the fake passport, holding the document between his thumb and forefinger for anyone who cared to see, proffering it as yet another proof of what he had always said about his daughter—that she was no good. 'No good, no good, no good!' he exclaimed with his usual propensity for endless repetition. These two vignettes from the larger story were then played out endlessly.

He also made his way to a police station in spite of Monty's mother's efforts to stop him. Once there, he attempted to describe the crime committed by his daughter. He even filed two separate First Information Reports for the moped and the daughter.

But the police were living in horrific times. They were attuned to much more grisly stuff. They were having to keep a daily count of the dead on their fingers and then on their toes—but the numbers often exceeded both—and they were required to line up the dead for photo sessions. (The jobless photographer they hired for the purpose had learnt to fit half a dozen heads into one frame so that he could sell one for the price of many to the newspapers and the police. It required only an adroit application of a pair of scissors to the negative.) Confronted by this daily dance of death, the harried uniformed men could not really get worked up over a moped or for that matter a passport that had been fraudulently made in another country, in the name of somebody who lived in a third country and, finally, lay unused in a wooden wardrobe in the heart of this small town. They tried to look concerned when Lalli spoke to them, but they did not know under what head to list this travesty of law. They were very sympathetic, though. Fed on the same diet as Lalli, they could appreciate the horror of the father who had a daughter in flight. It took a lot of convincing to persuade Lalli that bygones were, after all, bygones. But to look at it sympathetically from his point of view, letting bygones be just that, would only deny the past to a man who had no future to look forward to.

To add fuel to fire, Karuna called a few weeks later from somewhere on the globe. She wouldn't tell him where she was, but that she was in another country and that he should stop looking for her. 'Why did you leave the moped at the workshop?' he thundered into the telephone receiver. Her words came through, clear as a bell across the vast distance, except for the potholes of silence created by the lag in voice transmission. That was when he learnt that she had done the first lap of her journey on her moped. Needless to say, he was enraged. After that, he did all the yelling while she maintained an immunized silence. Distance made it so much easier. She could disconnect the line at will.

13

Street Processions

Monty, however, had successfully disconnected the communication line right here. Surrounded by people, fretted over by his mother and sister, a cacophony of concerned voices investigated the depths of his silence only to be met by dead silence at the other end. The written word, though, was not taboo for him as he went about clearing the last year of his exams. He wrote and wrote and wrote, offloading words that must have been cooped up inside him. His was the first hand that shot up to ask for a supplementary answer sheet and after that it just kept springing up every fifteen minutes. 'Sheet,' said his raised hand, one accusatory finger pointing heavenwards and the other four cramped into an unrelenting fist. Fifteen minutes later, there it was again. The rest of the occupants of the examination hall threw covert glances his way, their minds ticking by this subsidiary clock. 'Now,' they thought, anticipating his hand going up, yet again, and freezing there till the sheet had been supplied. The supervisor moved base within the immediate vicinity of Monty's seat. He hoisted himself on to an adjacent table, all 120 kilos of him, placed his size 11 shoes squarely on the seat of a chair and glowered down at Monty, willing him to stop writing. When Monty did ask for the next sheet, however, he only had to lean across and hand it to him, instead of huffing and puffing his way down the hall.

Other examinees began to feel inadequate in the face of Monty's effusions on paper and spent considerable time flipping over their sheets to see what it was they had missed out on. The nervous rustling of paper never once penetrated Monty's myopic concentration on his own answer script and he just scribbled on, regardless, his head bent so far forward that his nose missed a rubbing only by a few inches. No one knew what he wrote, since the secrecy of the examination system would not allow such detail to emerge. His weighty answer script and its contents would forever remain buried under burdensome files. But, in what can only be considered a lucky break—one in a series of three—he made a surprising entry into the ranks of engineers in the country. Equally mysterious was the second instalment of the trilogy: a job offer from a pharmaceutical company because the on-campus interview could not have been a game of dumb charades.

But Monty had quit the job even before he joined. And no one could ask him why, since they knew, by now, that no answer would be forthcoming. All conversation with Monty was a monologue of repetitive questions with varying emphasis—cajoling, pleading, imperious. And the ultimate, exasperated one was launched, invariably, at an angrily raised pitch. 'Why do you want to leave a perfectly good job? You have not even gone and joined! At least, go and find out what it's like. You cannot just *not* go. How the hell does one get through to you?' That was how it always ended, but Monty never rose to any bait. Even the anger did not register.

Minnie's family, and in fact the whole town, was of the considered opinion that she should arrange to take her brother with her when she did leave the country. A change of scene might finally release him from his silence, they felt. The confident volubility of the West just might act as the catalyst.

'You should take your brother with you,' Lalli said to Minnie in a commanding tone. He was, perhaps, beginning to miss the satisfaction of wielding power, since Karuna and Michael were no longer there, and his wife, of course, lived in a different world, where she grappled with the past, the present rarely filtering in. So he used his now-out-of-practice tone of authority with Minnie which, needless to say, did not go down very well with her. She answered in the shortest possible way.

'No,' she told him.

'Very rude, you girls are,' he said, trying to back off gracefully.

But to her mother, who posed the same question, Minnie had more to say.

'Ma, how can I?' she retorted. 'You know I'm going to have a difficult time as it is. I have a bank loan to pay back. I don't know where I'll be staying. I don't know what I will eat. In any case, he will not get a visa.'

'But what will Monty do?' The question was directed more at the elements in general.

And the answer came in Monty's third lucky break. A classmate from school was setting up a factory and he decided to take on Monty as his partner. On paper, Monty was the technical hand in the partnership, the qualified unemployed engineer who would be entitled to a loan from the government. And that was all that was required of him. His business partner would do the rest.

Government loans were easy to obtain just then because it was part of the look-good exercise to counter the image of a state splintered by its encounter with guns. There were self-employment loans available for dairy farming in rural areas, particularly in the border districts that touched the neighbouring country, since a steady supply of arms and disgruntled terrorists was supposed to be coming in from there. In urban areas, the arrival of the fresh entrepreneur would have been welcome—a key to improving the climate of the state. But there were no takers. It was only the oddball who would want to set up a factory there, when everyone else was contemplating moving their assets beyond the reach of guns and extortion.

In one factory, there was a row of lifeless, migrant industrial workers in a shed. They had not been sleeping in neat rows of course, but in the careless disarray of fatigue, arms and legs askew, thrown out at tangential angles to the body. Their bodies had been lined up for the headcount only afterwards. This horizontally laid out ladder of dead bodies stretched all the way from the little patch of light that sneaked past the door at the entrance to the dark interior. And as the eye tunnelled into the darkness, it became aware of the repetitive image of death, as though reflected in parallel mirrors. The image, ricocheting off the dank walls of dingy industrial houses, sent a tremor down most spines.

Moreover, these hooded men occasionally came round for a collection, their begging bowl jingling bullets, and the message was clear. Those running big business houses knew that they had to set aside some money for this bowl when it came round. Thus, the idea of setting up a factory in these 'bad days'—as the policeman at the check-post had told Karuna—was foolhardy. It was time for people to pack up their capital and move out. Although, in some cases, fortunes were being made by boldly swimming against the tide, there would be very few who would, in these times, want to put all their money into the pretence at normalcy. As such it was no surprise that loans were more easily available than those willing to take them.

Yet, Monty could not sustain that for very long either.

He went through all the motions of signing applications, detailing his qualifications in appropriate columns, standing by while the official pored over the proposed project, evaluating it for feasibility. Monty behaved himself, silent but immaculate, each time the jobless engineer and budding industrialist were asked to present themselves at the head office in Chandigarh. His award-winning performance only came later. No one wanted to give them the loan after that. Aghast officials backed off from the spectacle, taking their money with them. There was no space left for assessments and evaluations, nor, indeed, for any second thoughts. Not even the politely dismissive, 'We will think about it. Keep in touch.'

It so happened that Monty suddenly lost his awe of the officials, the loan dispensers. Having stood by, nearly at attention, on numerous occasions, he burst in one day in a state of undress on a room full of officialdom. There he was, all brown bums and pink willy, as hushed whispers struggled against thick carpets and rich drapes. Besides, Monty in the buff wasn't a pretty sight. It only prompted an open-mouthed officialdom into instant reverse gear. They backed all the way to the exit from where they turned around and fled. They did it in a dignified, three-piece-suited way, of course. The factory became a non-starter.

Monty took to wandering the streets. Over time he managed to befriend a whole army of dogs that faithfully followed him everywhere he went. Monty's company suited his silent nature, although it was rumoured that he occasionally spoke to the dogs that followed him around. They said he was declaiming verse, but that might well have been a part of the myth that was developing around him.

The procession became a familiar sight, an air of purposelessness hovering over the man and his canine retinue, its direction dictated by a whim, be it of man or dog. It could turn left to satisfy a dog's desire to pee against a particular tree or go straight across a road screaming with traffic, when a single-minded canine led the way, its jaws firmly holding on to a battered plastic bottle and its features set in a look of unrelenting determination, as though to say, 'There are some things in life one has to hold on to.' At other times, the procession took its direction from Monty's impulse to take the road going right.

Most other processions had retreated indoors long since, gone into hiding. There were no longer any protest marches, no frenzied, hymn-singing religious marchers either, who startled sleep from its depths in the early hours of the morning, no slogan-shouting students who had wanted a reprieve from the bus fare hike, nor virulent, motorcycle-riding fanatics of the All India Sikh Students Federation, who wore the colours of religious fervour—flaming saffron turbans—as they rode in formation through the streets in a display of might, with people waving to them from rooftops, either because these men in black looked so grand as they went by on black motorbikes or because the people identified with the separatist sentiments of this 1000cc charge. There were not even those sorrowful, silent marches. People did not want to attract attention by being part of a gathering. Nor did they want to take any sides, lest they inadvertently be identified with a group. Also, in these times of fear, there were state laws in place that did not allow for congregation. Of course, that rule did not apply to Monty and his dogs. This was not an assembly of five or more than five, forbidden by the law, because the numbers in the statutes probably referred only to human beings. And so Mad Monty's cross-species procession, silently winding through the streets, was even more singular. At other times it might even have evoked derisive laughter. But not now.

In the midst of this silent parade, Monty continued to visit the city library, for books were a habit with him. He did not seem to be reading them any more, though. He would get one issued and carry it back home, keeping it next to his pillow, as though planning to read it in the night. But he would be back at the library the next day to return the book and have yet another one issued. As soon as he entered the arched doorway of this period building with its inbuilt sense of space and silence, word would go round that Mad Monty had come and heads would begin to peep out of offices along the corridor. The story of his performance before the loan officials had also travelled from one tongue to another and people were, perhaps, expecting to see him walk in naked. Gradually, everyone got used to his daily visits, which entailed nothing more eventful than the exchange of a book. So, after days of watching out for that odd thing, which Monty might do, they all went back to their work, a little disappointed.

'How are you today?' the lady behind the counter would ask.

He would only smile back.

'Would you like to return this book?'

Monty would nod in response. He would then disappear between the rows of shelves. After prolonged sounds of rummaging, he would appear laden with a whole pile of books which he would carry to the seat nearest to the window. A close scrutiny of each would decide his book for the day.

'You want to take this one?'

And he would nod.

'You like reading?' she would ask.

And he would nod, yet again.

She took pains to ask him a different set of questions each day and was careful to phrase them so that a shake of the head could suffice for an answer.

The dogs would wait outside, making the most of the extensive patch of green that skirted the façade of the library all the way. They dug through innocent-looking flower beds, peed, raced around, quarrelled and barked furiously at the sound of the train.

The railway track ran right across town and rattled the windowpanes of the library as it made its way almost through its backyard. Poring over his books, Monty would look up, momentarily, his fevered mind excited by myriad possibilities which came to nothing. In fact, the strange procession of man and dogs did often stop to watch the train speed past. At other times, walking alongside the tracks, it would simulate the sinewy movement of the train.

For all practical purposes, Monty was lost to the world he

lived in, which didn't make things easy for his family, though his mother had managed to cultivate a resigned acceptance of the wanderers in her family. They just breezed in and out. Her husband was the most ephemeral of them all, here one minute, gone the next. 'Gone?' she would often have to ask her daughter. He would appear as suddenly, startling her out of her afternoon siesta. He never carried any baggage, not even of the metaphorical kind. He just used whatever was at hand—shirt, towel, soap, toothpaste, anything—even toothbrush, which was why Monty's mother's toothbrush (she liked to give her dentures a vigorous scrub before putting it back in her mouth) was a closely guarded secret. It was tucked away into the inner recesses of the steel cupboard that stood next to her bed. That did entail considerable effort when she herself wanted to use it, since she had to begin by looking for the keys to the cupboard. Other than the possessiveness about her toothbrush, she was finally quite at ease with her husband's comings and goings. In fact, it left her pretty much mistress of her own time and energy. She had only to somehow fit Monty's wanderings into this framework of departures and arrivals. Then she could live it down, just like she had a lot else.

Minnie too had become a part of this to and fro. She came to Patiala every weekend and was back on the bus Monday morning. Through the week, she taught English in Punjabi, translating a simple English text into even simpler English and then into Punjabi because that was the only way it could be understood by students who were completely unfamiliar with the language. Over the weekend, she tried to speak Monty's language. It was a language she found difficult to fathom. At college, the preparation for a lecture to be delivered involved a close consultation with the English-Punjabi dictionary. But with her brother there were no dictionaries she could refer to that might give her the exact equivalent of an expression. She had to read sorrow, pain, hunger and laughter in his face. It was so easy to get mixed up. Hunger was just about the only one that did not come in shades. It involved no subtle nuances like laughter tinged with sorrow, or pain with a funny bone. Hunger was simply hunger. So, in the hit and miss of this guessing game, hunger was always the first option to be offered. In any case, hunger was bound to be a predominant sentiment, given the distances Monty walked on an average day. Minnie and her mother would often be heard saying, 'You must be hungry. Shall I get you something to eat?' and heaving a sigh of relief each time they felt they had got it right.

When Minnie came into town, Monty was usually not home and she would sometimes try and locate him. Monty, however, traversed distances that were well beyond the confines of the normal notion of a walk. He and his doggy procession could be anywhere in town. So, she would just put her bag down in the room that she had made hers and wait. Her mother would want to sit down with her and complain about the way things were, but Minnie did not want to verbalize anything. She did not want to talk about Monty's odd behaviour because it only made her feel depressed.

'You're on the right track. Don't push him to speak. Don't rush him,' Sadhana, her psychologist friend, advised her. Sadhana was teaching psychology at the university. 'Going to the shrink' had not yet caught on as a trend and there were none to go to, so the comfort of the couch was not available to Monty. It was only Minnie who could provide him with whatever cushioning she could.

'I really don't know what to do,' she confessed, helpless before a state of ill health that was not curable with a tablet. There were no antibiotics that could be administered to purge the virus of silence.

'Just give him a lot of non-verbal sympathy and support and build up his confidence,' Sadhana told her. 'Things will sort themselves out. There is, obviously, some sorting out going on inside him. After all, he is not actually dumb.'

So, with every weekend, Minnie pushed the frontiers of communication beyond the spoken word. She learnt from her psychologist friend to smile with her eyes and say 'Chin up!' with her shoulders. These were sentiments that had to be silently and subtly conveyed because a loud expression of encouragement might merely have ended up making Monty nervous. Minnie became good at this body language, even as she fine-tuned her verbal skills in the college classroom, while all the time waiting to wing her way out.

Unlike Karuna, she walked out the front door. She had worked hard to earn that exit. But she had not been able to pry open the door to Monty's mind. And as the academic session beginning in the fall drew near, she realized that she would have to go or abandon the thought forever. It was a dilemma, but she did not want to become a hermit in penance, rooted to one spot, while her hair grew into the soil she sat on, and her nails, untended, became longer by the day and curled in. She would have to go. And though she had influenced Karuna to travel light, her own bag was heavy. It was lined with a guilt she could not leave behind.

14

Spilt Blood

In the same Sphinx-like silence that made Minnie carry her baggage of guilt all the way to America, Monty had his first full-blown sexual encounter. Ruby, the pretty young thing, happened to be the last of Old Man Sekhon's companions. With aspirations inspired entirely by the image in the mirror before her, Ruby had thought that getting herself a comfortable sinecure as the keep of a rich, old man would be easy. But it had, in fact, proved to be very difficult. She had become fond of the old man and all he did ask of her was companionship. He was one of those young-at-heart old men who do not like to feel that they have been forsaken by youth. She was, probably, a part of his feel-young drive. And her very presence was enough to give him the boost he needed. It made him a happier old man.

'Come and sit here with me,' he would invite her, as he settled down to a drink before dinner, which was a meal shared across a huge table for twelve. There had been a time, long ago, when he had eaten off silver plates. So he took grandeur for granted, as a part of everyday life. He found nothing out of the ordinary in sitting at the head of an empty table for twelve, as the gloved waiter served him his meal before bringing in hot chapattis which were delicately transferred to his plate with a fork. He ate only one and very small portions of daal and sabzi. But the ritual of the meal had to be gone through with all the attendant frills. After all, he was a man who had eaten off silver plates. That was when he was the young Old Man Sekhon. In those days, life was lived king-size and he had never had to long for anything. He had eaten plenty, drunk plenty and also had a surfeit of sex to satiate him for the rest of his life.

The meal across the table for twelve, with Ruby by his side, was followed by each of them retiring to their respective bedrooms. In short, this whole thing with Ruby was not about sex, although that was the very area which lent itself to the wildest speculation.

'What must the old man be doing? Do you think he can get it up at all?'

'Couldn't be pleasant, doing it with such an old man. But then he is a very rich old man.'

But sex was not the problem, for it never really happened. In fact, it was this very lack of anything at all happening that had begun to weigh Ruby down. She realized that she was not at all ready for this rich and retired existence. She had absolutely nothing to do because an army of servants ran the house. And Old Man Sekhon was out very often. So, even as she struggled with the legitimacy of her own existence in the present situation, she had to fill the yawning time that stretched before her on an average day. Yet, going away was not an easy choice either because Old Man Sekhon, though well past the prime of his emotions, was bound to feel bad.

She met Monty at one of the family dinners where he seemed quite out of it. He was, moreover, part of the extended family, being the son of the old man's daughter-in-law's sister. In the Indian family pantheon, a relative is a relative, even if it be through a convoluted route. With the older generation, these relationships were more an article of faith. 'He is my sister's father-in-law's nephew's wife's brother and such a fine boy,' an old aunt would say, though the boy, in this instance, might be well into his fifties. But the young were no longer willing to swing by this chain. Besides, Monty was the outsider by temperament. Since that was Ruby's status too in the family equations, she felt an immediate empathy for him. She hated these get-togethers where she felt like a little insect under a microscope, writhing and uncomfortable, but pinned down to it. It was always the men who looked harder, adjusting the eyepiece to get the right focus as it were. But none of them could ever meet her eye, because theirs were always lowered to the region below her neck. 'Deference,' she had initially thought to herself, but soon found that she came away from each such party with metaphorical holes bored into her breasts. The old aunt, whose sister's father-in-law's nephew's wife's brother was the subject of such effusive praise, was also not sparing in her scrutiny of Ruby, except that she studied her from head to toe, unlike the menfolk who had narrowed down the focus of their area of interest.

'Will you be staying long?' the old aunt would ask, apparently accepting the polite story of her being the daughter of an old friend who had come visiting, but letting Ruby know with her arched eyebrows that she believed not a word of it and approved even less.

'Yes, I will be here for some time,' Ruby had learnt to say without going red in the face.

'Where are your parents now?' she would again ask pointedly.

'They are not here,' was the neither-here-nor-there reply.

'But they must be missing you,' she said, suggesting a quick departure.

'Only my mother is there, and yes, she must be,' said Ruby, not willing to detail her mother's struggle for survival after her father's death.

The old aunt would turn away, disgusted at this shamelessness, and go back to the pleasant business of enumerating the virtues of her sister's father-in-law's nephew's wife's brother.

'Such a good boy! He is so fond of me and comes to see me every few days to find out how I am doing.'

This would afford Ruby the escape she was looking for right from the moment the old aunt had lowered herself into the chair next to hers.

But Ruby could not afford to be indignant. She had got into this situation only to secure a decent future for herself and did anticipate the disapproval with which polite society would eye her.

Monty, however, did not fit into any of these categories of lecherous men and disapproving aunts. So, Ruby, who had nothing to do, decided to make friends with Monty and that is how it all started. She had gone up to him during one of these occasions and found that with him things were always quiet beyond the smile. In fact, all subsequent exchanges or 'conversation' were also carried out in silent mode. She would smile at him whenever someone said something funny and he would smile back. They would also exchange smiles to indicate their amusement when a family argument broke out. They just sat silently side by side. That suited Ruby fine, since all verbal communication with the others usually resulted either in uncomfortable questions or a barb thrown her way.

How she and Monty got into bed involved another sequence of unsaid sweet nothings. It is a little difficult to make suggestions or gauge a response when no one is going to say anything at all. If the two of them spoke different languages, it might have been possible to consult the two relevant language dictionaries, put across the keywords and arrive at the reasonably safe conclusion that both were inclined the same way. But in the absence of all such aids, it was a guessing game.

One afternoon Ruby had spotted Monty at the Baees Number Phatak, walking past the shops, closely watching his footsteps on the pavement. She had stopped the car and invited him home with her. He had smiled happily when he saw her. She had driven home with him and the two of them had sat in the balcony extending out from her bedroom. The noise of the bazaar was only an indistinct murmur in the distance. He had visited her often after that and occasionally even managed to say things like 'nice place, this', 'you look pretty' or then just 'tomorrow?'. Ruby's instinct to nurse the wounded had brought them closer and she would cradle him in her arms.

The bedroom sequence with Monty proved to be hard work for her. She had to get Monty worked up, which was achieved after considerable and painstaking effort and frequent, encouraging exclamations. 'Come on,' she had to say, time and time again. 'You can do it. I'm sure you will like it. Just relax, let yourself go.' By which time, she was beginning to feel like a nursemaid. So, she had to slip into her slinkiest silken nightdress and writhe in front of the mirror. She twisted and turned to caress her own back where all her erotic flashpoints were located. And finally, she felt the resurgence of her sexuality. Fortunately, Monty still had an upright penis, although he seemed entirely surprised by its presence. In fact, he looked as though he had seen an alien sitting in his lap. Having arrived at a coordinated turn-on, however, things did eventually come to a head.

But then, Ruby suddenly upped and left. Just like that. One fine morning she was gone. She had gone to Bombay to push her luck and her looks in the glitzy world of cinema. At least that was what the grapevine said. She had this long, lithe figure and well-positioned breasts with the right degree of projection. She even had an attractive face, so the grapevine had promptly sent her where it thought she should be. Her mother had been a keen movie enthusiast. On many a hot afternoon, when her husband had left for work, she would hitch a ride on the office peon's bike to get to the movie hall. In fact, her claim to fame was the resounding slap she had given the usher in the darkness of the cinema hall. All attention had suddenly swung from the stars on the screen to the real-life drama unfolding in the third row. Many in the audience had clamoured for silence. Speculation ran through all the rows in a ripple of excitement. Had he molested her? What had happened? The nervous usher, the slap still imprinted on his left cheek, had then deposited her on the seat of her choice, irrespective of what her ticket said. Ruby's mother had only wanted a clear view of the screen, uninterrupted by big heads and big turbans. And then she could sit back and enjoy the movie, singing loudly to the accompaniment of each song on the screen.

It seemed only right then, and natural, that Ruby should head straight for the movies, as though directed by a genetic propulsion. Though no one saw her in a movie, the rumour of an impending Ruby starrer was always in the air. In some accounts, her beauty was said to have blinded the producer. In others, she was supposed to have slept with him to land a role in his forthcoming venture. It might have taken the gloss off all the gossip if it were known that Ruby was, in fact, working as a receptionist in a hotel in Delhi, living in a room over a garage where the toilet bowl also sat in one corner, separated from the rest only by a thick plastic curtain. When the curtain was pulled aside, there was an absurdity to the setting which laid bare everything. It was like lifting the roof off a doll's house and seeing the rooms inside in one all-encompassing glance. The chair at the farthest end might well have formed a cosy twosome with the toilet bowl if the curtain had not intervened. And while the analogy with the doll's house might make the entire arrangement sound cute and quaint, it was not so. The morning session in the loo had to be accompanied by sundry other necessities like switching on the fan and throwing open the single large window that overlooked the main house. Post-loo operations involved a generous spray of room freshener or, when the spray ran out, a sprinkling of talcum powder. In the event of a visitor being in the room, preliminary preparations also required that the two-in-one music system be set at full volume to cover up the embarrassment of explosive sounds from behind the curtain.

After her disappearance, a surprised Monty made many trips to the tennis courts, hoping to find her there. And though she was not there, he maintained a vigil, keeping an eye on every train that wove its way through the town, trying to discern in its beat the possibility of an arrival, as it pounded past the tennis courts where the players waited for the reverberations to die down before they regained their lost concentration. But, Ruby, when she came back, did so on a bus, even as poor Monty stared hard at the lighted compartments whizzing past him. It had never occurred to him to turn around and check at the bus stand across the road.

Ruby's return owed itself to the fact that Old Man Sekhon was no more. He had died a quiet death. There had been no warning signs. He had not complained of anything at all the previous day—no chest pain, no breathlessness, no sweating—nothing to alert anyone to the possibility of death. Nor had he stared into the distance and talked of death. The day had been an ever-so-ordinary one, boring enough for Old Man Sekhon to claim to have died of boredom, had he so chosen, but that being the prerogative of the younger generation, he had merely succumbed to life's inevitable conclusion. However, having established for himself a reputation of invincibility, no one could believe that he was actually dead. He only looked like he was asleep on his side, his left hand still resting under his head and the right one thrown carelessly over the covering sheet. When Lalli had been called in, he had tried to wake him up. He had asked the servant to bring in a hot cup of tea, thinking that all his father needed was his usual pick-me-up to begin his morning. It only struck him later that the situation might call for a doctor. Though the doctor would not make any difference either, since Old Man Sekhon had died some time in his sleep.

The will he left behind promised plenty to all. Such was the generous vastness of his wealth. The two sons, one of them being Lalli, had the bulk of it equally divided between them. However, there was something in it for Ruby, though she no longer predicated her existence on a possible mention in a will. But like all things that come unbidden and will be elusive when they are hoped for, the inheritance fell into her unsuspecting lap.

She came back to claim the small farmhouse on the outskirts of the city and some money in the bank, willed to her by Old Man Sekhon. The house was not palatial, but large enough for somebody who had started out with nothing. The details of the will had reached her via the grapevine and so she was back, leaving behind the surreal existence of a toilet bowl in the drawing room. It was not an easy homecoming, though, since there was marked disapproval of her wayward habits, particularly now that they had resulted in her becoming a beneficiary of a will that had plenty for all. Everyone made sure of directing a few meaningfully sarcastic observations at her.

'You have finally got what you wanted,' said a leering Lalli, not too unhappy with what he had got himself.

'Yes,' she affirmed, deciding that it was better policy, perhaps, to be candid instead of coyly righteous.

'Come and see me sometime,' said Lalli, although now he was not being sarcastic at all, but merely suggestive, working on the assumption that what had been his father's would now be available to him—a deduction based on the simple laws of inheritance.

She never did go and see him, though. But nor did she leave town. It was expected that a girl like her—which essentially meant somebody physically endowed as she was, with an added emphasis on her bust size—would pocket the money left over after paying the taxes, sell the house and stash the money gained from that too into her pocket, before sashaying out of town to the first film producer in Bombay.

But Ruby did not go away. She stayed right on. And with that the 'film star Ruby' myth finally had to be discarded. After all financial settlements had been made she went out looking for Monty.

They made an odd couple, he the silent type and she vivacious. Gradually, they came, to be a part of the partying circles in town, each with a hand tightly clutched around a glass. With that kind of diet, they usually observed the wasted world around them with a beatific indifference. The occasional toast would also be made to Williampal Singh who was very much a part of the happening set in town. From Monty's point of view (this is pure conjecture, though, since the expression of such sentiment involved prolonged verbalization, which would have been entirely outside the ambit of Monty's self-defined capabilities), there was no getting away from certain things even if you chose to adopt silence as a defensive weapon.

Back in the old days, when Monty was still at school, Williampal Singh used to sit next to Monty. While Monty was forever at odds with his surroundings, Williampal Singh was completely at home in them, the swagger in the name corresponding with the swagger in his personality. His lineage went back, perhaps, to the list of Griffin's *Rajas of the Punjab* for whom the school had come into existence. Or so he claimed. He perpetuated the family tradition of being a gentlemen-at-large, a kaka.

Williampal Singh endured most of the lessons in the

classroom with a fortitude that could even be deemed commendable, given his wider propensities. He had never read a book in his life. Not even a war comic. Reading just happened to be an activity beyond his world-view. So, the classroom was an enforced interval in the progress of his life. Williampal did the world a favour by being there at all, almost looking around for applause each time he made it to the classroom. But he would usually add the finishing touch to the largesse implied by his visit by tilting his chair back and simulating a fall—just when the teacher was deep into the profundities of history. That would put an effective full stop to the lesson, because the entire class would, by then, be wholly occupied in making sympathetic noises, dusting him down and checking for broken limbs, if any. He was careful to introduce variations into the act, so that he could not be accused of subversive intentions. And he was a hero each time he did it.

He had somehow managed to scrape through school and had spared himself further tortures inflicted by education. So, he had merely sat around and grown into the town till he was old enough to get married. And now, he and his wife just sat around, then went out every evening. And, here was Monty, once again sitting next to Williampal, the differences of personality ironed out by the shared bonhomie of liquor. It was in this haze of many toasts offered to everyone around that Monty and Ruby got home in an old Fiat that sputtered its way across town in the very early hours of the morning.

In the turmoil of the late eighties and early nineties, this was not the best time to be making your way home, particularly now that Ruby was going to have a baby, a discovery she had made only the previous morning after a month of imagining that her menstrual cycle had dried up for want of blood. But the discovery had pumped more blood into her veins and she had arrived home with flaming cheeks to tell Monty about it. Monty's initiation into sex had been slow, but had not always stayed that way. They had a healthy sex life, though Monty continued to be a man of few words. Words, in any case, would not have added anything to the process of procreation. So, Monty's silence was no handicap. They had not thought of having a baby, though. Now that it had happened, however, they were rethinking their evenings of revelry as they drove home.

'I think we will have to slow down,' Ruby was telling Monty.

'Yes,' Monty agreed, and that was as good as it could get, because this too was uncharacteristic verbosity on his part. Besides, there could be no disagreement on the point, since the two of them would have to allow for Ruby's body to recoup for the big event. No liquor, no late nights, and a healthy diet.

This inebriated couple had made their way home through a hundred evenings before, but this time, it was with a cold, sober Ruby holding on to her abdomen each time they went over a bump, worried that the potholes would disturb the configuration inside her. She was the one who usually drove the car. But somehow, this evening, she had felt different in her mind and, therefore, in her body too. Caution was all of a sudden the keyword in all her actions as she spent the entire evening at the party nurturing herself, taking each step gingerly, seating herself down gently, holding her plate carefully away from her tummy. She had built up a momentous nervousness in the course of the evening, till the everyday world around her seemed fraught with nameless dangers. It was the newness of the experience that had engendered all these frightening monsters, which seemed to have broken free of her imagination and were suddenly standing on the lonely stretch of road that led to Ruby's acquired farmhouse. A car had pulled over to the side, gleaming an eerie white in the distant darkness. The moon did not help. It was only a thin sliver in the sky. The vista ahead was a whirlpool of darkness with the white car as its vortex. And try as they might, they were hurtling towards it at uncontrollable speed.

That was the only route to their home and under normal circumstances there was a certain romance to it. The trees that lined the road would catch the light from their car, preen a brief while in the spotlight, then as quickly bow out into the darkness as the headlights moved on, perhaps even shake their heads sadly, regretting the brevity of their star performance and that it was time to leave the stage to the newcomers. But tonight, they had encountered an audience preoccupied with its own fears. The silent trees were merely sentries at the gatepost, saluting the passing dignitary who did not notice their ramrod-straight stance or the sweeping grace of the salute.

As Ruby and Monty neared the luminescent white car, a dark figure with a sombre blanket wrapped around him, stepped out of the far side of the vehicle and made for the centre of the road. The blanket is the usual garb worn in rural Punjab as protection against the harsh winter. Therefore, it was not that Monty and Ruby were startled by the novelty of the blanket as a drape. It was just that the blanket no longer evoked the image of a family huddled together on a cold winter holiday, chatting the morning away. The blanket now had to live down a reputation it had acquired over the past few years. It symbolized the terrorist's favourite dress code. While that might seem like a cumbersome choice for people whose job profile involved the use of a gun, scaling a wall, taking cover in the fields amidst tall, standing crop, and fleeing on a motorcycle, there was a perfectly logical explanation for this seeming absurdity. The weapon that this blanket-wearing brand of terrorist carried was slung over the shoulder and sat snugly between the shoulder blades, cosying up to the spine. An assault involved the single sweeping act of shrugging off the blanket and swinging the gun out into firing position.

That was why Monty and Ruby were taut with tension when they saw the blanketed man. He made as if to flag them down, but they did not wait to see him complete his action. They had merely watched a movement under his blanket and stepped on the accelerator of their old car, which could only respond as much as its wizened years would permit it to. Ruby felt the hysteria slowly rising from the pit of her stomach to her throat. She saw the man as their car approached his. She saw him stride across the road and come abreast of their car. She saw his dark blanket with a muted maroon checkered pattern. She saw his face with the eyeballs ablaze. She saw the fire rising from there consume his face. She saw the smoke billow upwards. She saw it engulf the trees that had lined up for their dance. She saw their foliage wither. Her panic translated into a series of uninhibited screams which filled the car with an electric charge. It took the car hours to traverse the distance between the initial stride of the man to his appearance in the rear-view mirror. And all the while, she screamed. She screamed for fear of the man who might have shot at her and at her stomach. Her scream acquired a momentum of its own, surging into the night, lifting itself out of the present context and moving into a sphere of timelessness—a scream for all sorrows, endured before and after.

She continued to scream even after they were well past the striding man. They drove home at that same speed, aware of a pair of headlights behind them. The rear-view mirror brought these blinding lights oppressively close and followed them all the way till the last turn to their house. It could have been that they were only party-goers like themselves who were also on their way home. But Patiala was too small a town for two sets of party-goers to be living in the same neighbourhood without discovering each other. And finally, it did not matter either way because she had gone home and bled. It had been a night out for her monsters who had howled at her through the car windows, draped themselves across the windscreen and hidden the ribbon of road from her sight, had hurled stones at the fleeing car, made the journey home a nightmare, and did not let go even after she finally got home, legs still trembling with tension, and lay down doubled up with stomach cramps. The sheet on which she lay had a spread of red and in the toilet bowl there were two small pieces of flesh that were the embryo she had so carefully protected against any jarring impact. Cramping with pain, curled up on her bed, she had herself become the foetus she had lost. Blood had so many ways of spilling itself.

15

Washing it Down

But then blood also finds as many ways to reassert itself, creating bonds that never let go. A few years later, the dust had settled on time and Minnie had managed to quell the migrant's feeling of alienation, which rises like bile in the throat in those first few years of being far from home. She had fought it with adequate doses of beer, quaffed down with admirable speed at the numerous bars in town. She had discovered that not only did a good, healthy deluge of beer drown all such unwanted sentiments, it also expelled them altogether with a long, salutary pee. Once all such emotions had been flushed down the toilet, one could get on with one's life. These twinges of loneliness then continued to float in the deep, subterranean dungeons of the psyche until it sprang a leak. However, even that netherworld could not obscure the two pieces of flesh, the embryo-that-might-have-been-a-baby. Occasionally, it stared up at her from the toilet bowl.

She had learnt of Ruby's pregnancy and abortion all in one go. For Ruby and Monty too it had been a reality that lived only for a day—though for that one day, it had been their only reality—from the appointment with the doctor to the encounter with the blanketed terrorist. Even before they could share the information, their child was gone. And by the time Minnie was told about it, they had become twin events, like death superimposing on birth so completely that it would not even allow a peep into life. It resembled yet another story narrated to the persistent child by a harassed adult about the king and queen who lived and died and so the story ended.

In the split second that Monty's child lived in Minnie's mind, a whole lot of possibilities had opened up before her. She had seen herself as the aunt abroad: 'My aunt is sponsoring me. I will be doing my engineering course in the States.' She could not bring Monty with her, but now she could bring his baby. She could begin where she had left off, with the intervening years providing the advantage of hindsight and multiplying options. Even as Ruby told her, over the phone, of the visit to the doctor and of finding out that she was pregnant, Minnie had visions of redemption. The guilt that gnawed at her could possibly be purged after all. But she had only had time to exclaim an excited 'Really!' as Ruby drew in a breath to continue. Then the rest had followed—the man in the shadows of the road, the blood on the sheet and the embryo in the toilet bowl. When Minnie told Karuna about the events back home, she had to drink several glasses of water in the telling of it to swallow the accompanying emotion.

Minnie had discovered that the guilt that was part of her baggage refused to get washed down, even with the best beers. In fact, this gnawing-at-the-heart guilt was something only Karuna could understand, since she had a fair share of her own, which she too had carried with her in spite of all the sifting and filtering that was done to accommodate her life into a bag. She had carried her compunctions with her, riding on her shoulders and that was what had given them that slouch. But, perhaps this guilt was not so new either. It was endemic to them. It was the guilt of being born at all and went on from there to encompass anything and everything. 'I'm sorry,' said each of the two girls, ready to acknowledge their fault for Michael breaking a leg, Monty leaving home without breakfast, things going wrong. And, of course, they were guilty of the deaths, one in the prime of life, the other even before it could take shape. The two cousins met often because a collective guilt was easier to deal with. Ponytail was a tolerant enough husband but even he could not cope with the remorse that was Karuna's. He encouraged her to visit Minnie frequently, hoping that it would help her chase away her ghosts.

And so Karuna would cross the Canada-US border to spend weekends with Minnie. Sitting in Minnie's bedroom in the ranch house, which she shared with so many other Asian students, they would tell each other how neither of them was to be blamed for the lives they had not lived.

'You would have been a dowry victim and we would have been doing the rounds of the law courts trying to have your in-laws convicted,' Minnie would often tell Karuna. 'Much good that would have done anyone.'

'Maybe it would have made everyone happier to see me moping around and miserable.'

'The world does, of course, love victims and hates those who get away,' agreed Minnie.

'But I don't think I would have survived there. Though I am not sure I feel that I've got away,' sighed Karuna.

Karuna had become a permanent exile. There was no going

back for her. The glamorous legend of the visiting NRI was forever to be denied her. The perfumed, nail-varnished, leather-bagged and high-heeled descent into the airport foyer, trailed by the aura of an acquaintance with worlds beyond was not for her. She could not go back to talk to those at home of things and systems that worked, of the dust that was missing, of the stores that sold everything. Besides, there was no one to whom she could go back and say, 'You know, one never really needs to do any dusting, because unlike here, there just never is any dust.' Her mother had stopped listening a long time ago and, in any case, she was constantly raising dust as she picked up pieces from the past. Karuna's return was thus bound to be different. No eager friends and family hanging around, willing her to open up a suitcase of goodies. Instead, a father waiting at each turn with a ready pair of handcuffs. The never-to-be scene of a return was, therefore, obscured by her usual nightmares, which conjured up horrible images of manacles, alive, hungry to swallow, snapping their jaws in anticipation, shaped, perhaps, by her recent surfeit of exposure to the monsters of Hollywood. Her nightmares ensured her exile.

The cousins tried to assuage their guilt and alienation by filling their lives with a frenzy of compensating gestures. They had even gone looking for Aunt Veer's brother who was somewhere in this Western world, living here as an illegal alien. He had recently sought asylum on the trumped-up grounds of being a member of a minority in his own country and, therefore, discriminated against. They were told that he now called himself Paramjit Singh and claimed to have escaped with his life from an armed encounter with the Punjab Police. A letterhead of a separatist organization operating in Punjab, given to him from the underworld of the gurudwaras in the States, certified his identity as the poor, persecuted Paramjit Singh who had just entered the country. Karuna and Minnie had discovered this on the gurudwara-going social circuit and had abandoned the search for someone who had deliberately sought alienation.

Apart from talking a lot about nothing and everything, the cousins would also take endless walks. It was on one of these obsessive walking trips that they had come across the dimple-cheeked, curly-haired Shanne. At least that was how he had introduced himself in a lucid moment. It was his dimples and sense of discomfort with the world that had drawn Minnie to him. 'I see the world in bits and pieces,' he told them, 'a nose here, a moustache there.' That too not in their rightful sequence, one below the other, but as disjointed objects floating around without a context. That was what he saw of people. He never apprehended the entire human being. At most other times, he seemed to abandon the effort at lucidity and just parroted everything that was said around him. He picked up the tail end of each sentence that carried through to him and repeated it.

'Would you like to eat something?' Minnie would ask him.

'Eat something,' Shanne would say, the question becoming a statement by the time he echoed it. He would fill the gaps in the conversation, drawing in the last bit of each sentence to fit in with the next words uttered. At other times, he was the poet, reciting verses from Urdu poetry with a coherence and fluency that were missing in his cognition of the world around him, where moustaches existed in a void without the corresponding upper lip. Minnie and Karuna had found him sitting in a park with a big fawn dog curled up at his feet. He was laughing to himself when they first saw him, entertained, perhaps, with what his partial perspective on the world offered him. Voluble and amused, he was the antithesis to Monty, but his dimples, his obvious homelessness and the dog at his heels threw up echoes that were disturbingly familiar.

Minnie had asked him if he would like to have some coffee.

'Have some coffee,' he said.

'Won't you join us?'

'Join us.'

'Come,' she said.

'Come,' he said.

That was, of course, before she had figured out the echo effect, assuming a compliance on his part, which was only an illusion. She had to ask him again and put out her hand to help him up. He did get up and follow them for coffee. The fawn dog waited outside. The cup of coffee became a ritual. Minnie and Karuna would stop at that particular bend in the pathway and look around. Shanne would either be there sitting on the bench or striding up with his fawn dog at his heels. Coffee time, and both Karuna and Minnie got used to the presence of Shanne as a subtext to their conversation.

Of course, he was Shanne the poet, and not Monty the engineer. But Minnie and Karuna were trying to right the wrongs that were part of another world—a world they had left behind in Patiala, yet carried with them everywhere, a world in which one brother was a photograph on the mantelpiece and the other unsteadily made his drunken way home.

'Shanne reminds me so much of Monty,' Minnie would say sometimes.

'He does,' Karuna would reply. Once, in a reflective

moment, she added, 'You know, about Shanne—do you think in a different sort of way we are being as silly as Dazed Uncle's father? Remember him?'

'That's absurd! We aren't doing the horrible things *he* did.'

For as long as they could remember, Dazed Uncle had lived in a fog of incomprehension. In his youth, he had very nearly been decapitated when he trekked with a group of friends from his college in Lahore to the Indian side of the border in '47. A sword held to his neck had suddenly been withdrawn because news had filtered in just then of a much larger migrant caravan moving in that direction, which had to be stopped and slaughtered. When he had finally made it to his family home in Delhi, babbling incoherently about blood and headless babies, his father had gone out and killed a few of those others making their way to Lahore. His act of revenge had not helped his son, who wandered about distractedly for the rest of his life, till he disappeared during the riots of '84.

It was a skewed world. The past never got resolved and it never left you. But Minnie and Karuna wanted to set the record straight. They had survived, so they would make amends.

When Minnie got an apartment of her own, with a kitchen where each utensil had a proud sparkle and each room was primed for use unlike the house she had grown up in, Shanne and his fawn dog became a part of the household. He would wander out into the streets every morning and return without fail every evening. And just as Minnie had once learnt to understand the language of silence, she now learnt to decipher echoes. On the weekends when Karuna visited, Shanne would follow them on their long walks, repeating their words behind them. They would, occasionally, turn around to respond to his echoed participation in the conversation.

Miles from home, their tireless steps matching each other's, the cousins sifted through the past, recycling it as they went.

Remember *to* Forget

1

The iced whisky in the glass had numbed Tejpal's hand into a talon. He transferred the glass to his left hand and blew hard on the right one. The fingers gradually woke to life when his foggy breath touched them.

As the evening shivered on, the air above the nearby Sirhind Canal condensed into water droplets. They gathered in a puddle on top of the tent that had been pitched for the party. When the tent could take no more, it slowly started letting down its burden. A number of drops squeezed through the canvas and suspended themselves there, waiting to gather strength. Then one droplet took a tentative plunge into the plush seating underneath, and others, sure of finding a soft landing, quickly followed suit. The pearly procession began to make a joyous descent.

There was a noisy rout underneath. The women went 'Eeeee' and jumped up; the men went straight to the point with a series of 'sisterfuckers' and 'motherfuckers' muttered under their breaths. Guests scattered looking for cover, or at least a place near the numerous coal fires placed for the women to warm their hands and the men their frozen posteriors.

It was not a great time to party, since November is a

cold month. The sunshine is only a decoy. At night, the cold is real, becoming gooseflesh on naked arms in party clothes on garden chairs. Most people had forgotten the cold of last November and the November before that and the one even before that. 'It was not so cold last November,' they told each other, even though it had been just as cold if not colder. However, it was important to forget, to move on.

And one way of doing that was to run a party relay, a series of parties, each edging the previous one out of the frame with the spectacle that it offered. Insurgency in the state was in its dying throes and what better time than this, to celebrate? They had just lived through ten years of police clampdowns and curfews. Men with long beards and equally long names—names that carried their addresses, following the nineteenth-century edict on using the name of the village of birth as the surname—and an even longer list of dos and don'ts, had curbed the natural excesses of the Punjabi spirit. Their dos had included carving Khālistān out of the Indian state. And their don'ts had forbidden liquor, among a lot of other things. In fact, there were a hundred and twenty-two 'thou shalt nots', proclaimed from mikes at religious congregations, posters on gurdwara walls, press notes that landed on the newspaper editor's table with a warning—print or else...

They proscribed make-up and nose rings and earrings and bangles for brides. They proscribed salwars for boys because boys must be boys and wear the pants in the family.

They prescribed veils for the women to cover their heads with.

They proscribed shedding tears for the dead. Or bowing before the dead.

They prescribed telling on those who were telling on them to the police. They also prescribed food and shelter for themselves if they were to visit villages in the dead of the night.

They proscribed girls dancing on stage.

They proscribed Hindi and the national anthem.

They prescribed death for policemen, informers, dogs that barked in the night, stubborn newspaper editors, men who did not wear turbans… It was a long list.

In these ten years people had been dying of fear rather than in the appropriate Punjabi way—of high cholesterol induced by a desi ghee diet… Until the long-bearded ones themselves began to party and decay. Some of them were discovered living under false identities, in houses equipped with twenty-four televisions and video players, twelve mixies, ten air conditioners, thirty-two cameras and on and on, a long list of gratuitous greed.

However, the state police kept suggesting that it might be wiser to wait a while before celebrating. They said so to the industrialists of Ludhiana specifically, one of them being Mr Bakshi, owner of a hosiery factory. But Mr Bakshi's event managers had suggested 'Snow' as a party theme. This idea would have been a bit incongruous in summer. Of necessity it had to be done in winter, and then, better November than December when it would become even colder.

The venue was Mr Bakshi's home, which had been modelled on a house that he had seen in Europe. Reigning local architectural taste had been added to it—Gothic columns and Roman domes, modernist angularity and Georgian windows, Islamic minarets and English roofs. One dish of everything on your menu, please.

This evening, very little of the house was visible, with

the rising fog clouding it out of existence. The fog had risen from the fields drenched in irrigation. It usually hung above the experimental fields of the Punjab Agricultural University before slyly spreading its reach in whispered movements. Mr Bakshi's house had been swallowed whole.

Lights, with their outlines untidily rubbed out by the fog, lit the way. Pebbled pieces of thermocol formed a snowy carpet all along the driveway from the gate to the doorstep. Rectangular strips of cotton wool hung like limp bandages from the branches of trees and plants, which were otherwise bare of foliage. Attempts had been made at providing the sloping English roof with a thermocol and cotton cover, but most of it had just roller-coasted its way down to the ground.

'Enjoying?' Mr Bakshi asked Tejpal when he spotted him standing alone, flexing his fingers.

It was a usage Mr Bakshi had picked up from a prostitute he had visited in his youth. He had been reluctant to give her his name for fear of having it sullied and had introduced himself as Pappu, a name that gave away absolutely nothing, a name that had neither prefix nor suffix. He was just one pappu amongst thousands of other anonymous pappus out there—who were anything from waiters in dhabas to insurance agents to big industrialists to politicians.

'Enjoying, Pappu?' she had asked at the height of his ecstasy.

And since then it had seemed such a well-worded question, so fulsome. Now he omitted the Pappu, though.

'Enjoying?' he asked Tejpal again. 'Have a drink-shrink,' he added. At other times, or earlier in the evening, it would have been 'tea-shee'. The doggerel came from effusive heartiness, from a hospitality that pinned you down and forced food down your throat. Just the offer of a drink was an inadequate, pale statement of intent.

Tejpal was not 'enjoying', because November was that one month of the year which he did not like. He did not like most months, but this one in particular was where his nightmares were temporally located. It was always November when he was startled awake from his sleep and had to wipe a film of perspiration from his forehead.

'Yes, enjoying,' he said, though his tongue involuntarily, yet again, sought and probed the cavity in his molar, and his senses waited for the familiar pain that would jangle through his head. I really must go to a dentist, he thought; but that required concerted action and he had, in any case, got used to the pain. It was only occasionally that the pain became loud enough for him to think of the dentist. It was a bad moment to be asked if he was 'enjoying'.

Perhaps it was also Mr Bakshi's attitude and his distracted, disinterested air that prickled under Tejpal's skin. But then these moments don't have a single trigger. They come from an accumulated backlog of resentments and memories, from the last word you never got in during an argument, from the up-yours sign that the speeding motorist left with you before he became dust in the distance. One of those moments may choose, maybe, 10.20 p.m. on the first of November to erupt.

'Good, good,' said Mr Bakshi, rubbing his hands together in the certainty of a thing going well, already on his way to the stage to catch some of the limelight.

'You could not find any other day to have this party?' Tejpal said, grabbing Mr Bakshi's retreating shoulder just a shade roughly.

'Is there something wrong with today?'

'You have forgotten the riots of November 1984, when so many Sikhs were slaughtered?'

'That was ten years ago, Tej beta.'

'They split open our skulls, they gouged out our eyes, they poured kerosene on us and burnt us alive. Thousands of Sikhs died that day. Just because it was ten years ago does not mean you…' Language was beginning to desert Tejpal. The sentence completed itself in a number of popping sounds that must have approximated a sentiment.

'You have to learn to go on with your life,' Mr Bakshi advised him. This was his favourite counsel, the one that allowed him to go back to the miracle of his own rejuvenation. Once upon a time, his mother had always apologized for having to entertain without carpets. 'All ours have gone for dry cleaning, you see.' The sorrow of not having any carpets killed her. How happy she would have been today to see all the carpets in his house. Even in the bathrooms! Carpets with foam lining underneath, like padded bras. She might have been happier still with the swathes of marble that formed white vistas in his house, with the pearl and satin-finished woodwork and the golden cornices.

He was about to say more. 'To be very frank…' was going to be his next line, as it so often was. But Tejpal's brow was much too thunderous and his eyes too raw red for any 'frankly' friendly chats. He was not in the mood to hear any preaching. He was in the mood to sock someone in the jaw. He made a wild figure just now. His open beard was flowing down to his chest, his saffron turban looked like it would ignite from the spark of his anger. This had been his new look after November 1984, when he had begun to see himself as the keeper of his religion, and the groomed corporate image had given way to the Punjabi Wild West.

There was a time when he had sported a close-cropped beard and short hair, quite against the tenets of his religion. But that was long before everyone became jumpy about matters of religion; before they lost their sense of humour. Before the capers of the comedian in Sikh garb in a Hindi film evoked not laughter, but indignation. Travelling by train, he had happened to be sharing his compartment with a lumdarrhiya, a longbeard, an irreverent reference to a very devout Sikh. The lumdarrhiya had quizzed him about his religion.

'Beta, you must not trim your beard or cut your hair. The guru had created the Khalsa, the Sikh, in his own image. "Khalsa mero rup hae," he had said.' The lumdarrhiya had quoted him scriptures. 'You have committed a grave sin. A very grave sin.' He shook his admonishing finger at Tejpal, then topped it up with some wisdom. 'You know that each hair of the head, each pore that houses that hair, receives signals from the guru. When you cut off that hair, you cut off your direct connection with the guru,' he said, stroking his own beard with a flourish that was designed to provoke envy of his high connectivity with the heavens. He then leaned over and whispered to him that women who shave their underarms similarly destroy these celestial transmitters.

Tejpal had punctured the pompousness with a strategically told untruth.

'Singhji, I was born a Hindu and was in the process of converting to Sikhism out of a belief in its tolerance and modernity, but listening to you today has convinced me that

I might as well go back to the faith of my ancestors.'

That had deflated Singhji, who had then practically prostrated himself at Tejpal's feet, asking to be forgiven for his unbidden tirade and begging him not to revoke his decision to convert to Sikhism.

The Singhji would be happy to see him today, with his flowing beard, each hair receiving godly messages, though reason had become bits of flying debris from the fiery explosion inside his head.

Tejpal made a lunge for Mr Bakshi, saying, 'Doesn't matter to you, does it? You are a mona, a Hindu.'

These days everyone was trying to negotiate the narrow spaces between religious identities, talking about the weather instead of counting the number of Hindus killed by the long-bearded Sikhs through the years of insurgency, or the number of Sikhs killed by Hindu hooligans in the riots of November 1984. There were official statistics for each of these categories. Statistics to prove that the terrorists had killed as many Sikhs as Hindus; others to prove that the riots were as much an expression of the distance between those who were flush with effete and those who would like nothing better than to be that way. Interpretations could absolve one side and indict the other or vice versa. Statistics were putty but life was not.

To give the acrimony a voice and form was luring the snake out of its hole. And maybe sticking one's own finger in it too, for good measure.

Tejpal had clearly crossed a boundary.

An irked Mr Bakshi said, 'What is this Hindu-Hindu? You are not the only one to have been in the middle of riots. I have seen enough riots in my time.' He said it as though it were a well-cultivated virtue.

Mr Bakshi knew, though he did not know how to say it, that you could not feed off God. No matter what the promises of the afterlife, God was not going to get up and cook dal makhni and top it up with a desi ghee tadka when your stomach growled. These Sikhs, he thought, they really could be a bit dense sometimes. It was from the perpetual weight of the turban maybe. But he did not want to be caught with that thought and quickly shook it out of his head.

By now Tejpal's voice had risen many uncomfortable decibels while various pairs of hands tried to restrain him. He bellowed a series of sputtering incomprehensibles about discrimination against the Sikhs, about Punjab's river waters flowing into other states, about Sikh jokes.

The male half of the gathering congealed around this sudden sore, rushing in emergency measures.

⁂

Tejpal's wife, Harpreet, was sitting with the women at the far end of the lawn, on chairs that ringed a coal fire like a voodoo circle, heads straining inwards, the shadow of a conspiracy rising out of the fire as they measured against each other for all the things that their spouses did or did not do. They tapped into the passing spirits. A white-gloved waiter with his battered tray, both veterans of many a raucous party, was summoned quietly, with an inaudible psst. Double pegs of whisky sat in each of the glasses that trellised the tray. A quick spike in the cola, like a propitiation rite.

'He fights his sleep,' said Harpreet, 'like a baby.'

She had no idea why she was offering these confidences. She did not have to. The gathering was full of the diamond-clad. Diamonds were like regimental gear. You wore it, you were saluted. Harpreet never wore the right uniform. Her plain look was too severe for her surroundings. But confessionals were in the air like an infection.

The most resplendent of the women was now talking. 'Initially I was very upset and tried to make him break off with her. But he stuck to her like glue. She is not even nice looking. I decided that I might as well make myself happy. I just buy plenty of clothes and jewellery whenever I want and give him the bill. Every month I buy. Part of the monthly ration.'

'These men, I tell you, they are terrible.'

'It is only because of us women that marriages survive.'

Not all complaints were in the same league as a mistress in the closet though. There were also grumbles about the mundane. They ranged from the dripping wet bathroom that he left behind to the ill temper that accompanied even a mild fever to the fuss about food and the plateful of alu gobi flung against a wall, leaving behind a turmeric yellow bloom.

Harpreet added hers to the growing pile of grouses. 'The television in our bedroom is blaring all night. The minute I switch it off he wakes up.' It did not sound horrible enough even to her own ears, and she let it hang there unacknowledged.

She looked around and noticed the commotion near the stage. Craning her neck to try and spot the source of the disturbance she thought, we Punjabis love a good fight. A bam-bam fight in which there are a few displaced turbans and jaws and then everybody is ready for a good, hearty meal amidst a resurrected bonhomie, which is even more effusive after the battering it just suffered.

But then she spotted saffron at the centre of it all.

'I think that is your husband,' the resplendent one said to her.

'Don't worry,' said Mr Bakshi's daughter-in-law, Sarika. 'Harish is already there.'

Harish, her husband, had his arm around Tejpal and was walking him towards the house. 'Come. We will get a drink from the bar inside,' he said, removing Tejpal from the scene.

Balli hurried to catch up with them.

'Try taking deep breaths to soothe anger,' he said. 'It works like gargles. A nose-full of breath circles around in the brain, touching all the raw spots.'

Yet another diversion came by way of a recall.

'Oh! I nearly forgot. I had bought some cars today. I wonder if they were brought in,' said Harish, looking alternately green and red standing behind the counter of the bar, as the coloured lights that made up the canopy blinked in sequence. He spoke casually, as though he had picked up bags of peanuts and should have offered them earlier to his guests, to go with the drinks. No one was surprised at the absurdity of the purchase. He went out to check and came back to say, 'Want to come and see? I have asked them to bring the cars round to the front.'

In the driveway stood four diesel-run Mercedes.

'Mark my words,' said Harish, proudly eyeing his new acquisitions, 'ultimately we will all have to switch to diesel. Petrol prices will keep going up with these oil-rich mullahs dictating terms.'

'I should have been born an Arab sheikh. I wear a turban anyway. Could just as well have worn a flowing veil held in place by that ring. Much easier actually,' said Balli.

'You could also have had many wives. Expensive to keep them in good wifely humour though,' was Harish's response, though Balli had no wife at all.

With more money than he knew what to do with, Harish was always obsessive about its buying power.

The men walked around the cars, patted the bonnets, caressed the flanks, fiddled with the door handles, fussing over them like paranoid mothers.

In Ludhiana there were a couple hundred Mercedes plying the roads.

'How this town has changed from the little village it used to be when we were growing up,' Tejpal told Balli, his anger now merely winking bubbles after a smouldering effervescence.

He was not referring to Mir Hota, the village that it was in the sixteenth century when Sikandar Lodi's chief, Nihang Khan, settled in the region, patted it into shape and named it Lodiana. Tejpal was referring to the Ludhiana of the early sixties when cars did not sell like peanuts.

'We were idiots in our youth. We would chase after the occasional car on our street like village children, fascinated and amused by the urbanite and his gadgets.'

'I would even let out blood-curdling yells,' said Balli. He had used the Punjabi word badak to describe his cry—a cry which emanates from lips held loosely together and sounds like a challenge thrown to the world.

Tejpal continued to reminisce. 'Do you remember, on the other side of the Sirhind Canal there were only forests and witches and we had this crazy story about the baba with the long beard. It was so long that he tripped over it but became fleet-footed the minute he spied little children.'

'I think we had come up with that one only to discourage Kaka because we did not want him hanging around with us since he was too little to fit into our scheme of things. But

I had begun to believe my own stories about the baba and was quite scared myself.'

'So was I but I would have hated to admit it then.'

The forest had since disappeared. It was called South City now, and had rows of farmhouses equipped with their own golf courses and swimming pools.

Tejpal had been for a walk along the canal, hoping to resurrect some of the magic. The bushes that lined the canal on either side had looked menacing. That is where those witches came from, the ones with their feet turned inwards and their breasts so pendulous that they had to be thrown over their shoulders like a casual scarf. They would never have been able to walk if the twin udders had been allowed to hang loose in front. But he was not looking for witches or babas; he was looking for the sparkle from those days—the moon staring up at him from the water, surrounded by a protective army of a million stars. He would look up at the sky and expect it to have emptied, since the occupants had made their way down. And then he would be amazed at the endless supply up there.

'Run, run. He is right behind you,' Tejpal would shout to Kaka.

Harish would offer practical advice, 'If he can't see you his beard will get entangled in his feet. Run so fast that he won't be able to see you.'

'Run, run Kaka. Disappear,' Balli would shout.

And all the while that they were urging Kaka on, they themselves were running that much faster, well ahead of Kaka, so that if the baba were to grab a tail, it would be Kaka and not them. Ultimately everyone would get away—

because childhood monsters are always much kinder than adult nightmares. It helps for monsters to have cumbersome breasts and overgrown beards.

In the harsh light of adulthood, the dusty walk along the canal had less romance and more discarded polythene bags. It did not look like the appropriate setting for mystery and adventure. The town itself was choking, houses following each other at a breathless pace to catch up on any gaps or open spaces, cars dovetailing into each other, motorcycles, scooters, rickshaws, autorickshaws, cycles and pedestrians crowding like an undifferentiated, crawling mass. The city had no lungs even for that occasional breath. But it was also said of the city that no one slept hungry here.

⁂

In any case, no one at this party was likely to go to bed hungry unless liquor got the better of them. Most would make it to the dinner table around midnight. The guests had arrived only at about ten o'clock from a series of other parties and white-gloved waiters were plying them with food. You waved away one and another appeared almost at his heels. 'Fried fish,' he said. 'Chicken tikka,' said another. 'Mutton kabab'; 'French fries'; 'Honey-soaked cauliflower'. They were like persistent summer flies—the more you waved, the more they descended on you. Tejpal moved out of range of a proffered plate of tandoori paneer and asked Harish, 'Have you sold that house in Ghumar Mandi where we used to visit you?'

'Long ago,' said Harish.

As Mr Bakshi, Harish's father, had moved up the financial ladder, they had shifted house, changed furniture, acquired imported goods and altered their self-image. Mr Bakshi now stood tall, definitely taller than his five-feet-eight-inches, when he looked into the mirror.

Tejpal stuck a toothpick into a piece of boneless chicken, having succumbed to the onslaught of food, and asked Harish how they had managed when the Russians left the Ludhiana market.

'That was a tough phase but we changed our products and found other buyers,' said Harish, colouring a little with the blush of memories.

In Ludhiana there were many stories of new beginnings and dogged perseverance, of Kashmiri shawl-makers who came here during the 1840 famine in Kashmir and went on to create a carpet-making industry. Or the migrants of 1947 who started out by knitting socks on small machines installed in the house. Backyards would echo with the rat-a-tat sound of these machines—tak-tak-tak-tak-a-tak-tak. They went on to become exporters of hosiery, making huge sweaters with tea saucers as buttons, till the city came to be known as the Manchester of India. Tatters-to-tycoon stories. Russian buyers would arrive in large numbers, but housing them was a problem since the city had only two hotels. In the early sixties the hotels were always full of thickset Russian men and women with sturdy ankles descending into comfortable stomping shoes.

'How do you celebrate your birthdays if you don't drink vodka?' they had wonderingly asked Mr Bakshi over tea at his house.

'We eat pineapple pastries,' Mr Bakshi had told them. Gobind Sweets made them with a six-inch layer of shaving foam on top, designed to leave behind a white moustache of sweet stickiness.

Mr Bakshi's mother had told the Russians all about the missing carpets. And little Harish had pretended to be looking for his non-existent pencil by writhing around on the floor in the hope of catching a glimpse of what was under her skirt, never having seen a skirt, or for that matter what was under it, ever before in his life.

Then the USSR broke up and the Russians disappeared from the Ludhiana market. Harish had hoped that that would be the last he would hear of his juvenile endeavour to get under a skirt. However, Tejpal's reference to the Russians had been inadvertent and was not meant to be a wink and a nudge in the direction of skirts and what they veiled.

Just then the crackle of a mike coming alive drowned out all conversation.

'Hallo, hallo. One-two-three testing. One-two-three mike testing…' was followed by the sound of hammering, which was only the speaker drumming his fingernails on the mouthpiece and complaining, 'This is not working.' A fainter voice was heard telling him that it was and he only thought it was not working because the loudspeakers were placed at the far end of the lawn.

'Achha okay. Shall I begin?'

The speaker began again, but this time in his mike-worthy voice.

'Ladies and gentlemen, please come to the drawing room,' said the voice. 'The ceremonies are about to begin.'

It took several more announcements along the same line—with the voice on the mike going from measured, deep and cadenced, to desperate, screeching and persistent—to dislodge people from their groups and propel them in the desired direction.

He varied his calls.

'Please come, one and all,' he said, taking his cue from the announcements that he made for Saturday tambola at the club and at the annual fair.

'Come one. Come all.'

'Come and get your seats in the front row for the big event.'

The event was the release of Mr Bakshi's book. He had hired a scribe to ghostwrite the story of his life. It had been difficult to find somebody to perform the onerous task since the job required skill in rhetoric and bombast.

'I knew in my heart that I could climb the highest mountains and reach the peak to plant the flag of my victory. It is my strength of character that has made me what I am. I buffeted the storms of my life with a determined mind and heart. Each step was a struggle. But at every step there was achievement. So, step by step my journey went on. And now, I am plucking the fruits of my effort...' There was this and lots more of the same.

Dictation mornings were an arduous affair for the scribe. Mr Bakshi would push his chair away from the desk, lean it backwards, stretch his legs out in front of him, clasp his hands behind his head and stare at the ceiling for inspiration. The lone lizard in the corner would become self-conscious and scurry away on little legs; an eavesdropper in its last life, it had to be a lizard in this one with its ear to the wall. The scribe would doodle in the margins of the page and wait.

Mr Bakshi would say, 'My life has been such a success'—and complete the sentiment with a sigh of satisfaction. The scribe would write down the sentence. Other times Mr Bakshi would rattle off chronological details of births and deaths within the family or in his social circle. He had no doubt about their historical significance or of his own important place in the march of time. Meanwhile, the scribe would be rummaging through his head for flowery figures of speech, for sentences that would curl into pretty daisies at the end.

The Story of My Life was to be an inspiring account of Mr Bakshi's life, and everything one wanted to know about starting afresh. It worked like a hot-air pump on his ego, sending him floating above the skyline. However, shorn of all the self-congratulation, it was an honest account of his life. Though the book left everyone, or at least those who rifled through it, wishing that he had pretended some humility, even if he felt none.

It was a coffee table edition, with Mr Bakshi staring out of coloured photographs. 'Mr Bakshi enjoying in a swimming pool', 'Mr Bakshi enjoying on the streets of London', 'Mr Bakshi in different moods' said the lucid captions. Occasionally, in a burst of generosity, the book conceded print space to other members of his family and towards featuring his houses. The books sat in enormous piles on a glass table in the centre of the drawing room. On the lower shelf of the table a number of magazines lay casually strewn around. These were usually bought by Mrs Bakshi through the window of her car. She would roll down the window when the car came abreast of the magazine vendor's stand, and ask for a few glossy periodicals.

'Give me ten,' she would say. 'Preferably imported. I have a party tonight.'

But these magazines were obscured today, their pride of place having been taken by the home production. The guests were each going to get a return gift—their own prized copy of the first edition of this glorified family album.

Mr Bakshi gave a speech.

'Ladies and gentlemen,' he said, with the flourish of a man who had finally got hold of the mike and did not intend relinquishing it without a fight. 'Let me start the ball rolling, as they say in cricket, and tell you all about my life. Let me be frank with you: I came here with nothing, litter-ly nothing, and now you all know what respect I enjoy in this town. Last year the Global Punjabi Conference called me. I was given a very befitting honour. Some of you have been to my office, no? There you must have seen my photographs with prime ministers, presidents and so many other important people. And now those pictures will be with you in this book. Thanks God that I have been so successful. But mind it, it is not without hard work.'

He was right though. Behind the ornate office chair in which he sat was a wall of photographs of himself: receiving a gift, receiving an award, giving away a gift, giving an award, snipping an inaugural ribbon, standing in a group with a bunch of somebodies.

'I was in Rawalpindi when Partition took place. And as I was telling Tejpal here, we were in great danger there when the riots began. I got away from there in a truck. My entire family came here that way. We all—my family, my father, my brother and sister—we lived in a huge haveli in Rawalpindi.'

He took advantage of the liberty that is available to the migrant to assume an identity and a past. If he had said that they once ate out of gold plates studded with diamonds and embossed with their own coat of arms, there was no way of verifying it, their past having been left behind in another country. So a mansion it was.

'We lived in a haveli,' he said. 'It was known as "Bakshian

di haveli", a landmark, and people pointed to it as they went past. My father was in the trading business.'

There were not many in the audience who were interested in Mr Bakshi, and even less so in his father. But then, he had the mike. A microphone in the hand makes the audience irrelevant and the speaker self-sufficient. He hears only his own voice as it comes back to him magnified, laden with its own echoes. He does not hear the disinterested buzz of conversation, the desultory applause, the unsaid 'boo'.

'He, my father, was a very respected man in society. Any important function in town was not complete without him. Even Englishmen came to take advice from him. To be very frank with you, when we left and came here in August 1947, we came with nothing. It was August twelve, I still remember. It was raining so much all the way that even my underwear was also soaked. We came to the Jawahar Refugee Camp here. The government gave us money every month to live. Three years we lived like that only. Then the government decided that families with men must earn themselves. They started giving us less money. So we came to Model Town and rented a room. To be very frank with you, we all lived in that one room. You see my house now,' he said, waving his arms expansively to encompass it all—the house, the chandeliers, the minarets, the domes, the gardens. 'And you will not believe that at one time my father did not have thirteen annas to send me to school beyond class seven.'

He repeated the last sentence to emphasize the enormity of it all.

'He did not have thirteen annas to send me to school!'

'Thirteen annas!' he said again, like a rendition in Indian classical music in which the artist improvises a threefold repetitive musical sequence.

'You will not believe that I sold peanuts from a rehri and even went from house to house selling newspapers early in the morning, before going to school. And see how successful I have been. I wish my father was here to see me today. He would have been a proud man. Apart from making a flourishing business, I have now also written a book. The area from where I come, Pothohar, which is now in Pakistan, is known for its literary people. All literary people in English literature or Punjabi literature come from Pothohar.'

He proceeded to list all the biggies of the industry and established for himself an exalted literary lineage. 'And now, not the least, myself.'

The gathering was beginning to lose patience with the Bakshi saga. The clusters standing right in front of him found it difficult to move, pinned to their place by the Bakshi eye. He was addressing them directly. They looked around shiftily, trying to avoid direct eye contact while rapidly sipping their drinks, parched sponges into which whole glassfuls disappeared; hoping to project their hurry on to the speaker. The rest of the party was discreetly becoming vapour. By the time Mr Bakshi held up his book to indicate its release, since he was doing the honours himself, the flashbulbs of hired cameras exploded but the backbenchers had already bolted. The loudspeakers burst into song:

Congratulations and celebrations
When I tell everyone that you're in love with me.

The DJ had selected the song with an eye on the first line.

At the far end of the room, conversation was in full flow, unmindful of the passion and perseverance of the speaker. Balli was saying to Tejpal, 'A Singh after all! You had to land up in the wrong place at the wrong time.' He was attempting to cheer Tejpal by drawing on the self-deprecating humour of the Sikh community. 'You heard about the Singh in Kerala. There was a fire in a tea factory and while everyone else was running away from it, he was running towards it. And I am not joking. Even the papers, *Malayala Manorama* it was, carried a story about him. H. M. S. Pannu, I think his name was, and he was running towards this raging fire in the hope of rescuing some documents,' said Balli.

Tejpal laughed. 'And why not Santa Singh or Banta Singh who are the regulars in Surdi jokes? Why H. M. S. Pannu, like a ship?'

'You think I am joking? You think I have cooked up the name, dreamt it up?' protested Balli. 'This one is for real.'

But all Tejpal dreamt of was marauding hordes. He was running... Always running. Breathless but running. Panting and running. Wheezing and running. Terrified and running. But the futility of action in dreams made escape impossible. The mob always caught up with him.

'Try using a car in your dream,' Balli said to him. 'Maybe you can ask Harish to park one of his new Mercedes' there.'

'Won't work,' said Tejpal, warming up to the image. 'It will involve too much reversing and changing of gears.'

⁂

He would be running for miles through little lanes and by-lanes and each time he would emerge at the same square. By then, the crowd bearing down on him would have inched still closer at each successive appearance. He would turn around and run. The background score in all his dreams would be a combination of a drum beating time to a marching drill and the steadily heightening roar of a mob on rampage. Looking back down the length of the road he had run, he would see a tea shop where a huge aluminium teapot sat on a clay oven, in which the flames just kept rising higher and higher till they were slurping on the leaves of the tree overhead.

⁂

The large clay oven, the tandoor at Mr Bakshi's party, had grilling rods standing in it, strung with chunks of cottage cheese and pieces of onion and capsicum like gigantic emerald and moonstone necklaces. The tandoor stood in one corner of the lawn where a few of the more adventurous women had strayed with their dinner plates. Among them was Harpreet. There was talk of designer clothes and the futility of buying them in Ludhiana, since that would compromise their exclusivity.

'Every party you go to, somebody is bound to be wearing the same clothes as you,' lamented one.

'I always buy my clothes in Delhi or in London when we are there,' said another.

There were also philosophical observations about simple living and high thinking. This had come from Sarika, the gold bangles on her arm jangling, the diamonds on her finger emitting sparks, as she declared the motto of her life. It was unclear how she would achieve it in the plenty of her surroundings. In fact, her brand new diamond ring just happened to be visible in each photograph that featured her. No happy coincidence that! (Post-party photograph browsing revealed that she was wearing it alternately on both hands, keeping a careful eye on the hand that was likely to be exposed to the camera.)

Harpreet wandered off to look for Tejpal in a preliminary move to leave for home.

Tejpal resisted. He always did. It was part of his epic battle against sleep. First he would cling to his glass. Then he would linger over his food. Once home, he would put off the evil moment of getting into bed till sleep overcame him on the sofa in front of the television. His head would droop as though attached to his torso by a particularly tensile rubber tube.

He had to keep awake because the moment he would fall asleep he would step right into the sword-wielding crowd that he had been trying to dodge the night before.

⁂

This headlong plunge into trouble in his dream had to do with that November morning of 1984 when, clad in his red turban, he had stretched, yawned and stepped off the train on to the railway platform at Old Delhi station, at a time when everyone else with the burden of a turban was trying to hide. But he had had absolutely no idea about this. He was fresh with the innocence of a sound sleep that had been induced by the gentle rocking of the train. Newspapers were told to blank out news of the violence that came on the heels of the assassination of the prime minister. There were blank spaces in newspaper columns with 'Censored' boldly written across. Behind the words that were never written were stories of mass killing and looting. But Tejpal did not know.

The morning before, he had been standing outside a government office in Chandigarh for an eleven o'clock meeting where he was to be evaluated for the grant of a loan of six lakhs. This was seed capital for first-generation entrepreneurs.

He wanted to start a factory and already had his patch of land on the outskirts of Chandigarh. He had been through a series of interviews to qualify for this final one.

But the government office was strangely quiet and empty on what should have been a working day. Officialdom has its own rhythm of laxity and activity, he thought with resignation.

'Someone will show up some time,' he assured himself.

'What's going on?' he asked a uniformed peon who had sauntered in, seated himself on a bench, kicked off one shoe and folded his leg under him.

'Go home,' he said. 'Nothing is going to happen today. In fact, nothing at all is going to happen for many days. Indira has been shot dead.' He was referring to the prime minister of the country, but he spoke of her as though they had been on first-name terms.

Tejpal looked blank.

'Who?' he asked, his mind still preoccupied with the possible outcome of the forthcoming interview and visions of the factory that was already going up brick by brick in his mind's eye.

'Indira. Indira Gandhi. You don't know her?' the peon said with impatience.

'Oh, I thought you were referring to somebody in this office,' Tejpal replied lamely.

'No, no. I am talking of Indira. I know she is dead, though All India Radio is trying to pretend she is not.'

It was a first-name familiarity born of heated political discussions amongst the peon and his friends as they sat awaiting the next bidding from their bosses in the secretariat. Political bigwigs were household names.

'Rajiv broke down and cried,' he added. He had perfected

the art of adding just that little bit of home-grown spice that would remain within the realm of the credible but would give him an edge over the others. 'Saab was here but he went home to listen to the news. You better come after a week or so. No one will be working here for the next few days.'

He should know what he is talking about, thought Tejpal, given the fact that a bench outside an office is a vantage point. In any case, Tejpal was booked on the Kalka Mail that left Chandigarh at midnight and arrived in Delhi at daybreak. A brief halt at his camp office there, a bath and breakfast and then he would board the train to Gwalior. It was a journey he had taken many times over, ever since he decided to set up his own outfit, having worked as the manager of a factory in Gwalior. He walked out to his waiting cab and directed the driver to the site for his factory.

The land had been purchased many years ago. The to-buy-or-not-to-buy debate had closed with his father's conclusive remark: 'Beta, God has stopped making more earth.'

Any piece of land was therefore bound to become more valuable with time. Tejpal spent the afternoon tending to the saplings that he had planted there. The seed capital for the factory would, however, have to wait.

By evening he was back at the railway station. He spread his bedding in the single coach to Delhi that waited on the tracks for the rest of the train from Kalka, and went to sleep, his body still warm from the afternoon sun and tired from the exertions of the day.

The Chandigarh railway station did not offer much by way of activity—two desultory bookstalls, a loud chorus of birds chirruping in the overhead rafters, bird shit that came flying through the air and had to be dodged, a few tired boxes sitting on the platform waiting to be loaded. It was a good place to catch up on any appointments that one had with oneself. Tejpal usually caught up with missed sleep on this leg of his journey. He did not hear the Kalka Mail arrive nor did he feel the shudder when his coach was attached to it. When he woke up, the train had just reached Delhi and he cheerfully stepped on to the platform, bag in hand.

At the wrong place, at the wrong time.

2

Jasmer Kaur's house was an anachronism in time. There was an endless brick path from the gate to the house. A field of matted weeds threatened to swamp the path. A forest of fruit trees shaded it. The house had a cantankerous bell that rang only sometimes, after repeated jabs at it. The noise of the traffic outside was a muted murmur. And growing old with her house, her wrinkled hands now matching the knots in the barks of the trees, her chin sprouting unwanted hair like weeds, Jasmer Kaurhad become 'aunty' for the English speaking and 'mataji' or 'beeji' for the hawkers with their pushcarts full of vegetables. But she had been Jassi when she was young and she continued to think of herself as Jassi.

The gentle tinkle of a spoon in her afternoon cup of tea was suddenly interrupted by Kailla's rant. 'Kaille da kalesh', she called it. It had to have a name because it had become institutionalized. It happened every day.

'Just you wait. I am coming,' he was shouting to the children who had crept in to steal the fruit and to seek entertainment in the chase that inevitably followed, in which they were always at an advantage. Kailla hobbled along behind them. He was a wiry man with eyes that started out of his head. The clumsy swirls of his turban usually came unstuck the minute he moved. The bottoms of his pyjama flapped as he hastened after them.

'You just stand right there. I am coming to get you,' he said, trying to tuck in the loose ends of his turban while negotiating his walk, both at the same time. There was hardly any likelihood of the children waiting around to be thrashed. They sped away shouting out to him, 'Chacha, we will see you tomorrow. Can't wait just now. Have business to attend to. We are in a hurry.'

'Just you wait,' he shouted. 'I will watch out for you tomorrow and then you won't get away.'

Kailla lived in the outhouse from where he kept one sleeping ear cocked for the giggles of the children creeping in. He even went through the ritual of locking the gate every afternoon, but the younger ones climbed over the barrier and the older ones vaulted over it.

When he was younger, he could occasionally catch one or two of them. He would raise his hand and threaten them with dire consequences, but all he did was give them a vigorous shaking. He grew old but the children remained young, one generation having handed the baton to the next, passing on information of a house with lots of trees loaded with fruit, of a man who merely shouted, gave ineffective chase and threatened but did not beat, of a kind-looking woman in the house whose face appeared at the window sometimes but who did not say anything.

Jassi had been averse to renting out her annex to young couples because the one time that she had, the experience had been surreal. She would be drifting into the sweat-drenched sleep of a summer afternoon when her half-awake mind would catch the sounds of a violent quarrel. She would look out of the window, and her tenant, a tough young woman, would be dragging her husband by his hair and appealing to the world for justice. A Sikh in a physical fight is always at a disadvantage since the turban is easily toppled and the long hair unfurling from under is a proffered weapon, handle first. The young wife invariably made a grab for it. The few times that Jassi had stepped out, she had been asked to 'look, *look* at the wretched man'. She had never been able to understand what to look for and just what was so evil about the man who was being dragged by his hair, other than the wretchedness of being dragged by the hair. She had decided then not to risk young couples and their raw emotions.

However, the first impression that she had of this other couple, who had been in her annex for about ten years now, was that they held together; and though they seemed to carry around some sort of a burning ember, it was so deep within them that it was not likely to spark into a display of pyrotechnics down the drive. Besides, they had come here after the anti-Sikh riots of 1984, and that resonated in her being. Even now, when she reached deep inside, there was a point that hurt dully.

The morning after Tejpal and Harpreet had settled in, the children spotted a new face at the window when they were hoisting themselves on to the gate. Should they go in? The split second of indecision was, however, automatically resolved in favour of a halla bol, a continued charge, since the momentum that carried them to the top of the gate also deposited them at the bottom on the other side. They barely had time to make it to the trees and Kailla was already out, shouting his lines: 'You just wait. I am coming.'

Harpreet was watching from the window of the annex, and Jassi from hers. Too many people, thought the children, and ran for it with Kailla in hot pursuit.

Harpreet had laughingly called out to Kailla, 'Why don't you let the children eat some of this overload on the trees? I am sure Jassi would not mind.'

That one sentence had won Jassi over—she herself kept telling Kailla to let the children be. It suggested a sense of belonging, as though Harpreet were already a part of the household. Also, she liked being called Jassi. That was the beginning of their friendship.

The day after the party Harpreet wiped the sweat from Tejpal's brow and said, 'Why are you sweating?'

A sleeping Tejpal was always more lovable than Tejpal awake. She would watch him negotiate his breath between snores and feel the urge to soothe him.

'Because I ran,' he said. 'Because I ran, like a mouse,' he repeated.

It was exhausting. He had to run even in his sleep, overpowered by the slow viscousness of dreams, by the inabilities that crowd them—the examination hall that cannot be reached as time ticks away and you stand in your underwear unable to find the right clothes, or the pen that refuses to write at the last minute. But Tejpal's dream was a labyrinth without an exit, peopled with a mob that sounded like a congregation of flies in conversation.

⁂

He had stepped off the train at the Old Delhi Railway Station in his red turban. There was a press of cabbies vying to relieve him of his bag and herd him to their taxis. He had instinctively picked one with a red turban.

'Where to, sardarji?' asked the taxi driver.

'Janakpuri,' he said, which was where his company had a branch office.

It was very early in the morning. On the way there was a campfire in the middle of the road. Or so it seemed. Furniture was piled up twenty feet high and was burning rapidly.Black smoke curled into the white, wispy clouds in the sky, dirtying them.

'Some sort of clearing up?' he asked the driver.

'This is a rowdy area. Lots of gundagardi. Could be anything.'

'Even if they are only trying to warm up a cold November morning, why in the middle of the road?'

As they skirted the volcanic mountain of furniture, they saw a human leg sticking out from the bottom of the heap.

'Told you this was a bad area,' said the taxi driver.

They shuddered and drove past. Amidst the smell of burning wood, a fleeting smell, quickly submerged, of burning flesh. A sudden waft again and then they had moved on.

Tejpal washed and bathed in the camp office, then read the paper, which was inked black with news of the prime minister's assassination by her Sikh bodyguards. He contemplated awhile on how the commonplace eludes extraordinary lives even in death. Dying in bed of old age would be far too tame an end for the daughter of the first prime minister of independent India. But he had never liked her and could not say that he was sorry. There was something to be said for a life that was routine. You wake up in the morning and go to bed at night. At least no one thinks of gunning you down. Amidst such philosophical thoughts on the ironies of life he called for a cab to take him to the station to catch the eleven-thirty to Gwalior. 'Come and get it,' each of the drivers said, when he sent his office peon to the taxi stand. None would come to the building. He was surprised at the sudden intransigence of taxi drivers. He walked to the stand, carrying his overnight bag, the picture of normality beginning to curl at the edges.

A busload of ruffians went by.

'Sardar, sardar, maro, maro, kill him, kill him,' they shouted, pointing to him.

He gawked. Just when he had thought the ordinariness of his life was his armour. They could not be serious. They were just a bunch of hooligans getting a laugh out of the stupid look on his face. He waited for the bus to be on its way. But it stopped. And then they were streaming out, armed with clubs and swords.

'Maro, maro.'

There was an explosion of blood inside his head. He scurried into a by-lane and ran wildly. Like a mouse, he thought. He did not look back as that would have slowed him down, but concentrated instead, on getting away from the hungry-eyed mob. That was the stuff his subsequent dreams were made of: the maniacal running, the attempt to keep his feet quiet even as he ran, willing them to fall softly on the tarmac, hiding behind doorways, cautiously peeping round a corner before plunging on.

He had run through a number of by-lanes when he finally felt he had outrun danger. In the distance he saw a small dhaba at the foot of an ancient banyan tree. An old sardar with a flowing white beard was kindling a tandoor, putting small pieces of wood into it and occasionally stirring its depths with a fireiron. Tejpal waited for the heavy pounding of his heart to subside, for his legs to solidify once again into bone and muscle before he made his way there. The sardar was a kindly looking old man. Maybe it was the sudden antithesis he offered, but even now Tejpal thought of him as the most handsome man ever. He went up to him and asked for some tea.

'Babaji, how long have you been running this place?' He was making small talk as the nearly viscous mixture of water, milk, sugar and tea leaves gurgled in the weather-beaten pot, reassuring himself that the ordinariness of life was still intact.

'Been over forty years now,' said the old man as he poured the contents of the pot into a glass through a tea-blackened sieve.

Tejpal rubbed his hands together in anticipation of tea and also as a closure to the cat-and-mouse game. He had just curled his cold fingers around the hot glass of tea when the mob appeared around the corner once again. He thumped his glass down on the table. The tea sloshed all over his hand, scalding it, but he ran.

As he looked back from the head of the lane, he saw that the mob had caught hold of the old man and was swinging him into the fire. That is where his visual frame froze forever.

⁂

When Harpreet wiped the sweat from his brow, he had woken up mid-stride. But he had also left behind an old man being roasted in an oven. And now that he was awake, he could not alter anything.

⁂

Tejpal had been to a school in Ludhiana where most of his class fellows were sons of industrialists—some petty, some giants.

His father was a people person, prone to unleashing practical jokes. His favourite one was from the time when India had neither independence from the British nor a national anthem. He was enrolled in an engineering course in London and when students from different nations were asked to sing their anthems he had gone on to sing a Punjabi folk song; standing at attention, hand on his heart and a grave look on his face, though he was singing about a wily old traveller who stopped for a night at a lodging run by a woman and left behind two counterfeit annas as payment after availing of everything she had to offer. 'Everything' was a matter of speculation and could be stretched as far as the imagination would go.

'*Nalle baba raat reh gaya, nalle de gaya doanni khoti*,' he sang.

The assembly of European students stood straight and stiff, whilst laughter gurgled silently in his chest.

To Tejpal he would describe the time, back in 1915, when he and others would meet at the Dewa Singh Sports Goods shop in Chaura Bazaar. His narratives usually came with appropriate sound effects. He could never mention the word motorcycle without an accompanying, prolonged 'zooooooo' which went from a low note to a high-pitched one, or a resounding slap that was always a 'phataak'. There were many others and the accounts always became a dramatic enactment. Tejpal's father's stories were foggy and exciting. Tejpal never understood everything.

'We would usually gather at the sports shop because we had to each collect our share of the pamphlets that were to be distributed. We would talk in whispers. Phus phus...phus phus. Not that it made any difference because we kept getting into trouble anyway. We would keep telling each other to shhh up because that had been our problem. We could never keep a secret. The angrez always knew in advance what we were going to do next.'

'Did they know you?'

'No. They just knew us as the ghaddaris—rebels. They also knew that in the February of 1915, we were all going to rebel against the British. I was very little then, only good for fetching and carrying. And that is what I did. But the others, the older boys, had plans. They were going to destroy railway stations and police posts, disable post and telegraph systems, cause disarray in military camps and set up their own camps in jungles and border areas.'

'But I am sure the angrez knew you were one of the rebels. They must have been afraid of you.' Tejpal could not imagine anyone not knowing his father.

'We had just picked up a handful of those pamphlets and were headed out of the shop when one of those English policemen gave us chase. We barely made it because my friend dropped some leaflets and stopped to gather them, and I had to run back and help him.'

And then in a philosophical tone, he added, 'Bravery came so easily those days. It was fuelled by a righteous anger and we would just surge ahead on its torrential flow.'

⁎

When Tejpal finally drove into Ludhiana on that cold November morning of 1984, after a journey on the razor's edge, he felt nothing, not even anger. After he escaped from the mob he had been refused help by a senior police official who had told him he was on his own. Terrified, he had hidden on rooftops, and had watched two Sikh men being hurled off a neighbouring roof. He had been partially reassured when he found shelter with a friend; and had finally dumped his pride and identity and removed his turban, taken his hair down, smeared his forehead with a red tikka, and become Swami Vidhi Chand. His friend did not recognize him as he held up his hand in blessing. 'Tathaastu,' he said, and his friends gawked at this apparition that appeared to have fallen in through the roof. It was in this guise that he had travelled to Gwalior, only to find that he and his wife had to flee from there as well, because the mob had names and addresses there, too, and were carefully, methodically, going from one house to the other, making sure to kill, burn and loot.

All through the drive his wife sat beside him. Two large suitcases were thrown carelessly into the boot of his car along with a random selection of household goods—cushions, crockery, cutlery, gadgets, linen. There had been no time for considered choices. A hasty inventory made in a fleeting glance, things picked only because they were closest at hand, a moment of indecision between two necessities resolved in passing; racing against the crowd that was even now arming itself with swords and petrol somewhere in town.

The baggage in the boot, the car that they drove and a healthy bank balance were all that he had to show for all those years spent as a busy executive. He had arrived in Ludhiana with a frown wrinkling his forehead, eyes shadowed under by sleeplessness, worry lines creasing the rest of his face, his chin firmly set, not in any display of determination but more from the emotional necessity of gritting his teeth. Arriving at midnight, they had parked their car in front of the gurdwara at Kichlew Nagar. The familiar sight of a gurdwara, any gurdwara, offered a feeling of relief which had nothing to do with religion. It just gave them a sudden sense of belonging.

The town was characterized by frenzied industrial activity with neither time nor breathing space for any ghosts, nor for any finer sentiments that might pass for culture. Tejpal had parked here quite instinctively because this was where his parents had lived in later years after his father's retirement from the Punjab Agricultural University and before their deaths. Harpreet and he had looked at each other and cried silently for a few minutes in homage to their lost lives. Before this, there had been no time to cry. They had then debated waking some friends to find a bed for the night but decided against it. Neither of them had the emotional energy to give a coherent account of the events to anyone, least of all to those who would wake up from sleep—those whose lives were still determined by the certainties of the everyday.

'We will just sleep in the car,' was all they said to each other, hoping that the morning would look different. And it did. They had woken up in the early hours and already the streets were beginning to fill up with traffic, the silence of the night broken by milk delivery men on motorcycles, the tinkling of cycle bells as labourers on early morning shifts made their way to their workplaces.

Once the immediate sense of danger diminished, Harpreet began to feel that there had been something strangely unfettered about their journey. Just a road ahead and they could have gone anywhere, any milestones past any green fields. But they had driven into Ludhiana.

The first settlers, the no-baggage itinerants, the Rajputs and later the Jats wandering in from the South, must have looked at the Sutlej river and said, 'Here is where we stop,' and may have gone on to say, 'we may as well put down our backpacks and seek permission from whomever it is that gives permission.' And no matter how dusty and tired those first settlers must have been, they had made an epic journey. The kind that creates castles out of thin air; when the dust clears, a whole city is in place.

Some said Ludhiana took its name from the Lodhi dynasty in the fifteenth century; others believed it dated back to many thousand years before Christ, during the time of the Vedas. But the romance of antiquity was soon submerged by the scramble for existence.

Into this city Tejpal and Harpreet had come, the skyline teeming with rooftops as far as the eye could see. They had been welcomed into Harish's house. His father, the honourable Mr Bakshi, had lectured them on the mettle it takes to begin again.

'Look at me,' he said. 'You will not believe that I started with nothing, just like you will have to today. Of course, it is not everyone who can do it. You have to be very determined.'

3

Tejpal's friend Balli had a problem. He did not know he had one though. Too much had happened between the genesis of the problem and its manifestation.

'She is like my sister,' he would say. That applied to all the women he knew as well as to the millions he did not. Perhaps the sentiment had been reinforced by his parents, who were always describing each little girl who visited their house—a friend's daughter, the housemaid's daughter, the pigtailed girl in his class whom he was great friends with—as 'your sister'. But then this was no different from most parents who unconsciously hope to put off the evil moment of the discovery of sexuality in their children. Balli had taken it to heart.

On rakhi day he would have an armful of rakhis, all the way up from his wrist to his elbow, each the size of a big dahlia that had to be tied at a breathing distance from yet another blooming flower. Some featured a layer of tissue over a petal-shaped sponge, a bulbous daisy with a silver butterfly in the centre, others were a flurry of gold and silver tinsel with red velvet shapes spreading amoeba-like on the arm. A whole line-up of these, from his tiny wrist to his bony elbow, professing sisterly affection, were secured to his arm by little girls. The thread of love seemed to have tied him in knots.

'They are not your sisters really,' Tejpal and Harish protested.

'But they are like my sisters.'

Oldest ploy in the book, this one. Boys in school would say this to worm their way closer to the girls, and film stars in Bombay modified it a little to 'we're just good friends' and used it as a cover-up for relationships.

What made Balli's case different was that he was entirely serious about his peculiar angle on one half of the population. Not quite half though, since the population in Punjab has a skewed sex ratio. Part of the responsibility for this rested with his ancestors from the nineteenth century, who would put a piece of molasses in the mouth of a baby girl and a skein of cotton on her breast, and chant as they put her in a water pot and buried her in the ground.

Eat molasses,
Spin your thread!
We don't want you
But a brother instead.

Balli moved on from those big orbs on his right arm to sober, single threads in college and onto a bachelorhood that was teetering on the edge of perpetuity. His father had not given up though.

'Maybe you can convince Balli to get married,' said his father to Tejpal. 'We have a girl in mind, but Balli refuses to go and meet her.'

Actually there was a range on offer for selection. There were four daughters in that household, each born within a year of the other, and Balli had been offered the pick of the lot. They also had plenty of money thanks to a massive slice of land that the family owned in the heart of Ludhiana. Land prices had gone up a near vertical gradient and all they had to do was sell a few crumbs that fell from the table and that would be enough to marry the girls. Enough to buy a marriage outfit at the price of a car, a car at the price of an aeroplane and a house at the price of a trip to the moon.

Balli decided to go and see the girls because he had been toying with the idea of getting married. The added impetus was that Tejpal and Harpreet had agreed to accompany him and his father. His mother was a ghostly presence, a sighing shadow that floated in and exhaled the chill of some deep-seated sentiment and sailed out. It was only occasionally that she participated.

'Shall we go?' Balli's father emerged from his room all trussed up, his pink turban matching the pink shirt under his coat.

'Let's,' said Balli without enthusiasm.

'And don't ask the girls to tie a rakhi on your wrist,' Tejpal advised him.

The house of the prospective brides was a series of sitting rooms. At the entrance two chairs flanked a carved wooden table, followed by a lobby with a flowery sofa set, an atrium with a leafy roof and garden chairs and then the drawing room. Traversing through the endless sitting spaces, Harpreet wondered if they had any bedrooms at all.

'Which one?' Balli's father whispered to him after the preliminaries. He was referring to the four girls and not the numerous drawing rooms. They had been ushered into the room reserved for the most important events.

Balli shifted nervously on the velvet sofa and carefully examined his shoes, which were black and shining. He even leaned over and dusted off a speck with the paper napkin he was holding in his hand. It was attention to detail in the hope that the larger picture would disappear in a poof, leaving only him and his black shoes.

He looked up to see that the girls were floating clouds of gossamer veils in different colours. The centre table was burdened with sweets of all kinds. Orange jalebis, barfi glistening with silver foil, gulab jamuns soaked in syrup, a darkly brown chocolate cake, sandwiches, cutlets. It was difficult to choose.

'Try some,' the girls said to Balli, holding out each of the dishes in turn.

'Which one?' said his father.

'*Akkad bakkad bambe bo, assi nabbe poore sau, sau kalota titar mota, chal madari paisa khota.*'

The elimination count went through Balli's head, the jabbing finger of his mind going from one girl to the other. And wherever it stopped at 'paisa khota', which in any case meant a dud coin, that girl was out and he could then start with the remaining players. It was only a game in his head and not meant to operate as the decider because he was already beginning to feel fraternal towards the girls. But the timing of his father's query happened to coincide with the conclusion to the counting rhythm in his head and the jabbing finger turned into an inordinately long wooden pointer. It was the pointer that his geography teacher wielded when she stood aside from the board to give her students a clear view of the map, and traced the journey of the river Sutlej in its westward drift, explaining Ferrel's law to them. But Ferrel's law was only black lines with arrows, capturing neither the personality of the river nor the drama of the journey. And he liked to think of the river as a horse in full gallop.

Just when the geography teacher's pointer had wended its way in and around the districts of Ropar, Samrala and Jagraon and had arrived at a confluence with the other galloping River Beas at Harike, Balli's jabbing finger declared Girl Number Two as the winner. His father chose that moment to pop the question to him once again. 'Which one?' he said, and this time it was louder, almost a stage whisper. Without realizing it, Balli's flesh and blood finger pointed to Girl Number Two though he was merely indicating the winner of the last elimination round and not his choice.

But the place erupted into an explosion of celebration before he could contain his finger. 'Mubarkan, mubarkan, congratulations, congratulations'—they all said to each other. It all happened so quickly but in his mind it was a slow dance of deliberate actions, of people hugging each other and offering the silver-foiled barfi, clicking photographs of Girl Number Two and him seated side by side on the velvet sofa, feeding each other a piece of barfi, standing with her parents, then his father, then with Tejpal and Harpreet. They gave him five gold coins as an initial offering, sealing the contract to marry. *We put our money down on you.*

The other girls had now melted into the background like participants at a beauty contest who had recited their lines for the camera and were now gradually bowing their way out. The moving finger writes, he thought, and having writ, moves on.

The journey back was a sombre affair. He did not want to get married.

He examined various excuses to call off the engagement. Should he tell his father that he had a girlfriend? But then he would be required to produce her immediately with the added responsibility of explaining why he had kept her hidden all this while. Nor would it mitigate his crime if attention were drawn to the fact that his father had bought a woman for rupees five hundred in the hilly resort of Manali, way back in the early fifties, and had kept her there for many years, hidden from everyone. His mother's occasional remarks about the uncertainty of her own status within this house, and the angrily spat out words—'that woman!', told him that it was not just rumour. Maybe some of her sighs took their chill from the cold in Manali, from the snows that capped the mountains that surrounded it.

But the only girls Balli knew were either his rakhi sisters or his friends' wives.

He could also say that he was impotent, which he well might be, given the fact that he continued to be in a state of blessed virginity. But impotence was an excuse that girls used to annul marriages that they wanted to wish away, and it seemed like self-flagellation to be accusing himself of impotence. Besides, it would put the shadow of unmanliness on him and he may just as well have said that he was a homosexual. So, he resorted to the ridiculous. It was only meant to be a facetious attempt at putting off the wedding and he wanted to see just how far things could be stretched.

'The girl's teeth were not well aligned,' he told his father.

'Her teeth!' he said. 'How did you get to see her teeth?'

'She smiled, didn't she?'

'Whom was she smiling at? I did not see you smiling even once. In fact, you looked grim enough to be at a funeral.'

'I was coping as best I could. I did not think there was anything to smile about.'

He had not expected his father to do what he did next. His father could be brash, aggressive and loud, the kind who could embarrass you in a restaurant (such that when Balli was a teenager, he would usually act as though he had no idea how this gentleman with the booming voice happened to be sitting at the same table as him). Yet he did not expect this.

As soon as his back was turned, his father rang up the household with the four daughters.

'My son thinks that the girl has crooked teeth.'

'That is no matter at all. This is your house. You are welcome any time. Come again and see for yourself,' said her father.

The offer was actually taken up by Balli's father, who discreetly made a second visit to their house. When told of the event, after his father made a triumphant return home, Balli squirmed each time he tried to reconstruct the scene. Before leaving for the house his father must have had his usual ten-towel bath—one for his hair, one for his face, one for his torso, one for his back, one for his underarms, one for his upper limbs, one for his lower limbs, one for his genitals, one for his feet and one for wrapping around his middle as he stepped out of his bathroom into the dressing room. This was not from a neurotic disorder but from a desire to luxuriate in excess, whether it be towels or turbans. His father must have pulled out his brightest shirt and carried it to a cupboard full of turbans. He must have run the shirt across all these like a shopkeeper trying to match a sari blouse, located the best approximation, and then proceeded to get ready. He must have left the house with a strut, his moustaches at a ten past ten on his face. And he must have been welcomed there with the same fanfare as before. The table must have been loaded with an equally exhaustive array of foods. Maybe pineapple pastries instead of chocolate cake this time, and rasgullas instead of gulab jamuns, a different filling for the sandwiches, but the menu of available girls must have been limited to Girl Number Two only. Would she have been instructed by her father to smile a lot or would they have manually parted her lips to see her teeth like the examination of buffaloes at a cattle fair? A toothless buffalo, her milk teeth having fallen out, would fetch a good price since it would mean that she was ready to give birth. The birth of each calf would result in two teeth sprouting in her mouth and after six teeth she was done and ready to be retired. But Girl Number Two had to show the presence of all her teeth to establish her beauty and youthfulness. The molars, the canines, embedded in the jaw in a curve well defined. Maybe her father had used that same wooden pointer to spell out the map of her teeth.

'Those people are so nice,' Balli's father said to him. 'Nobody is so nice these days, so accommodating. The minute I told them of your doubts, they were unhesitating in their invitation for us to visit again. You now have no reason not to marry her.'

'But how could you have gone there again?' said an exasperated Balli.

'You are the one who expressed doubts about her teeth, so I just went and checked up again. There is nothing wrong with her teeth.'

He would have to marry her now, not because her teeth had made the grade, but because he would have to atone for the second examination, the double display of the girl.

He stared out of the window of Shangri-La and said, 'I don't really want to get married.'

'But why not?' Tejpal asked. They were at their favourite Chinese restaurant where you could order noodles and sweet-and-sour but you could also ask for dal makhni and tandoori roti, with plenty of onions. Or then you could order them all together in the true spirit of a melting pot. In the old days they would even compete on the number of rotis each could eat. Twenty, then twenty-five and onwards. It was all on the house. Balli was the established winner. Even the owner of the restaurant, Meiyang, participated in serving the competition rotis. Meiyang was Chinese, but born and brought up in Ludhiana, and would qualify as a Singh on most counts except for a missing turban. He spoke Ludhianvi Punjabi, ate kadhi chawal on Sundays as did his children, and referred to his friends as 'Bhaaji'. His relatives in Calcutta accused him of speaking Chinese with a Punjabi accent.

Meiyang, Harish, Tejpal and Balli sat around a table, going over the events of the day. Balli said, 'I don't know, but something inside me revolts at the idea.'

Unlike most people, marriage did not throw up images of hearts and roses in his mind, or for that matter access to some robust sex. Instead, it brought to the fore hazy impressions of a hospital room and a wailing baby being tossed from one bed to another, with Balli trying to grab it, saying, 'My sister, my sister.' He did not know why these shadows danced in his mind.

'Maybe we need to purge you of this brotherly sentiment that does not let you get married,' Harish suggested.

'And just how are we going to do that? Light a fire and call in the voodoo man to use his broom to exorcise the evil? Beat it out of him?' asked Tejpal.

'I was going to propose that we take him to Dhakka Colony, where all those women wearing skimpy clothes come from. Those orchestra girls who are so visible at weddings, they are all there. Let's just push him off the deep end. He will have to swim for it and we will stand by and cheer.'

'How would that help?' asked a nervous Balli.

'You are not likely to see one of those as your sister,' elaborated Harish. 'Those ones wearing little, little skirts.' Harish wriggled his posterior to indicate the littleness of the skirt, the smallness of the bottom and the suppleness of both together.

The idea met with noisy approval all around.

'Wah, wah,' said Meiyang, as though responding to an Urdu couplet. 'Bhaaji, what an idea.'

⁂

Dhakka Colony was a colony by default. Like most parts of the town which had not seen anything like planned growth, it was not meant to have been there. Construction in the town was only a series of eruptions, which neither made any prior announcements nor followed any defined pattern. However, Dhakka Colony had the added misfortune of carrying a name that made its intent clear. It had pushed its way into existence but was not going to be a pushover either.

The unlit central road was a narrow alley with one-room housing on either side. The doors and windows of each of these rooms looked out on to the alley. Conversely, the occupants of these rooms provided a series of cameos to passers-by. Here was a woman in black buckling up her sandals; another one dabbing on make-up; a man emerging from his attached bathroom, wrapped in a towel with only a vest covering his torso; an oldish woman brewing a cup of tea; a little girl skipping out of the doorway. It was difficult not to see it all in one glance. There was also an urge to wait and follow the action through. To see the woman stand up in her sandals, to look at the made-up face, to watch the man pull on his trousers, to sense the comfort of hot tea coursing down the gullet as the woman sipped it. It was idle curiosity but fuelled by the manner in which these everyday people stood out in relief, in their lit up interiors, engulfed by the blackness around. And in spite of the seeming ordinariness of their lives, they became characters whose actions evoked interest, though they themselves remained oblivious to the transparency of their existence. They had a work-a-day equation with the street and therefore, did not see it as an intrusion into their lives. They neither pulled down any curtains nor kept the door shut, their quarrels and friendships unfolded under the spotlight of their sixty-watt bulbs.

There were signboards posted outside every other room. One said 'Sweet Star Musical Group' with a silver star dangling by its side, another said 'Golden Bell Orchestra', and yet another was home to the 'Melody Orchestra'. The woman who stood up in her sandals and the other who was readying her face would ultimately head out to one of the numerous weddings in town. They performed choreographed dances on stage, in groups or solo, to Hindi film songs while the wedding guests hung around and watched. They wore flashy, glittering clothes—the kind that were on display at the tailor's shop in their colony.

The tailor's shop stood at the head of the street and was the first thing that greeted you on entering Dhakka Colony. The shop did not have a name. It did not need one; it was the only one there. And it was unmistakable. Two armless mannequins stood outside. One wore a sheer black sequined skirt barely covering her plastic buttocks, and a short wrap-around choli of the same fabric on top. The second mannequin was in orange see-through, tight trousers, which too were all aglitter, with a choli to match. The tailor would haul both of them into the shop at night at closing time. He would put his arms around each one's middle and lift her just an inch above the ground. He did not want them rubbing their heels in the dust. He could not manage more than that because he was not a tall man. However, it did not involve more than a 180 degree spin around and one brief unsteady step into the shop. He would lower each mannequin on the left side of the door. Both would end up facing the back of the shop till the next morning, when they would be dusted, and their clothes straightened. Arms around the waist, the spin in reverse, one shaky step out and they would be back on their vigil, right next to the doorway. These two were the first personages that you met at Dhakka Colony, their faces smiling beatifically, their arms outstretched in a come-hither.

The flesh and blood women slept during the day and woke up late in the evening to rehearse or innovate dance steps, ready their clothes and prepare their faces for the stage. The street came alive only in the evening.

When the four friends walked down the street they felt like voyeurs caught in the act. They walked down one way and then walked back, pretending to look straight ahead most of the time though their eyeballs were dancing from side to side, catching glimpses of the women. They were not sure of their next course of action. Should they just walk up and knock on one open door or were there bouncers around who would toss them into space and send them into orbit? But if not a knock on the door then how else did one approach them? And then, what exactly were they looking for? Were they commissioning a dance performance for Balli's bedroom?

'I'll tell you what we will do.' It was Harish taking charge. 'We will walk up and down a few more times, identify the best-looking one and then approach her.'

'We should let Balli decide,' said Tejpal.

'Balli is being called upon to make far too many decisions in a single day.'

'But then it is he who has to watch the girl dance and feel something stirring.'

With uncertainties dogging each step, they made a few more trips. By this time they were beginning to get curious glances. The idlers and elders sitting on jute cots outside the rooms were following the movements of the strangers through narrowed eyes. They had once beaten the income-tax collectors out of their colony because, as they said, they were paying protection money to the don and that was as good as paying tax. Who were the taxmen to come and make demands on them? Their narrowed eyes narrowed a little more with each tentative step the quartet took.

'Who are they?' they were asking each other. 'Shall we ask them what they want?' 'Wait. Let us see what they do next.' But since the four men did not do very much other than walk up and down, a consensus started building up towards accosting them. The women were the bread-earners in this area, and the older among them began to roll up their sleeves. Even the stray dogs spread-eagled on the muddy sidewalk were now sitting up and growling under their breath. The four began to feel that they should just leave—and quickly. They would have to defer the knocking on the door to another day.

'Shall we run?' they asked each other.

None waited for the answer. They just sprinted.

'Why did you have to run?' asked Harpreet later.

'Even the stray dogs were beginning to growl. I did not want them getting a taste of my ankle.'

'Stray dogs are easily shooed away. All it needs is a pretence at picking up a stone and flinging it at them.'

'Not these. They were obviously born and brought up in Dhakka Colony. They were quite at home.'

4

Sweety of the Golden Bell Orchestra had no idea that she had been the subject of much discussion among four men who had gone past her window, examining her from the corners of four pairs of eyes.

Eyeballs left as they walked from the tailor end of the street to the vegetable vendor.

Eyeballs right when they made their way back from there to the mannequins.

A vision squeezed out of squinted eyes.

Even if she had known, it would not have made much difference. She was used to being eyed by men in that certain way. However, she may have seen a novelty in the oblique angle of the quartet's stare, since the usual gaze featured moustache-twisting, naked aggression. That macho kind of gaze was a guided missile that would bore down to the very marrow of her bones. She could sense it before she saw it.

Her feet ached because of the high-heeled black sandals in which she had danced the previous night at a wedding where guests refused to let the party wind up. Considering that many of them had just come in close to midnight, carrying gifts in shimmering paper with elaborate flowery toppings and cascading ribbon ringlets, it seemed only fair that the celebration be extended till the morning, to accommodate them. And then it was only at night that a summer wedding did not reduce women to mounds of molten make-up and turn men liquid inside two-piece suits. Some of the men would even need to be carried out, though that was because of the quantities of liquor consumed.

'This summer is exceptionally hot. Oof,' the women told each other, fanning themselves, while the two-winged pedestal fan sounded like a monster that had been disturbed in its sleep.

'I don't remember it being so hot ever.'

Yet, like winter, it had always been that hot each summer. The dust chased wizened brown leaves, which in turn looked like they were going to burst into flames. Buildings trembled, refracted in the rising vapour. Colour drained from the countryside. Memories were not short. They were only erasing, abnegating, to begin again.

The men were too busy to notice the heat. They were generating some of their own.

There had been endless encores each time Sweety stepped off the stage. She had been Madhuri Dixit that night, with an intoxicated audience swaying to her movements. Drunken and delirious men with liquor glasses balanced on their heads waddled around, gyrating their forty-four-inch middles to a countdown in a film song.

Ek do teen…
Char panch chhe saat aath nau
Dus gyaran
Baran teran

One to thirteen went the numbers, as the beloved counts moments to a reunion with her lover.

'I count painstakingly, waiting for you,' sang the men to each other, and with the pronouncement of each 'you', half a dozen hands shot out, pointing to each other in drunken misdirection guided by filmed-over eyes. Others pointed her way. Glasses clinked. Some fell to the ground from the giddy heights of balding pates, where they had been placed for a display of balance. She swirled around in her black, diaphanous nylon skirt worked over with blue sequins patterned into a moon and stars.

She had been briefly upstaged when the bridal pair had made their entry. All other lights had been switched off as a pair of 2,000-watt beams shone on a wooden moon pasted over with silver paper and poised atop a sweep of silver stairs. A door had swung open in the moon, revealing its brown, wooden behind. The moon's bottom. The bride and bridegroom had appeared, then stepped through the door like visiting dignitaries alighting from an aircraft, waved to crowds below while photographers and video-wallas clicked and rolled. They walked down the stairs in a glare of flashlights and were briefly surrounded by friends and relatives, then immobilized for the rest of the evening into two high-backed, ornate chairs, which were placed on a stage that was part of the heavenly constellation. After that, everyone forgot about them and proceeded to party. The couple sat and smiled self-consciously at the video camera that was permanently pointed at them, their image projected on large screens that were placed around the venue.

Sweety was back centrestage while 'whishky'-soaked voices called out to her, 'Shhweety, you are the besht.' Some of them scrambled on to the stage, waved a wad of money over her head to ward off the evil eye and gave her the money. A man in a bowler hat had even whispered something to her about a film career as he tried to tantalize her with money that took the halo route over her head—'Come and shee me.' She had a secret pocket even in her most translucent dresses, which only hinted at anatomy without actually showing any. This was where she stashed the overflow from unbridled generosity pried loose by liquor.

The morning was different. She needed a painkiller, both for her head and her feet. Extremities were always a problem, she mused. It was difficult being astride two worlds, the fairy-tale fantasy of a wedding venue and the reality of morning. It was schizophrenic being Madhuri Dixit and Sweety. She wondered if Madhuri Dixit herself had the same problem when she did things that were routine, things that protagonists on screen never seemed to need to do. Go for a morning shit for instance. Did she fill up a mug of water to wash herself—washing the moon's bottom—and then easily reconcile this squatting image with the one on screen where she only moved in a swirl of music?

But at least she did not have to go to a bed in Dhakka Colony, and that reduced considerably the operational area for schizophrenia.

Madhuri Dixit was Madhuri Dixit for most parts of the day and night, when she reported for her shooting schedule, sparkled at an awards ceremony, twinkled before television cameras.

She did not have Kailla looking in at her window. And that was Sweety's immediate problem, other than the drum in her head that beat a steady, unerring rhythm. Who was this man, she wondered. And why was he stationed outside her window? The few strands of his beard were grass struggling to grow in the dense shade of an old tree, the folds of his turban like an uneasily balanced, lopsided rope basket about to reveal a coiled snake.

In the distance stood a group of grinning bystanders. Had she woken up as Madhuri Dixit, they would have been looking for an autograph. There would have been adulation instead of derision.

'What do you want?' she asked Kailla.

'I was sent,' said he, in the best traditions of a messenger. The carrier pigeon with a missive tied around its neck.

'By whom?'

'Somebody.'

'But who?' she said, the irritation of an aching head rising within her.

'There is a man, a big sardar.'

Kailla himself was not very clear since the instructions had come down to him third-hand.

'He might have a name,' she suggested.

'He lives in that white kothi.'

Big white mansions were many. There was nothing rare or distinctive about them. They were in Sarabha Nagar, Ranjit Nagar, Model Town. Rows upon rows of them, competing for space on the ground and in the air.

'And?'

But that was as far as Kailla knew.

⁂

The four men had sat down over chicken sweet and sour, tandoori roti and a propitiating plate of noodles out of deference to Meiyang's Chinese origin, and relived their peregrinations up and down the Dhakka Colony road. Up and down went their minds, peeping in at the different windows. Too fat, too thin, either too jiggle-jiggle or a chest of drawers with two knobs. The bra size worked like the auctioneer's mallet. *Thaak*. Sold.

But on the dinner plate it did not work. What is needed is the leg and not the breast. Caterers at Punjabi weddings profess that they are on the lookout for a four-legged chicken for their business to be viable. 'Everyone wants a leg piece. Wonder why chickens could not be mammals with four legs?'

The breast piece works in bed though.

It was decided that the girl who was buckling on her sandals under the banner of the Golden Bell Orchestra was the best option. There was something erotic about a pair of black high-heeled sandals. Women in pornographic films wore black stilettos and absolutely nothing else, never worried about exposed warts or unwanted bulges for all to see. In fact, they puffed out their silicone-filled chests with a pride of possession that was very seductive. So thought all the others, though Balli was yet to discover that sentiment.

'She was nice, don't you think?' they asked.

Balli cleared his throat, his mind still full of burrs, and his heart still holding down his brotherly effusions, his knee pinning them down in a wrestling manoeuvre. He drummed a nervous tune on his knee, a morse code telling it to keep his fraternal feelings at bay.

'Don't even say that she is like your sister,' said Harish, his admonishing finger up in the air to pre-empt any such excesses.

Balli had also thought that she seemed the most attractive.

This time he was making his choice based on a squint-eyed scrutiny of her features rather than a counting rhythm. He prefaced and suffixed his expression of approval with a lot of 'umms' and 'hmms'.

'I think, though...umm...I am not sure any of this makes sense...umm...but if you insist...I think, maybe, hmmm the one that...'

It took him a long time. In the middle of it all he even shovelled in an entangled mouthful of noodles, taking extra time out to slowly and noisily siphon up a particularly long noodle that hung all the way down from the o of his mouth to his plate.

He also delivered a short, hesitant speech on marriage, which mentioned companionship and the lack of it, love and the lack of it. He spoke about the gap between love and compatibility. A gap so wide that a couple could fall through standing shoulder to shoulder. He spoke without the disadvantage of experience.

But he also expressed approval.

A cheer went up.

'Here's to the woman in black,' said Meiyang, raising the bowl of sweet and sour—capsicum, onions and chicken pieces slapping around against the dragons in the bowl.

That particular matter having been settled, there was yet the awkward business of contacting her and negotiating terms.

'You go and talk to her,' each said to the other.

'My wife will lynch me.'

'You obviously survived the last visit.'

'But that's precisely it. I can't tempt fate again and again.'

It was soon apparent that none of them would go. Dirty business. Round splatters of cowdung on the Dhakka Colony road of the same odour as the social grime attached to it. A societal pothole. Noses wrinkled in disapproval. Much easier to ask somebody else to negotiate it.

'I'll ask Kailla if he can do something about it,' said Tejpal.

'Who is Kailla?'

⁂

Kailla was a pre-partition fixture in Jassi's house. He was called Shafi then. His father had worked in a hosiery unit, while his mother worked in the house. They were devout Muslims, offering evening namaaz every Friday at the Jama Masjid in Field Ganj.

Religion then, like now, like always, was a whole meal—a bit of god, a bit of socializing and a bit of politics. But for three-year-old Shafi, god was yet an abstraction, politics was only a lot of excited talk and heated speeches meant nothing. The only thing that made sense was the presence of many other children at the mosque and the games he could play with them. Yet there was some sort of charge in the air, which even the children could feel. Not all the time, but at sudden moments when an adult face went red, with bulging eyes ready to pop or an odd tremor in the voice, like the twang of a taut wire.

In the December of 1921, a rumour had gone round that Maulana Habib-ur-Rehman Ludhianvi, great-grandson of Shah Abdul Qadir who had been at the forefront of the 1857 mutiny against the British, had been put to death inside the jail. People were already in protest mode. Mahatma Gandhi had addressed a huge gathering at Daresi Ground earlier in the year exhorting the people to adopt non co-operation as a means of protest. The Daresi Ground was a circular clearing in the middle of a teeming bazaar and the entire area had once been a part of the Ludhiana Fort. It was in the Daresi Ground that the British assembled Indian troops. An English General would command his officers to give the Indian troops a dressing down—'Give them a dressing down, give them a dressing down,' he said, and the ground came to be known as Daresi Ground.

In 1921, crowds had poured into the Daresi Ground to listen to Gandhiji, and as revolutionary words like non-cooperation and satyagraha filled the public address system, the assembly stirred to the call for change. Thereafter, the people fine-tuned satyagraha into strategic action in accordance with the resources available to them. At the end of that year, a hundred blind students from the madrassa raised slogans in front of the clock tower, led by their teacher, Muhammad Yasin. Then the Muslim, Hindu and Sikh women marched in the streets to protest the killing of Maulana Habib-ur-Rehman Ludhianvi. The police had to bring the maulana out of jail and show him to the public. But a handcuffed maulana was even more incitement to join Gandhi's satyagraha. The Muslims of Ludhiana stayed firmly with the Indian National Congress even when there were calls from other parts of the country demanding Pakistan.

Perhaps that is how Shafi had chosen to stay on in this sprawling house when Partition finally took place.

He was a jaunty young man working in the same factory as his father, where he learnt the art of weaving fabric on a loom, which became his specialization. As part of his duties for the day, he was also required to escort Jassi's sister-in-law, the daughter of the house, to college and back. He would carry her books and follow her faithfully, perhaps half in love with the idea of being in love, imagining for himself the role of a persecuted lover who dared to fall in love with a young girl from a rich family; his fancy fed by the many love legends of Punjab—Heer Ranjha, Sassi Punnu, Sohni Mahiwal, Mirza Sahiban.

He would usually be slaying monsters as he followed his charge, clearing his beloved's way of any dangers that beset her path. A swipe from Vincent A. Smith's *Oxford History of India* would catch the monster square in the middle of his forehead and it would collapse in a heap. His beloved walking in front of him would be oblivious to the flurry of events behind her.

When she got married and left the house, Shafi had mooned around for a bit because that was a requirement of the role he had assigned to himself. In the main house, when they noticed, they thought he was missing her just the way a brother should. But by then he was playing the role of a jilted lover and the agony of separation had turned into indignation.

Therefore, it was not for the maudlin demands of love that he did not leave when the nations got divided. It was for the drama in his head. Monsters climbed out of it and walked up the Ferozpur road to Bharat Nagar Chowk and on to the Mall Road where he slayed them. He addressed phantom gatherings at the Daresi Ground while on his way to the Ludhiana Fort where the British had set up a textile-weaving unit and a massive boiler with 'John Thompsons, Wolverhamptom 1924' written boldly across it. The fabric that came off the looms was also called 'Ludhiana', shirting material which was a muted, almost mousy mix of white with very dark grey, and which formed most of Shafi's inexpensive wardrobe. He would be cutting across Daresi

Ground whistling a tune of his own making, when the vast expanse of the ground would suddenly draw his attention and the temptation would be too strong. He would succumb.

The blink of an eye would raise a rostrum and he would be standing next to the Gandhi and Nehru that he pulled out of his head. He stretched out his arms to the people in appeal, then raised a finger to make a point—'Khaddar, wear only khaddar. None of this foreign-made mill cloth'. 'Shafi amar rahe, long live Shafi!' he heard in his head. There would be wild cheering. He would make an even greater impact than the national leaders. Next day, all of Ludhiana would be talking about this rising star on the political horizon, or so he imagined. The flesh and blood Shafi would make his way to the textile unit only as Shafi the weaver, the rhetoric of his long speeches sitting like coiled recording tape in his head, ready to be rolled out when it was time for play.

His mind was the landscape of the city. It swirled outwards from Chaura Bazaar and made its way down all the narrow lanes. He was in his late twenties when the rest of his family left for Pakistan, though his spirit was still skipping down the exciting pathways of his teens. In any case, he had not thought that the choice was so final, that the divide would be so absolute that he would be parted from his family forever. Later, news floated back that everyone had been massacred, apart from an uncle and a cousin.

He had to hide in the house like a fugitive, licking the wounds of his sorrow, till the killing of Muslims abated. For a while his mind was a snowy screen where there were no images. He would climb the fruit trees and sit on one of the branches, hiding amidst the leaves, his chappal-encased feet occasionally giving him away, as he swung his legs to his own rhythm. The household absorbed his withdrawal with a quiet patience. But gradually, the mischief in him resurfaced and he would fling the missile of an unripe fruit to announce his presence when he spotted someone in the backyard. When things stabilized, he resumed going to the Jama Masjid, except that the masjid was now a gurdwara. Shafi, having grown up exposed to both religions, made his peace with this new Jama Masjid where he did not offer namaaz but listened to kirtan instead. He grew his beard, rubbing camel piss and onion juice into his cheeks to get a more luxurious crop. He did not want to be a khoda sardar, a turbaned Sikh without a beard, the object of social ridicule. He then wrapped a cloth round his head in the semblance of a turban, and from Shafi he became Karnail Singh. The name was a derivative from the army rank of a colonel and the most appropriate choice for Shafi, who was a belligerent guardian of the house.

The day he made the formal transformation he travelled to Anandpur Sahib, the hub of Sikhism. Wearing the five accoutrements, each beginning with the letter 'k' and therefore referred to as 'kakaar', he appeared before the priests. He was checked for his steel bangle (the kara), for his uncut hair (kesh), the little comb that held the knot of hair in place (the kanga), the sword (the kirpan), that was slung on his side, and at last the long underpants (kachera) that he wore under pyjamas, which lay folded at his feet as he faced the inspection team.

He wondered if the women, who waited their turn behind the men, would also be asked to strip to their underpants to prove their allegiance. In that case it might have been a better idea to have let the ladies go first. But as it turned out, the women were taken into the fold fully attired and on the assumption of compliance on the length of underwear.

The bhai, as part of his priestly duties, examined each of the men like a nun in a convent school checking for bloomers under skirts and for clean fingernails. It took a whole sweaty day and was enough to discourage the weak-hearted from any pretensions to Sikhism. Karnail Singh was then administered the sweetened water which signified his official entry into the Sikh fold. Since there were no rough edges to his adaptability, Shafi had fused into Karnail Singh much before the clamour of this ceremony. And even though the Jama Masjid once again became a mosque in 1956 at the insistence of the prime minister, Pandit Jawahar Lal Nehru, Shafi continued to be Karnail Singh.

And from there on to Kailla was easy.

By the time that Jassi came into the house after her marriage, Karnail Singh was already Kailla. When a stroke left Jassi's husband paralysed, Kailla gave up his job at the textile mill and for four years bathed and changed him, massaged his legs and arms with warm oil, and carried him to the toilet and then the open veranda every morning and evening. But the evening entertainment was Kailla's specialty. That was when he was at his creative best, uninhibited by convention, innovating as he went. He would pull on Jassi's cast-off petticoat and kameez to perform a mujra—swinging his hips provocatively, rolling his eyes seductively and celebrating the ridiculous with complete abandon, while a tape recorder belted out sexy film numbers.

Jassi's son and daughter also grew up on a Kailla diet.

'I can make people disappear. I can turn a man into a broomstick, a jhadu, and stand him in a corner of the room,' he would tell them. 'That is what I do when big people misbehave.'

The children were sceptical. 'How can you do that? You are not a magician.'

'Remember when I went away last year for six months? I had gone to a magician and lived with him and learnt his magic.'

Kailla had indeed gone away for six months but it was only to learn swordplay from the martial nihangs. In those days he wore the designated blue robes and a two-feet-tall turban, which hid many talismans in its folds and which was so heavy that his neck sometimes tilted over like a stem loaded with a double dahlia.

'Then do some magic for us,' the children would plead.

'No, no. It is not a game. I perform magic only when the occasion demands it.'

The children would once again challenge him. 'You are saying this because you can't change anyone into a broomstick.'

'Why would I lie to you? Come, I will show you.'

And he would lead them to the kitchen.

'Do you see all those huge kundi sottas on that shelf?' he would say, pointing to the black stoneware mortars and pestles that are part of every Punjabi kitchen.

'They were all men once but now they have turned into stone because they were wicked.'

The black mortars and pestles, against the backdrop of a white wall, may have looked innocent in the day but in the dark they were just shapes. Admittedly not human, but they were nevertheless poised for action, as the pestle stood upright in its base. They were personages with potential.

Kailla had a story for each of these.

'This one you see, this pestle. It is smooth at the top. Feel it. This used to be a bald man.' The pestle was worn silky smooth, having been worked for years grinding rice for phirni, wheat for angoori barfi, lentils for making the batter for bhallas.

The children, more exposed to turbaned heads than bald heads, felt it and marvelled at it.

'Was he really? And what did he do to become a kundi sotta in the corner of the kitchen?'

'He ate children. He is, actually used to be, the King of Sunet. You know the one that I told you about.'

'The one who lived on that mound near Ludhiana and ate human beings and burped loudly? Then the old woman whose child he swallowed cursed him and upturned his kingdom into the mud like it was a bowl of porridge?' The horrible bowl of porridge, the dalia they had to eat every morning, was the easiest thing to upturn without any qualms, thought the children.

That was the thing. Bad deeds brought cataclysmic results. Rubbed the nose of civilizations into dust. Actions did have their consequences.

'What did the bald man do this time?' asked the children.

'He continued to eat human beings. So I had to turn him into a kundi sotta.'

That then was Kailla justice.

'Should I turn him into a sotta?' Kailla had thought when his uncle from Pakistan came to visit him many years later and had boasted about how he had avenged himself by killing many Hindus and Sikhs on the other side of the border in that bloody August of '47. Kailla had happily forgotten him as soon as he left and had gone back to teaching the children a song.

Come children, let me give you a window to Hindustan,
Mark your foreheads with the mud of this land,
This is the land of sacrifice.

And the song went on to list the heroes of India's struggle for independence from the British. However, in Ludhiana the history of Indian Independence was rapidly becoming the history of its industries. Stories of the meteoric rise of big industrial houses were becoming folk legend. The heroes were those who chartered planes, holidayed abroad, weighed down their women with jewellery. The trouble with this galaxy of heroes was that they were not from the past and were therefore subject to the vagaries of time, and so on occasion, one would fall through, bankrupt.

In the bazaar, shopkeepers were slowly hammering down the thick walls of the Ludhiana Fort to increase the sizes of their shops. They had to wet the walls and keep them soaked to soften them for slaughter. The walls would not give way otherwise. These were no ordinary walls but had once been the stronghold of the mutineers of 1857 when they seized the Ludhiana Fort. But now the remnants of its ramparts stood like the one odd tooth in an old mouth.

'No veer rasa, no juicy heroism,' Jassi would tell her children.

Over the years, the children grew up and went away to other lands; the elders, their grandparents and father died, leaving behind Jassi in the house and Kailla in the outhouse.

The textile unit where Kailla worked also changed character. When he had worked there in his teens, the weavers usually broke up for namaaz. Then came a time, after Partition, when the unit was starved for workers and Kailla had become a master craftsman at the knitting machine. Of late however, there was a new influx of workers, who were coming in by the trainloads from Bihar and Uttar Pradesh. There was a 'kisan special' that came from Benaras to the Ludhiana railway station twice a week and each time disgorged hundreds of labourers. In the seventies they had come in response to a changed cropping pattern in the fields of Punjab, where there was a seasonal need for extra hands. They came and they went. But now they were manning the power looms and lathes in the Ludhiana industries. They stayed in their own colonies, the cloth shops selling saris, the sweetmeat shops selling gujiya, the general merchant selling 'chokra sabun' and 'sri gange tel', a rail reservation agency catering to the home visit once a year. This was the Hindi heartland in Punjab.

Kailla was a frequent visitor because his friends at work lived in Indira Colony. He would also periodically fall in love with one woman or another in this locality, fascinated by the rings in her feet, believing that he was still young enough to get married.

So Kailla acquired yet another layer to his persona, of the Bihari from Bihar. He took to speaking a mix of Punjabi and Hindi and added Chhat puja to his list of propitious days to be celebrated. He would join the kilometres long procession that slowly made its way over the Phillaur Bridge with the river Sutlej flowing below. Vendors would sprout up alongside—balloons and baubles, chaat and channe bhature, tea and pakore—as the devotees made their way to pay obeisance to the setting sun; then again in the morning to catch the rising sun, setting afloat lighted earthen lamps on the water body. The town would turn up its nose in disdain at this collective visibility of an alien culture. Travel advisories would suggest that motorists should not attempt this stretch.

Kailla would be there in the middle of it all, carrying a basket-load of raw coconuts, sugarcane, home-made puris and earthen lamps on his head. Born a Muslim, practising Sikhism and now a Bihari among 50,000 Biharis. These were not layers that were a protective covering for the kernel. They could not be peeled off to reveal an entirely different Kailla—one that had been well hidden, one who had to offer namaaz. The layers themselves were the essence. The layers were Kailla. Like an onion, each peel was part of the whole, each were integrally the same.

⁂

Today, Kailla had walked down the Dhakka Colony road, past the puncture repair shop—'Pancher fix', past the meat shop—'taaza murge ka meet', also translated into 'frash cock meet', and stopped at Rajhans Studio—'photografs in 20 mint for Rs 20 only'. Life-size cutouts of Madhuri Dixit and Sridevi, even if a trifle stunted, their necks deep inside their shoulders, stood just inside the entrance. He stuck his right arm around one and smiled down at the woman in his embrace. She is smiling in the other direction, he thought. He moved to her right, his left arm around her. She smiled up at him.

An amused audience gathered outside the shop, entertained by the incongruity between an old man and his teenage sentiment. Some looked, laughed and went away. The idlers stayed on, waiting to see this through.

Nobody thought of getting me married, thought Kailla. His resentment against fate was only a mule track in the landscape of his mind. He had strayed onto it just now because the cutout had smiled at someone else even as his arm encircled her. That was the thing about fate. It always smiled at others and reminded him that he might have been married but for the workings of chance. It reminded him to grumble. He murmured to himself.

'Want a photograph?' Ramesh asked, peering through his lens, his left eye tightly shut, double images edging their way into unison. He had a winner there. His cutouts were inspired by the tailor's mannequins, which, he had noticed, seduced even the most casual passers-by. After an analysis of its benefits, the idea was executed in cardboard and topped with faces of film stars powdered over with dust from the road. It worked. He had only recently put his tentative toe into business, swirling it around to test the waters from scalding hot to comfortably cosy. Only two years ago the Khalistanis would have shut his shop, might even have killed him in a fervour of propriety. In those days it was best to minimize your visibility and seem as though you were not there even when you were. Those men with long, flowing beards would not have approved of this new hussy face, one that compelled a gaze.

Kailla hesitated. Became coy. But then, had his picture taken in a sudden rush of brazenness.

'Chadi jawani budde noo,' said one of the idlers derisively. An old man trying to be young.

'And why not?' said the youngster who wore a visor backwards. 'Look at all those oldies running our country. You have to be eighty plus for life to begin.'

They all grinned broadly, their teeth gleaming in the sunlight.

'Keep at it, keep at it, lage raho,' they advised Kailla.

They were waiting outside for him when he emerged from

the shop, and followed him to his next destination. They had nothing else to do.

They were part of the background when Kailla approached Sweety's window. They watched the mute show from a distance, scripting dialogue, providing their own soundtrack for the exchange, betting on possibilities and guffawing loudly with a distinct desire to give offence.

5

Gurjant Singh was a dud firecracker, sputtering in situ, never really blazing into the sky. He was a leftover of the insurgency, a bad aftertaste. He survived when others died at the hands of the police. He had remained on the fringes then, when all the others, similarly wired, had been wielding AK-47s. He only liked the posturing that it allowed him. He liked the aspen fear that it evoked. He liked the sense of commitment he could subscribe to without having to make a heavy investment. It only involved growing an untamed beard and configuring a fierce face.

When all his armed comrades were talking the language of the gun, he was getting into wordy disputes. At one such incident he had sprung out of his chair in the very last row during a seminar on Punjabi poetry and objected to the speaker referring to Guru Nanak as a poet.

'He was our Guru, the founder of Sikhism and a saint. Not a poet. If you make this mistake again,' he told the speaker, 'you will be eliminated.' The term resonated with memories of lucid letters, hand delivered, signed by 'generals' of the Khalistan Liberation Force, Khalistan Commando Force, Babbar Khalsa International, threatening dire consequences if...

Gurjant strode up to the mike, past the seminarians, whose arms burst into pimpled gooseflesh. He stood towering over the dark little woman with short black hair who had made the blasphemous statement and already felt a little ridiculous for having used a hammer to swat a fly. It spurred him on to greater heights of threatening rhetoric.

'Our panth, our religion is not to be tampered with. When we form our own nation, people like you will be done away with at once. At once!' he shouted, his voice cracking up, raggedly torn asunder into different decibels and tonalities to let through the force of his emotions.

'It is not an insult to be called a poet. That too is an exalted calling, consciousness at its most evolved, capturing the silences that lie between words,' said the little lady looking up at him from somewhere in the region of his belt, holding to the square inch of ground under her feet and using seminar language as though responding to an issue that had been thrown open to the house.

'Actually, both poets and saints usually sit on the fringes of society,' she added as an afterthought. 'It is only the offal of religion that tries to push centre stage,' she said, hinting at Gurjant's grabbing of the mike and his ungainly thrust into the limelight.

'A poet is of this world. But a saint is different,' he shouted. He too felt those intervening spaces that she talked about, though his were filled with grime. But he did not have the pretty words needed to contend with the little lady. His sensibilities needed a mysterious god up there, even if it took a certain amount of shuffling around of gods and saints to install one. He did not want God becoming the next-door neighbour. He repeated himself, 'A saint, not a poet'—in that same loud voice of a defeated argument.

The firmament is Thy salver
The sun and moon Thy lamps;
The galaxy of stars as pearls strewn.
A mountain of sandal is Thy joss-stick
Breezes that blow Thy fan;
All the woods and vegetation
All flowers that bloom
Take their colours from Thy light.

—The little lady recited Guru Nanak's verse and asked, 'Is this poetry or is it not? Devotional poetry, but poetry all the same.'

'If he was a poet and only human,' said Gurjant, thumping the speaker's rostrum, 'then how come he performed all those miracles, wringing water out of stone, getting Mecca to move around?'

She was not to be moved.

'But the gurus were at great pains to emphasize their humanity, not their other-worldliness. These saakhis are to be understood as metaphors. When it says that he moved Mecca around it was only to point out that God is everywhere, not just in temples, mosques and gurdwaras.'

'You are trying to downsize our religion.'

'But I too am a Sikh.'

'Then why are you wearing your hair short?' His pitch was still at rafter level and he no longer knew how to bring it down without losing face.

But the more he ranted, the more did the difference in their heights stand out in relief—and the more foolish he felt. The audience was transfixed. At other times they would have sniggered, but not now. Would he pull out an AK-47 and spray the assembly with bullets? They waited, minimizing themselves in their chairs. Is this how they would die? Seated in their chairs, at the verge of making a point and then going up in a cloud of pointlessness? Should they crawl under the hoof-shaped seminar table? But that might only mean precipitation. They waited for Gurjant to pull out his gun.

Suddenly, he stormed out like an angry husband crossed in argument. Just like that. He was followed by his assorted collection of hangers-on who tried to wither the gathering with their looks as they swept out in a burst of indignation. The last of them turned around to deliver a final, over-the-shoulder killer glance, like a ramp model just before disappearing between the curtains.

Gurjant and his team had been similarly belligerent when an Odissi-dancing husband-wife duo had performed an oeuvre piece, choreographed to the strains of a shabad. They had prepared this one especially for their Punjab visit, selecting the hymn with care to evoke a propitious opening, the man had said.

The man's bare upper torso glistened with sweat and necklaces, his red-spangled lungi sparkled under the stage lights. He did not know that he was severely underdressed for this particular undertaking. Heads had to be covered for the rendering of a shabad, combined with a stillness of stance. And here is this shamelessly naked head threatening to dance to a shabad, thought Gurjant.

And that too in a state of undress.

And definitely no dancing.

And not with that hairless chest.

His sense of manhood was clearly defiled by the sight before him. A man had to walk as if he had a lemon wedged under each of his armpits. Of course, that is not how he put it to himself since he took a much more serious view of the entire business of being a man. But since messing around with the attributes of manhood only took him into dark depths—some known, some unknown—he leveraged his faith instead, putting it into gear for confrontation.

He is even wearing necklaces and rings.

Kohl in his eyes!

Bloody homosexual!

It made his stomach turn to see a man, a topless one at that, dancing in this effeminate way. A topless woman he would go with, but this was gross. Sisterfucker, thought Gurjant.

He and his non-playing team stormed into the wings, even as the dancer was reciting the verses to which he would perform.

From the perspective of the audience, the dancer's subsequent behaviour remained inexplicable. Every twenty words he looked into the wings, then every ten. Five. Two. One. His head was on a spring, bobbing up and down and left and right. Finally his gaze was completely swallowed up by the curtains. A half-sentence ricocheted in the hall, looking to complete itself. But, for the dancer, his audience had ceased to exist. He himself became the audience, transfixed by that which only he could see.

Gurjant was performing what appeared to be a war dance, in the wings. He was gesticulating madly to convey his affront. His actions mimed a neat slicing of the throat, a display of bare nipples as he twisted two points on his shirt front into little knobs, and the firing of a gun. The dancer got the message and hurriedly walked into the wings, his ghungroos setting up an agitated tinkling as he went.

The performance was cancelled in the interest of all concerned and Gurjant had achieved this with his bare hands, without AK-47s. But that was then.

Now that wearing a gun was no longer fashionable, put out of vogue by the police crackdown, Gurjant had taken to carrying one. A countrymade pistol, the kind that would explode in the hand of the shooter. Or it could be jammed and create a comic villain who clicks and clicks and clicks, but never fires.

He had threatened Sweety with it, exhorting her to stop dancing on stage.

Sweety had thought, in a perverse sort of way, that this might be a good way to die, alive one second and dead the next. No death throes. You could die laughing.

'If you do have to kill me, then you might as well put aside that gun of yours and plant a bomb on me instead,' she told Gurjant.

His gun was not loaded. That was his sinister secret. Not even his hangers-on knew this. His countrymade weapon was only a cosmetic intervention, false boobies deployed in the industry of sex. His entire existence centred on a display of bravado. His dream was to watch the world quake as he strode past it, to see all of humanity tremble before him, to see people on jelly legs letting down a quiet trickle of fear.

'Don't give me smart answers,' he said, shaking the pistol in her face, starting up a delicate breeze with it.

'Why don't you do something else for a living?' she asked him.

'That is my business,' he said righteously.

'Then how come everybody else's business is your business?'

Sweety was being facetious, and Gurjant did not like

it. Threats had to be taken seriously in order to be threats, otherwise they were not worth the breath expended on them. And he was beginning to suspect that he and his pistol were not having the desired effect. In fact, he had the distinct impression that they were working like a feather duster, gently tickling the senses. Sweety looked like she was about to smile, but it was quickly siphoned up by her eyes, before it could burst at her lips. He would have to do something more severe to evoke gravity.

That was the trouble with these guns.

His own had always been undersized. When he was little and a keen participant in the 'shoot a piss' competitions, his pee would invariably rain down on his own toes. And, since then, there had been a steady lack of adequate growth.

One could grow out of the habit of eating candies and into the mature desire to eat the much-despised vegetables of the gourd family; one could grow into the desire to go early to bed; one could just simply grow fat or thin, as the case may be, each in opposition to the intended end.

But in Gurjant's case it had been that he had not grown at all in that one area of concern. Rather, so little, as to be seen as not having grown at all. He could now aim past his toes and just clear the inner rim of the piss pot.

He had even gone to one of those men who offer miracle cures. The ones that offer to increase a penis to the size of an elephant trunk; promising the sexual prowess of an acrobat.

The hakim, his head crowned with a tall turban, sat on the floor in a colourful, makeshift tent which had the dimensions of a little room. Nath Baba claimed that he was from Himachal Pradesh, and it was from the mountains that he brought all the herbs that went into the making of his medicines.

'From far up in the mountains,' he said. 'Sometimes you have to stay in the forest the whole night and wait for the first rays of the sun to fall on this medicinal plant, through the early morning dew, before you pluck a few leaves. It is not easy.' These were no dime-a-dozen popping-pills that pharmaceuticals churned out in industrial quantities, which one could buy off anonymous shelves in chemist shops. They were custom-made. The hakim not only knew just when to pick the first leaf warmed by the first rays of the rising sun, but also knew the problem that you were coming to him for.

'A small one? Yes?' said the hakim.

And Gurjant was completely overawed.

Gurjant had hoped that the cure lay in that line-up of jars that stood poised for a group photograph—little ones in front on the ground, taller ones on a shelf that ran right around the tent and still taller ones on pedestals at the back. Little globules like pinheads, bigger ones like ball bearings, still bigger ones like table tennis balls, floating in brine or rose water or sitting cheek to cheek in jars.

'Yes, small,' said Gurjant, losing some of his inhibition, since the secret was already out. 'Sex is a problem.'

'I know. I could see it on your forehead when you came in.'

What did his forehead have to do with the size of his penis, he wondered. Was the smallness of his member advertised on his forehead and had he been walking around all over town like an open book? Did people laugh behind his back when he had gone by? Did they jerk their thumbs his way and say 'did you see that'?

The hakim gave him ten little packets with ten little globules in each of them. He had asked him all kinds of questions. Do you shout when you get angry or do you only grumble under your breath? Do you go for a shit as soon as you get up or does it come only later and what colour and consistency is it? Do your palms itch? He had then meditated for a while to arrive at the right globules. Gurjant had fidgeted with his hands, his buttons, his watch, his turban, his moustache, all the while that he waited. Finally he was told that he was to swallow the contents of one packet of the pinhead variety, each day, on an empty stomach, before he went at the fried paranthas. On the eleventh day he would be a new man, with a brand new penis. After the visit, he would carefully open one packet every morning and funnel the globules into his mouth. When the occasional one got away, hiding amidst the sheets or bouncing its way under the bed, he would be down on his knees, groping, then coming up for air and a torch, since it was pitch dark under the bed; and then he would dive under once again. He could not afford to lose that tiny but potent bead. It might well be the source of that extra micro millimetre.

However, he woke up as Gurjant Singh of the little wee wee even on the twelfth day. That made it all the more necessary for his countrymade one to find veneration. He, Gurjant Singh of the 'short'-gun fame, needed to take a more perilous route to recognition.

6

The road to Mr Bakshi's house was winding strangely. The last they knew, and that was not many days ago, just six as a matter of fact, it had kept along the Sirhind Canal and was straight as an arrow. But here it was, meandering so, almost like a mountain road to an inaccessible peak.

'Keep to the centre of the road,' Tejpal told Balli.

Balli was driving with the vigour of a truck driver, swinging the wheel, his hands flying over it as he alternated his grip to take the turn, first left and then right. His wheels would kiss the edge and Tejpal would shout, 'Watch out, watch out!' Balli's hands would go into a desperate retrieval dance, as though shaping ladoos in the air, forming perfect globes out of sweetened dough.

'This sisterfucker road,' he said.

But as it turned out, the road was quite as straight as ever, it was just that Tejpal and Balli were negotiating it through brains that were swimming in scotch whisky.

Balli had insisted on driving. 'Of course I will drive. Why, why can't I drive? I am perfectly in my senses. You think I am drunk?' he had asked, taking great umbrage at Tejpal's hesitation to ride with him. 'I am not drunk. Don't think

I am drunk,' he had said, the alcohol sloshing from side to side in his cranium.

'No, no. You are my brother. I will go anywhere with you,' said Tejpal, hidden tears in his eyes and voice, his loves and hates greatly sharpened in his mind over the last few hours with the repeated clinking of glasses. They had had to do the last few cheers very studiedly and carefully though, since they were beginning to miss each other's glasses. He had been everywhere with Balli. He had gone to Dhakka Colony with him and now he was sitting in a car that was only inches away from diving into the Sirhind Canal or flying off the embankment into the entangled undergrowth. This, most certainly, was anywhere or nowhere.

The wheels of the car once again negotiated the tightrope between life and death. In this state of mind it was not possible to distinguish one from the other, to tell between the hullabaloo of life and the hoo-ha of death, or between a man and a bush, a tree and a truck. The road too kept appearing and disappearing like an illusion. The twilight made it worse. Danger was no longer danger but exhilaration. It only strengthened the belief in the drunken lore that an invisible cushion lay under one's butt in case of a fall.

Believers presume that god, or those of his ilk, have a special love for drunkards. This lore grew and prospered because those who had driven off the embankment had not lived to tell the tale. And those who survived were that much more convinced of the existence of that eight-inch foam which miraculously appeared under their falling form, unrolled straight from the heavens.

Balli and Tejpal made it though, without any emergency celestial intervention. Past the lone, lost cow. Past the man on a cycle. Past the truck loaded with ugly aluminium chairs that boasted red velvet upholstery for a large wedding somewhere in the vicinity—a man sitting atop those chairs, ready to unload them when they reached the venue. They could see the glow from the wedding lights burning into the sky. When they arrived at Mr Bakshi's gate a party was in progress. They swept into the driveway as though on the trajectory of a mountain bend and on that same elevation of spirit.

They had started drinking early in the evening, much before the sunset hour. It had all started with the arrival of a government notice that threatened to take over Balli's father's land for the development of an industrial estate. In Ludhiana the industrialists were envious of the tax exemptions that the agriculturists were given and agriculturists, in turn, felt that they were being circumscribed by land ceilings whilst the industrialists expanded unchecked. The two, farmer and factory owner, were always threatening to edge each other off the earth. As Tejpal's father had told him, there is only so much land on the planet. Only that much space for everyone to exist. Back then he would not have known about land reclamation though, about boulders being dropped into the sea to create land and landing strips, about man playing god. About god abdicating, trounced out perhaps, by man's upward aspirations.

Initially, Balli had laughed about it, saying, 'Good enough. Ultimately we can all eat cycle parts instead of wheat.... or then, penis,' he said as he spotted Jeeta, the old family retainer, coming in to serve a bowl of peanuts. Jeeta never got 'peanuts' right, though he could have just called them by their Punjabi name—'moongphali'. But Jeeta wanted to be able to throw in that odd English word. And so he offered 'penis' to Balli's guests. While the men guffawed, the women burned with embarrassment.

Balli's father had, in fact, attempted to set up an industry for cycle parts in the fifties because he was convinced that ultimately, the man at the driving wheel would be the businessman.

He had named his outfit Zygon Industries. The name had come from his desire to be contrary. Most people wanted names that began with an 'A', because that ensures first place in a line. The line at the estate office, at the registrar's office, at the magistrate's office. However, the line was only in the head, if at all, since most places that required a queue usually degenerated into a moving mass of jostling elbows, a press of bodies and eyes peering over shoulders. No one stood in a line anywhere. But Balli's father had thought of going to the tail end. 'Z,' he had thought. And then, since he was already at that end of the alphabet, he had tried both 'X' and 'Y' to go with 'Z'. But the former offered only impossible tongue twisters, zxytic, zxotic, zxmon… He had finally arrived at Zygon.

It was a false start. He had no idea of how to keep track of the nuts and bolts that keep the axles in place. He had piled them high like stacks of wheat in the single room. There were no inventories. The workers went home with pockets full of nuts and bolts. They sauntered in when the morning was well on its way. No one knew how many axles should be produced in the course of a day to ensure a profit above expenses. The production rate was whimsical.

The factory had to be shut down while others went on to become cycle tycoons. Thus Balli's father had gone back to growing wheat with the resignation of a martyr and an air of superiority about the wholesomeness of his occupation compared to the stinking sleaze of business.

In any case, agriculture was looking up just then, looking up to the US from where a Ford Foundation team had arrived on invitation from the Indian government to study ways of increasing wheat production. Ludhiana was chosen as the prime location for their pilot project. They were introducing Mexican seed, which was slated to give three times more yield than the local stock.

Balli's father had been fascinated. These Americans come equipped with everything, he had thought. Years later they even went to war outfitted with television and chewing gum and popcorn, where they sat in their tanks, watched television and ate popcorn, apart from going out there to kill and be killed.

When they arrived in Ludhiana they had their beer bottles. Budweiser. The American researchers and farmers had lunch together everyday. A working lunch. And out came the beer. Jeeta, a lot younger then, would carry Balli's father's lunch to him on site. In those hot summer days, when the sun would burn holes in their heads, lassi would be the essential starter to lunch. His wife would send a huge thermos full of buttermilk for him.

'What is this you drink every day?' the Americans asked Balli's father.

'Lassi,' he said, but then realized that the word meant nothing to them. It did not conjure up images of languid summer afternoons, of cooling down as lassi coursed down the gullet, of headiness induced by two big glasses of lassi, a healthy drunkenness summoned out of the good things of life with no moral laxity involved, of the long siesta that was a must. He knew he had to explain. As the shortest explanation of all these delicious images in his head, he said, 'Indian beer.'

'Oh, we would like to try some,' said the Americans.

After all, they were exchanging technologies. They might as well exchange beers too. There was a ceremonial give and take of glasses. The Americans loved this 'Indian beer' and wondered why it was not marketed and why they could not buy it off the shelf. From that day onwards, they drank lassi and Balli's father drank Budweiser. The arrangement met with the satisfaction of both parties. It was only when the Americans asked for Indian beer at a party that the truth of it all emerged. They had refused to talk to Balli's father after that.

But his acres began to prosper by the seventies. His house on the farm had been a courtyard surrounded by an unbroken row of rooms with two fans ineffectively whirring away the heat as best they could. The toilet on the roof had been a bricked-in chamber pot. When the Mexican seeds became wheat in the market, every room had its own fan and plumbers were called in to install pipes and drains and flushing systems. Every room now had its own bathroom. These attached bathrooms were a measure of the good things of life. His farmhouse had become a palace from where a car carried his only child to school everyday.

His prosperity did not produce more heirs for him, though. Strangely enough, his wife's second pregnancy a few years later ran its full term but produced nothing by the end but a lot of hot air, gossip about how it had only been a tumour, or an illegitimate child, or a pillow tied around the stomach. Why would nine months of carrying around a distended stomach produce nothing, not even a stillborn child?

So Balli was the only son of a prosperous landlord, and was to inherit all those rich acres. But now he was angry that the government might inherit it instead.

That is why he had swung into the driveway of Mr Bakshi's house, though of course Mr Bakshi had nothing to do with the threat of it being taken away. Mr Bakshi was only tying up with some foreign buyers for the supply of still more pullovers and mufflers. He had no idea of the resentment with which two individuals were riding to his house.

Balli and Tejpal stepped out of the car and were immediately swallowed up by the swirling party. But not for long.

Initially they had mingled with the guests and made not-so-polite conversation since they were on a wavelength that lifted them above the usual niceties of life. But soon enough the issues about land were rising up from their stomachs like an ill-digested meal, threatening to discharge a burp with an offensive odour.

They had gatecrashed, but Sarika was gracious nevertheless, insisting that they stay for dinner. Balli bowed low over her hand, almost kissing it, though that would be a gesture entirely alien to his Punjabi sensibility. Guests were beginning to look his way from the corners of their eyes. There were suppressed sniggers. A drunk offers juicy dramatic potential.

'I would love to spend the night with you,' he said, 'but I have to go.' Loosely interpreted into more acceptable sentiment, he only meant that he would have loved to stay for dinner but was hampered by his own liquid state.

Just then he spotted Mr Bakshi.

'You, you,' said Balli, his finger pointedly sticking under Mr Bakshi's nose, 'you stop swallowing up our land. You are not satisfied with what you have. You want to eat up everyone's share. You leave my land alone or I will shake the teeth out of your head.'

'You farmers are a pampered lot. No taxes to pay and yet

you go around with an injured air as though someone has robbed you of your rights.'

'You know how hard my father had to work. And things were never available. He had to go all the way to Ferozpur to procure one can of diesel for the tubewell, tractor and thresher; plead for electricity, plead for water. You people keep a generator right in the middle of a locality, have thick red wires running into the house and start making something and money. An ice factory maybe. Dirty ice that makes people sick.'

'And what about the wheat you grow? What you finally sell has generous quantities of mud. Just listen to the rubbish he talks. I have seen him this high,' Mr Bakshi said, indicating the region of his knee. 'I have even seen him naked.' An indrawn breath from the goggle-eyed gathering, particularly the foreign buyers, who immediately jumped to the only conclusion that such a statement warranted, which was slightly misplaced since all Mr Bakshi meant was that he had seen Balli as a toddler, when nakedness is not shamefulness.

'Are you saying we purposely dirty our own wheat?' An angry Balli was incredulous.

In 1885, the Deputy Commissioner of Ludhiana had conducted an inquiry and found that wheat was mixed with mud pellets and that there was a ready supply of these available in different sizes and colours to suit different kinds of grain. It was the traders, not the farmers, who made the blend. A hundred years later they were still talking about dirty wheat.

The argument got louder, uglier and more irrational with every exchange. The only sensible way of settling such arguments was a decisive punch to the jaw.

'You!' said Balli angrily.

But, like always, Balli's finger pointed in the wrong

direction, because Mr Bakshi was completely innocent of the alleged crime. Balli had then stepped forward to dislodge Mr Bakshi's teeth. The assembled company hurriedly stepped in to rescue his teeth from harm.

Balli and Tejpal were soon regurgitated from the party. Unceremoniously. And they once again sat in the car for a hair-raising ride back home. Balli's confidence was undiminished. Tejpal's faith in Balli's driving skills was a little rattled but propped up by the sentimentality of a childhood friendship.

7

'It's all these guns. Turns their heads,' Jassi said.

Harpeet had been talking about her husband's snoring. She usually became quite animated when she talked about it. It had such dramatic narrative potential. Much more exciting than just a story between book covers where one's imagination has to lift events out of the pages. She alternated the 'khrrrrrrs' and 'pheeeees' with the practised ease of a virtuoso.

She talked about how his cover sheet rose and fell, pitched on a stormy sea. Of the brief moment of silence when she would check to see if he was still breathing, and would then retreat startled, when he would roar back into the next round aloft a hungry lion. Of the whistles and trebles that emanated from him in slumber.

She had no idea how guns suddenly became a part of this exchange. But then Jassi had become hard of hearing of late and the conversation usually skidded along a giddy path, slipping into side lanes via homophones. Had she, Harpreet, said something about 'runs' or was it 'suns' or for that matter 'sons'? Any of those could have triggered the deviation. Especially sons.

They ended up discussing sons and the great Indian love for them.

Jagga jamia te milan vadhaiyan,
kevada ho ke daku ho gaya.

When Jagga was born there was much merriment,
And when he grew up he became a bandit.

This was Jassi's favourite ditty. And even though legendary, Jagga's banditry was not genuine villainy but revolutionary zeal, quantified into a large swathe of sand, nine maunds to be precise, getting soaked with his blood after he was shot dead by the British. Jassi still saw him as the boy who deflated the dreams of his parents.

'All this fuss about having a son and then when they grow up they are drilling holes in their parents' heads,' she said. 'Now look at that Inder. What she did makes my stomach turn even now.'

'Inder who?'

'Your friend Balli's mother.'

'Balli's mother?' said Harpreet, stupidly echoing Jassi.

'You seem to have caught the deafness from me,' Jassi said, her years giving her immunity against the social codes of pleasantry. 'Yes, Balli's mother. Two daughters were born to her after Balli. But where are they now?'

Harpreet had no idea of course. She did not know that they had ever been born and therefore was hardly likely to know of their present whereabouts. However, Jassi clarified things for her—one had disappeared from her crib in the hospital soon after she was born, while the other had died under very suspicious circumstances.

Harpreet heard the tale with growing horror.

The doctor at the nursing home where the first baby disappeared had told the story with great pride. 'Right here in our hospital,' he used to say, as though he had done the baby a good turn.

There were two beds laid out side by side in a private room. Two women lay there wailing. One because she had had a miscarriage and the other because she had given birth to a daughter. Both thought it was the end of the world. Both thought that fate had dealt them a tough blow and were shedding enormous tears, which were swamping their cheeks like a river in spate. But grief has a way of building walls around people, sealing them in high towers, making them feel exclusive—so that the women felt that their respective sorrows were far more potent than anything that had happened before. It was, therefore, after a while that each of them registered the caterwauling of the other. They removed their wet veils from their eyes and exchanged notes.

'But why do you want a girl?' said the one who had just given birth to one, amazed at the quaintness of the other's need.

They came to an arrangement.

The woman who had lost her baby would adopt from the one who did not want the baby. The dead baby would be Balli's mother's instead, to wail over and cremate. And that would set the record straight. The hospital and the doctors concerned looked the other way while an informal adoption took place. Little Balli watched his baby sister going away with the aunty in the next bed.

Harpreet said, 'Oh!' and suddenly understood Balli's vision of a world inhabited by sisters.

'Duniya rang rangili,' said Jassi. It takes all sorts to make the world.

They had reached that stretch of their morning walk along the rail line where it was necessary to hold a hanky to one's nose and wear blinkers over one's eyes. This was the slum settlement where parties of children organized themselves every afternoon to conduct raids on Kailla's fruit trees. In these early hours, the railway track acquired a scalloped edge from the many bottoms that sat there for a morning shit, facing the train, which was only a passing audience. Here one minute, gone the next. There was no shame in being seen by those who would quickly melt into the mass of undifferentiated humanity. The anonymity of their bottoms turned towards the settlement, they figured, would save face for day-to-day living.

It was this stretch that deterred Harish's wife, Sarika, from visiting Harpreet. The rest she did not mind, she said.

'You have such a simple lifestyle. It is so sweet,' she had said simperingly, clearly not meaning a word of it, and taking in the two rooms in a single glance. 'How do you manage, though,' she had said, in an inadvertent slip, which she quickly covered up with effusive praise for the three-legged stool, the four-legged dining table and the five-cornered makeshift kitchen.

'How different.'

But the smell en route she could not take.

Somebody with an irregular constitution had chosen to perform his morning ablutions at the exact moment when she was passing by.

'Why on earth don't they go do this somewhere else? No shame, really. Sitting there in full public view. I tell you we Indians have just no civic sense.'

'Actually they are from the labour colony across and I don't think they have much choice,' Harpreet had said.

Did she think they had an attached bathroom but preferred to offload under the sky just as they exercised their freedom to fart in public? If you keep it bottled up inside then you are likely to rocket forth into the sky at some point of time in your life—this was the subject of many Punjabi jokes in which Santa Singh finds himself deposited in Japan straight from a Punjabi village as a consequence of having expended wind. As children, a fart always occasioned considerable giggling as they lay under their mosquito nets beneath the sky and heard their grandfather's uninhibited fart. He would be half asleep, ensconced in his own mosquito net, many beds away in the line-up which followed the family hierarchy, the eldest first and down to the youngsters who made up the far end. They could even imagine him lifting one side as he let fly, and they would usually dissolve into helpless giggles and smother them in their pillows. They need not have bothered though, since this was a moment of such singular concentration and catharsis for their grandfather that he would hardly have noticed even if they had been rolling over with laughter. They might however, be admonished by their respective mothers, though in a conspiratorial, 'we understand' sort of way.

But exigencies in life always blurred the lines between private and public life. And the exigency of the lack of a private toilet was bound to take the shame out of a shit.

'No, no, these people just don't want to better themselves,' said Sarika.

'I wonder why,' Harpreet said sarcastically.

'They just don't have the sense. You remember Sarla? The sweepress? She is going to have another baby. Soon they will have taken over the earth and people like you and me will be looking around for some obscure corner.'

She then pulled out a bottle of perfume from her designer handbag and gave herself a generous spray even as she mouthed a disgusted, aspirated 'ouf'.

She had never come over after that.

The smell was quite offensive though, even if Sarika's reaction could be dismissed as the squeamishness of the rich about all things that smell less than Chanel. But both Harpreet and Jassi had learnt, this being their daily route for a morning walk, to inhale deeply just before, as though readying themselves for a stretch underwater. They did not want to change their route. At least here they knew exactly when they should inhale and when it was safe to breathe again. Smells could not make a surprise sally into their nostrils.

So all conversation ceased just then. That was the nice thing about these companionable conversations.

Having negotiated the smelly stretch, Jassi took a deep breath, more from the fact of having held it for so long than as an accompaniment to the sentiment she was going to express, and said, 'Boys are callous, girls are such a comfort.'

Her son had given her no reason to arrive at this particular conclusion. He was a doctor abroad and was as attentive to her needs as a twenty-hour flight with two stopovers would allow. Her daughter was her favourite though.

As they walked, the aroma of ripening mangoes filled the air. For everything that goes wrong there is always something that goes right, thought Harpreet. For every lungful of faecal breath there is the heady fragrance of chausa mangoes.

If you were not in films and only living life, then things fell back into the commonplace of ups and downs, the rhythmic see-saw of festivities and mournings, quite quickly.

Jassi did not agree though. She had seen enough drama in her life, she said, to have developed a chronic sense of anxiety. When her husband had developed high sugar she had dreamt that he was pissing sugar cubes. When she told the doctor of her dreams, he had only been pragmatic. 'What is there to do? Just gather up the sugar cubes and you have your month's supply.'

As a young girl she had packed her small tin trunk and come to the Indian side of the border when the country was partitioned. 'If you can carry a spoon instead of a ladle, do that,' her grandfather had said when she was leaving, as a sort of larger statement on travelling light, and from the certainty of coming back once things had settled down. It had rained incessantly that August of 1947.

They had spent the following winter as refugees, wrapped in cotton veils because their woollens lay layered with neem leaves in large trunks back home. Her brother, with a chapati in hand, had asked her mother, 'Beeji, have we become beggars?' They hadn't really, but they had pretty much scraped the bottom of the barrel.

Rain is something of a mood enhancer, thought Jassi, as she recalled that August drenched in blood and water. If you are happy you dance in it, if you are sad you cry with it. But when clouds do gather in the sky and the rain comes down all of a sudden on a nondescript day, there is panic, the danger of getting wet far outweighing the danger of being run over on the road—two wheelers will drive blindly, pedestrians will dash through the rain blind to the oncoming speeding car.

'In our time even the weather was much better behaved,' said Jassi, obliquely referring to the wayward ways of the young. 'It played no tricks. My mother used to tell me that when the British were here fifteenth of September was the official onset of winter. The manual operator of the fan would be put on another job.'

'He must have lost his job when electricity was introduced.'

'Maybe he was then employed to remove and put away the wooden wings of the fans and wrap the remaining stumps on the ceiling in cloth. And then on October fifteenth the angeethis would be lit up by him because that is when winter began according to official orders.'

The cycle of seasons too obeyed these official orders.

But in this August of '95, forty-eight years later, the monsoon had failed. An occasional shower, only good for dirtying feet and paws and for generating unsavoury smells. Wet pet paws on drawing room floors, mud-caked shoes drying in verandas. Not good for much else. Certainly not good enough for the crop in the fields.

'Too damn hot,' said Harpreet, grumbling and wiping the sweat from her brow. 'I could just melt away and would have to be collected in a bucket.'

'My grandchildren, when they visit in summer, think that I have turned on the heating. "Switch it off, nani," they tell me. I tell them of the man up there in the sky who has all the controls. And they wonder why they can't see him and appeal to him. "Who is this guy?" they ask me.'

Her grandchildren, in keeping with the expatriate spirit, struggled to keep up with the loaded business of being both American and Indian, of being able to say 'sat sri akal' and 'hey dude' in the same breath, of sporting underturbans as a mandatory part of their religion and yet regarding their headdress as the American freedom to be different. They had learnt the names of the ten Sikh gurus but if, when reeling off their names, they stumbled, then one would ask the other, 'Hey, what is the name of the eighth guy?'

Harpreet shared a name with Jassi's grandson. He too was called Harpreet. Sikhism was gender equal when it came to names. Other things being unequal, as in most other religions, societies, worlds.

Harpreet had been named even as her mother braided her hair into pigtails for her first day at school. Until then she had only been Baby, the youngest child in a household of many. Her eldest brother was Harpreet Singh. Running out of ideas and time, her mother had said, 'Shall we call you Harpreet too, Harpreet Kaur?'

She was quite happy to be Harpreet.

Playing hopscotch with their own thoughts, the two of them, Jassi and Harpreet, had reached the head of their lane when they noticed a figure standing at their gate.

'Can that be...?' asked Harpreet.

Jassi was equally incredulous.

'Your eyes are young; you tell me,' she said.

'It is,' said Harpreet.

Sarika had come, wading through the smells and slush.

'Papa has disappeared,' she announced, when they reached her.

Mr Bakshi had indeed disappeared. Her father-in-law had worn his favourite white shoes that morning. This pair was as white as his shiny white teeth. His shoes were a measure of his mood. He wore them when he was feeling on top of the world. In spirit they were his high boots, the kind that the hunter wears when he stands beside his trophy, one foot atop his kill, to be photographed in all his glory. But now he had disappeared, white shoes and all.

8

Mr Bakshi's white shoes were sitting on the floor next to the bed, one shoe lying across the other, like a fork and knife crossed in a plate signalling a desire for more food. The superstition was that one shoe riding another was a sign of impending travel. In the case of Mr Bakshi, however, the journey had already been made, quite against his will. He crossed his arm over his eyes and wished that he did not have to see the ceiling, where a crack in the whitewash wended its way right across and suggested a possibility of the roof caving in. What you could not see did not hurt, even if you were only pretending not to see it—a tactic that was part of his survival kit. Mahatma Gandhi had also told the nation, through the example of the three monkeys, not to see, hear or speak any evil, though his exhortation was more an injunction to steer clear of evil rather than as a means of self-deception. For Mr Bakshi, this instinct came from the hand his mother extended over his eyes to prevent him from seeing things she did not want him to see. 'No, no, don't look. This is so horrible. Look at all that blood. Terrible accident. Hai rabba…' And though he could not see the bloodied man as he lay there choking and gasping, she would feed the picture into his imagination. Which is why he now occasionally peeped at the ceiling from under the crook of his arm to make sure that it was holding out—seeing and yet not seeing.

The fan whirred reluctantly, hanging by a claw from that same cracked ceiling, groaning with the effort, hammering out an unvarying rhythm—khat khat khat khat khat, and kht kht kht, discarding its vowels when the electricity voltage increased. Hmmm hmmmm hmmmm went the mosquito in tandem. It sang persistently in his ear. He tried to swat it away, clapping his hands over it half-heartedly, but missed it altogether and watched it float with graceful ease up to the ceiling. The sound of the clap had startled the silence, like a gunshot in the night, and he thought he had best let the mosquito be. Would it survive if the roof fell through, he wondered. It was an idle thought, but then he did not have much else to do. Idle thoughts were all that were available to him and he was willing to pursue them so long as the burden of consequences fell on the mosquito. He did not want to speculate about his own fate because that would mean dwelling on the bloated form of the body that would be found floating down the Sirhind Canal. Some would say it was the police that had put it there to cover up its policy of elimination without trial, while others would say terrorists had got tired of lugging him around, from hideout to hideout, and dumped him there to get rid of excess baggage. If his kidnappers wanted to swap him for some money—a few lakhs maybe—then there was still some hope. He had no idea what he was up against or what he was worth.

One minute he had been strolling in his driveway, wearing his elevating white shoes, ready to leave for work, working up an appetite for breakfast and feeling an intense sense of well-being while his thumb lovingly caressed the amount on the cheque in his hand. The next moment he had become a portable bundle, parcelled into a blanket, stamped, labelled and posted to an unknown destination, journeying in a car boot on a potholed road. All this was conjecture on his part though, since he had no idea what was happening to him or where he was. The darkness was absolute. It was the kind of darkness that surrounds you when you wake up and grope around for the light switch, then find it is no longer where it used to be, and then realize that you are on an unfamiliar bed. It was a strange, unyielding darkness, viscous with fear. This is it, he thought. When the blanket was thrown over him at the moment of his abduction, he had quickly balled up and swallowed, after assiduous chewing, a cheque worth ten lakh, though his insides retched at the strangeness. His eyelids had automatically closed tight with the weight of the blanket. His eyeballs, pressured down with an unrelenting hand, had square stars dancing in them, little geometric shapes that appeared and disappeared, then winked their way to an exit and floated in yet again. He had been lifted off his feet, like a child, while his white shoes kicked the air.

As a child his mother had wrapped him in her veil and hoisted him on her shoulder to carry him across the newly defined borders between nations. Someone had lifted him and deposited him in a truck. Even as he had been dumped into that truck he had felt like a piece of cargo. He had clutched his mother's veil tightly around him and concentrated on its nearness. All the while that they had journeyed through seething fires and spilt blood, he had been tracing, with his finger, the diagonal lines of the lehriya on the veil that covered his face and form. The parallel lines ran down the length and journeyed to the edges of the fabric. He had stayed the course of those lines with single-minded devotion.

But travelling in the boot of a car was new and intimidating. The reassuring diagonal lines were missing. It hurt to be pushed up against hard surfaces, to feel the sharp edges of apathy, of unbending metal. His flesh endured the impact of the potholed road. His senses touched the blackness, longing for familiarity, but finding only a malevolent strangeness.

In the boot of the car, he thought he must no longer be alive. He lay there, a foetus in embryonic darkness, but without the promise of birth. He must be dead. And if he was not, there must have been some mistake somewhere. When they finally lifted him out of the boot, he realized that he was not dead, as he had imagined. I'm alive, he thought with a measure of disbelief. The bruises hurt and assured him that he was indeed alive. He felt no exhilaration at the discovery, because what do you do with an existence that is smothered in a suffocating blanket in the middle of summer, with sweat trickling down from the nape of the neck, along the spine and into clinging underpants, where it spread into a dampness onto the seat of the trousers? He was only a body that was being tossed around like a sack of potatoes, lifeless and unresisting. The kidnappers had then deposited him into yet another vehicle, but this time he was sitting on a seat, registering sounds of undirected traffic that lurched and swerved, screeched and honked, and missed you by the width of a whistle's breath. Were they driving through Chaura Bazaar, where vehicles treaded on each other's toes in an ungainly dance? It was not a spacious bazaar, as the name suggested, and there was hardly any room for negotiating a vehicle through the chaos that prevailed. It took nerves of steel and a persistent hand on the horn to carve out a path through it all.

All the while he was thinking about just how 'strugglesome' his life had been. This was a word he used often; its existence in the English lexicon was not of deep interest to him—in fact, he was singularly confident of its evocative powers to describe his travails through penury on to prosperity. Because, as he often said, 'I have got flow of English and good knowledge of English.' And that precluded any attempt at correction to a standard which had been set by someone else, somewhere else, and which did not recognize his personal equation with English. When he was spoken to in Punjabi, he responded in English with a generous sprinkling of 'sirs' and 'madams' in an effort to display his breeding. His use of articles and prepositions was peculiarly effusive. 'Myself the Mr Bakshi,' he would say, whilst introducing himself.

He hoped this was not his whole life flashing before his eyes in a sudden premonition of death. He had heard stories of how his grandfather knew that he was dying and how, days before his death, he had begun talking about his past, had begun to see his elders standing beside his bed and beckoning to him, while those attending to him had become invisible. They had been at pains to tell him that he was only seeing things and that it was a delirium of fever and that he should in fact, be acknowledging the reality of those around him. But he had gone quite firmly into flashback mode and announced to the world at large that he did not have very much more to do with this life; it was time for him to go.

⁂

Mr Bakshi was deposited on a bed in the room with the

cracked ceiling, after a long journey. The room was spartan enough to be the setting for a hermit's sanctum sanctorum. In a corner sat an armchair with one arm missing and a table with joints that quivered to the touch. The blanket that had, till recently, covered him and under which he must have passed out before he was deposited here, was carelessly thrown over the one-armed chair. Only the nail hammered into the door contested for attention with the crack in the ceiling, a riveting presence in the isolation of his incarceration.

He wondered what his family would be doing back home. His son and daughter-in-law must be asleep yet, working off the excesses of the party they were at the night before. They clocked a different sunrise from the one that was stated in the newspaper every morning. For them, the day began when they woke up. Even my children have not appreciated all my efforts, he said to himself. What is it to them? They got all this readymade. He was thinking of the wealth that made it possible for his wife to order around the many servants to ready his breakfast. The smell of paranthas being fried with oodles of rarified butter must be filling the air. His nostrils inflated as he inhaled deeply on that delicious aroma. But it only made him aware of the gaping hole in his stomach. Would they, the kidnappers, merely starve him to death? No loaded gun. No pressing down on his oesophagus with the power of a well-applied thumb. Just plain starvation.

'You are going through a bad patch, these are bad times for you,' the pandit had told Mr Bakshi. 'You must take half a kilo of black lentils, one kilo of wheat and a handful of rice every Tuesday and immerse the whole lot in running water if you want to ward off the evil that is now hovering over you, as indicated by your stars.' He was supposed to have followed this regimen for the next twelve Tuesdays. He wished that he had paid heed to this advice. After all, he had consulted this same astrologer when his son was to have been born. His wife went through a caesarean operation to make sure that their son was born at the right time, under the right stars. He had been meaning to get started from the coming Tuesday. The delay had only been the result of something as innocuous as the location. Should he go to the Budha Nala, which was a minor tributary of the River Sutlej and might therefore qualify as running water in the astrologer's book of abracadabra? However, in reality the Budha Nala, once a perennial stream of clear water, was now nothing but stagnant water and grime, layered over with pollutants from the factories and waste from the city. While the river gathered history on its shores, the Budha Nala gathered effluents. There he would have to hold his nose and discharge his celestial duties. He could also go to the Sidhwan Canal, a seasonal irrigation canal, which bifurcated the town and was the hotspot for all such immersions, though he would be at risk of breaking the law under open skies. The city administration had imposed Section 144, prohibiting easy movement in the area, precisely for all those unhappy worthies who had been to a pandit and were looking for heaven-born solutions. He could join the rows of early morning visitors to the canal, as they stood clutching their lentil-filled polythene bags, prepared to make a hammer throw as far into the waters as possible. Yet another option was to drive to the river, half an hour away from the city.

He had not gone and now he could not go.

He had tried the door with its wart-like nail to attempt an escape. He had pulled with all his strength. He had placed his foot, shod in its white shoe, against the wall, to give himself some leverage, and then he had heaved and tugged and cajoled and sweated and abused. The door had been immovable, obdurate. He had stopped a while to catch his breath. Then he had gone at it again. 'You motherfucker,' he told the door, not conversationally but with strong overtones of a challenge. 'You think you are smarter than me? Try this for size!' and he had kicked it with his white shoe. He was not, of course, offering his shoe to the door but was saying this only to emphasize the enormity of his kick. The door had been unmoved by the intensity of his frustration. Its nail-wart did not even quiver, and it had continued to look back at him poker-faced. No creak, no groan. He had made as if to kick again but then changed his mind because that pair of white shoes was a particular favourite. He did not want the point of its toe to cave in. He had waited to see if his exertions had been noticed by those who had brought him here, and who would certainly not look kindly on any attempt at escape. There was no sound. He had stared resentfully at the door for a few more moments and then gone to lie down on the bed, defeated. When he had removed his shoes they fell in a cross on the floor.

9

The police came to pick up Kailla, saying everything added up except perhaps his age, but they would have to overlook that for now since times were bad, and things suspicious were things suspicious, irrespective of mitigating factors. He was anywhere between sixty and eighty and hardly likely to be running around toting a gun and pressing it to weak vertebrae. He had looked the same ever since anyone could remember—eternally old or eternally young, depending upon where his years were pegged. He could be anything from a teenager to a prematurely greying middle-aged man, to an old man who had preserved himself well.But then he was also a Mussalman, dressed as a Sikh, behaving like a Bihari. It was difficult to reconcile all of these and still not notice any jagged edges that should have been there. They felt around for these, in anticipation of tripping him up on the facts of his ethnicity.

They asked him why he had stayed back and not gone to Pakistan with the rest of his family during Partition. He did not tell them about the giants that he had killed as he followed his charge to college, about the heroism in his head. Had he visited Pakistan? No? He must have, they said. No, he said yet again, bewildered by their insistence. You're lying, said one of the men in uniform, poking him in the ribs with his rifle. Did anyone visit you from Pakistan? Aha, your uncle? Your uncle indeed! They all say that… Uncles on hire, as many as you like. Did you go to one of those terrorist training camps they run there?

He had no idea what they were talking about and, therefore, an emphatic no seemed the right answer. Then you do know about them? He had to say no once again. They did not believe him. If you know that you have not been to one, then you do know that they exist and what they are. We will find out, they said. And then you have had it.

They asked him why he had become a Sikh. He had no answer. He had just become one. All he had to do was grow a beard, which was in any case an in-house affair, a simple matter of farming in one's own backyard. No land deeds, no title disputes, no labour problems. He had not shaved for a few days and the beard had followed its own growth logic, with very little help from him. They had not bought into the naiveté of his responses.

You went to Dhakka Colony the other day, did you not? You even had yourself photographed? Yes, he said, but he had not known that it was forbidden. How did they know that he had gone there, he wondered. The long arm of the law, or was it a giant eye in the sky? They had shoved him around a little as a foretaste of things to come. Don't you play the fool with us, they warned, pushing him in the direction of their parked vehicle.

It was a still day, so still that it did not even seem to be breathing, lest it reveal itself and be called upon to bear witness to the sequence of events. The scorched leaves were waiting for the rain to wash them down. Everything was taut with the tension of heat and suspended dust. Kailla stood with his sweaty shirt clinging to his back, and the dusty haze of the atmosphere reflected in his clouded, uncomprehending face.

They had wanted to know Kailla's date of birth. He had never felt the lack of knowing one so far. It had seemed fine enough to have been born. He had never gone to school where they might have asked him to write down his name, father's name, date of birth, religion and much else, squeezed into dotted lines too few to accommodate all this information.

'Happy Birthday to you' sung in an enthusiastic tunelessness and celebrated with candles and cake had not yet become fashionable, so there was no occasion for Kailla to notice that he did not have a 'happy birthday' date.

He had not needed a ration card because his name was added on to the family's card where he was listed as a domestic help, and that had ensured the half kilogram of sugar allotted to him during the days of rationing.

He had never wanted to vote either, not because he had any strong opinions on the matter but because the choices between contesting candidates seemed identical, where Sant Singh and Natha Singh were one and the same thing. He was not counted in the census when it happened every decade. He would usually go up into his trees when officials came round to note down the names and dates of birth of all the inmates in every household.

His date of birth was a matter of pure speculation, a derivative from many other things entirely unconnected with the matter at hand. His grandmother used to say that when Shireen, his cousin, started to make pigtails, he, called Shafi then, was only a baby, and she, Shireen, must have begun making pigtails when she was ten years old. And since Shireen was born about ten years before Mahatma Gandhi addressed the nation from Daresi Ground in Ludhiana, Shafi, being about seven years younger to her, must have been about three years old then. An assorted collection of disparate facts like these were strung together to form a sequence, much to the smiling satisfaction of all his relatives.

The month was a relatively simple matter. 'It was very cold when you were born,' she would tell him and the tone of her voice implied that it was somehow his fault. 'I had to carry buckets of hot water in for your mother.' Being his mother's son, he had obviously inherited her culpability. 'It must have been the month of Poh, or maybe Magh.' The year and the month, Poh being mid December to mid January in the Indian calendar, were trouble enough to calculate, so she never got round to pinning down a date on him. He could have chosen anything, from the first of the month to the Indian Republic Day on 26th January, anything from Poh to Magh. He had mulled the dates over in his head but had never fixed on any one because he had never felt the need to.

The absence of a date of birth in fact, was really a stroke of luck. It engendered in him an unshaken faith in the perpetuity of his youth. It gave him a certain free play with time. If Jassi occasionally, affectionately, admonished him, 'Kailla, you must act your age,' noticing that he was talking incessantly of some woman with toe rings on her feet, Kailla would look entirely unabashed. 'You should have found a girl for me and got me married,' he would say. 'It is still not too late. And in any case, what is my age?' he would add, more as a rhetorical question.

But just now it seemed very important to have a birth date to get these 'policias' off his back.

'Twenty-sixth January,' he said in a sudden moment of decisiveness.

It did not go down very well with the men in uniform.

'You are trying to pull our leg?' said the rib-poking policeman. 'You think we should be toasting you as a national hero just because you have given us this fanciful date of birth? Even Mahatma Gandhi was not born on that date, though he is the father of the nation.'

Kailla had obviously made the wrong choice in this moment of crisis. Would it have helped if he had said fifteenth instead of twenty-sixth? But now, it was not possible to take his words back.

The neighbours were out in their front verandas and gardens, trying to see and yet not be seen, to mingle with their surroundings, white kurta pyjamas merging with the whitewashed walls, eyes looking through the green hedge.

Jassi had heard the commotion and come out to see what was going on, although she expected to find only the usual—stolen fruit, fleeing children and Kailla in hot chase. But she spotted a load of policemen instead.

She tried to intervene. 'But what has he done?'

'That, we will find out,' they told her.

'I can vouch for him. He is a very good man, there must be some misunderstanding. He is really not the kind to mess with the law.'

'These are cordon and search operations, and we are instructed to carry them out with a thoroughness that cannot be compromised,' said one of the policemen.

'He has been lurking around in strange places,' said another. 'Places he should not have gone to. Times are bad and it is our job to examine anyone or anything that looks suspicious.'

One of them probed the nearest bush with the end of his rifle. The bush revealed a startled bird, which instantly flew away, resulting in a slightly awkward moment of embarrassed authority, which was quickly covered up by more bluster.

'Come on, you. Don't waste our time. We have not got all day.'

They were not going to take any chances with this bird in hand.

The 'bad times' referred to were, like the joker in the pack, useful to whip out when all else failed. 'Bad times' was the logo that had so far emblazoned all their transactions, personal or public, even though these bad times were gradually becoming a thing of the past.

They marched him to their blue matador, five policemen on either side with their weapons poised, anticipating an assault from some unknown quarters.

'In you go,' said the policeman, as though offering Kailla a secret door into a magical world, an exclusive entry into a club reserved for the elite. But he was only being pushed into the secured vehicle, the iron bars like a neatly woven handloom across the window. The doors were shut behind him.

He stared out at the checkered scene with a resignation that was not new to him. He had learnt, early on in life, to accept things as they came to him and make what he could of them, even if they appeared in the form of handloom squares. Kailla was not fighting the world. He was just living it differently.

There were more iron bars at the police station. These were not checkered but in even stripes like the pyjama from a night suit. But he could only feel them, since it was pitch dark, the day having gone by in extensive questions and answers.

When he had tried to grope around for the switch that would turn on the light, a voice had said, 'What is it? You can't rest in peace?'

He had instantly stopped, startled into momentary submission.

'What have you done?' the voice asked.

'Nothing,' said Kailla.

'You spend a night here and if you haven't done something so far, you will,' was the ominous reply.

'Will they kill me?' Kailla asked.

'You just stick to the rules and you will be all right,' continued the voice.

'What rules?'

There was no answer from the voice in the void.

Kailla had no idea what rules it was talking about. As far as he could see, or not see, in these circumstances, there were no rules of any kind. It seemed more like a free for all.

He found a wall, leaned against it, and slithered all the way down to the floor, waiting for morning to come.

10

When Kailla disappeared, the Bring Balli Back from the Brink of Bachelorhood Campaign came to a grinding halt. Balli had not been very cooperative to begin with, straining at the bit like a shy bride, both willing and reluctant, his ambiguity resulting in a gruff, disinterested manner, a 'hmmf' that was both consideration and disapproval. He had imposed so many conditions that it became impossible to locate the right place, to identify the right time and to create the right ambience for Sweety's performance.

'Not in my house. Not in yours either,' he had said.

'Try the moon, in that case,' his friends told him helpfully, taking their cue from old romantic songs that featured the moon when it was still a part of lovelore.

Kailla was to have been the ombudsman between the dancing girl and Balli, but after the police picked him up, the momentum was lost in a number of other pressing preoccupations. Finally, Balli's mother, Inder, the one who had traded her baby, was taken ill. So ill that Balli was completely diverted into the tasks of fetching and carrying blood and urine samples, collecting laboratory reports, consulting doctors, buying medicines and injections, and worrying till his head hurt. There was nothing ostensibly wrong with her, yet she was bedridden. Her already ghostly presence began to recede still further into oblivion. However, long-forgotten memories still asserted themselves, making her eyes appear as though they were trying to turn inwards, to spin around in their sockets and spot something infinitesimal, which she was straining to see. Her skin was like thin parchment stretched across her bones, so taut that a mosquito could break a tooth on it in an attempt to bite.

They took her into one of those hospitals that looked like a hotel, with potted plants and a café in the lounge, uniformed men and women as nurses, front office personnel, patient care specialists, public relations wizards, all of whom said 'please' and 'thank you' with unfailing regularity and a generous smile. Piped music, however, was of the religious kind, kirtans and bhajans, which gave the game away. This was no hotel but a place where disease and misery had a front office, where a smiling mask hid the dying throes of the patient and the devastation of those left behind.

It was at this smiling front office that they entered details of her age and the history of her afflictions, though they could only talk about the palpable ones—diabetes, blood pressure, arthritis. Balli's finger moved down the printed list in the form handed to him across the check-in counter. He ticked off her ailments, though none of those explained why she was their ghost-in-residence, flitting about the house with purposelessness; or why it was that she only came alive when it was cleaning time and she became a fiend with a broomstick and dusters; or why her hands were always moving to defend herself from something, which only she saw and the others did not; or why she said things which no one understood.

Initially they had rushed her to the Intensive Care Unit where the cardio monitor sounded like an electronic bird, an egret—ti ti ti teen, ti ti ti teen—persistent and unvarying, its monotone becoming a throb in his head. 'Ti ti ti teen,' sang the electronic egret in his head. It continued to sing for long afterwards.

His mother stabilized and was moved to a private room. She lay imprisoned in a bed with railings, and a nurse came in breezily at five every morning and suggested a bath, slapping down a fresh set of hospital attire on the bed. Even if there was nothing much that medicine could do, at least she could provide her patient with a bath. So thought the nurse, and in any case that was part of her job profile, so the sooner she got started and finished, the better for her. She could then sit down to a satisfying cup of morning tea. Balli's father would cheerily visit her later in the day, rubbing his hands with a gleeful air as though events had taken a most gratifying turn.

'So, how are you this morning? Had some breakfast?'

He was not of course, looking for an answer. They had lived their lives with words that only echoed back to each of them, cleanly bouncing off the other. When she told him of her headaches and backaches, he was not listening. When he told her of how the secretary of agriculture in the government had quaked before him, she had heard not a word, his vainglory entirely wasted. The hospital had only solidified this insularity into visiting hours, binding it down to that one hour in the morning and occasionally for one hour in the evening.

She has really become an old hag, thought Balli's father, his own youth being that magical secret between him and his mistress in Manali, which became a glow in his deepest being. He had to rub his hands now and again to release some of the charge which this glow had generated in him.

Secrets, like food, have good calories and bad calories, ones that add to the fat and others that work it off. However, the health quotient of secrets cannot be measured in terms of their acceptability, or the lack of it, by a stiffly moral society. In fact, the more unacceptable the secret, the greater its power to give off a radiance; the more secret the secret, the more its voltage. Balli's father's cheeks, though his beard hid them from view, flushed a sunset red each timehe thought of his mistress in Manali. His secret was doing him a lot of good.

Inder's was doing her none. It was, in fact, singularly responsible for her general decline.

Outside her room, they were washing down the hospital corridors, sloshing water all around and then drying it up with long-handled mops. This cleaning up, thought Balli's father, as he opened the door to make his way back, Inder seems to have brought it with her here too. Do they all have their instructions from her? I am obviously in the way.

Then he gingerly stepped over and dodged water puddles and swishing mops and was gone.

But he would have to be back sooner than he had thought, and much sooner than his mandatory morning visit when he would be bursting with its thoughtless bonhomie.

Inside the bathroom, Inder let the attendant scrub her back. She was too weak to protest about undressing before a stranger, too weak to mention that she found the water very cold on her back even though it was only September and real winter would only be here by November, or that her fingertips became like raisins in the cold water, dehydrated and wrinkled. In any case, she did not want to acknowledge the coldness of the water because it dredged up even more memories best kept dormant. The attendant was thorough, whipping up a lather that stood up in peaks like beaten egg white. Each new peak increased her sense of satisfaction and made her think of it as a job well done. The egg white then washed off on to the floor in a great mass of resistant foam, which gathered on the drain cover, waited a while there and then sank through, making gurgling sounds like a happy baby.

'You have only one child?' said the attendant, who had been watching the comings and goings of father and son.

The conversation never got any further than that because Inder, in response, fixed her with a baleful look and the breakfast trolley soon came rattling down the corridor. Ghosts did not eat breakfast but Inder got hers in a tray that sidled up to her on silent wheels astride her bed. Cornflakes and milk, egg and toast, butter and jam. She could not eat anything.

'I cannot eat,' she said, in a laboured whisper.

'Try a little,' said the attendant, coaxing. 'Your son will be here soon and he will want to know what you have eaten.'

Balli walked across the squeaky clean hospital floor and tried to introduce a spring to his walk in an attempt to lift his sagging spirits. His shoes squeaked each time he lifted his foot. It was embarrassing to be walking down the length in that hush-hush atmosphere, drawing attention to one's state of well-being. The floor that he was walking on had perhaps been paid for by Mr Bakshi, or at the minimum, its upkeep came from his pocket.

⁂

Mr Bakshi had made a generous donation to this hospital because it had earned him an income tax reprieve, and also because an act of philanthropy looked good, not only to the world at large but also to himself. He had got up from his chair after signing the cheque because he thought he heard applause. The mirror on the wall opposite, which offered a clear line of sight when he stood up, was the added incentive. He surreptitiously stole a glance at himself. Apart from the reprieve in income tax, donations could also earn a reprieve in heaven, an assured place for him amidst rivers of milk and honey. But according to the Hindu way of thought, there are no rivers of milk and honey in heaven. In fact, there is no heaven at all since souls are legging it from one birth to another, exhausting the 84,00,000 lives—all of which are a necessary part of progression, like a trainee who has to work his way from the front office to the top slot by going through the grind. The ultimate destination is only a state of beinglessness, a release from the cycle of birth and death. It is Islam that offers a honeyed heaven. Many centuries of coexistence had resulted in an osmosis of cultures, such that Mr Bakshi was not even aware that he was borrowing a vision.

This particular hospital had Hindu antecedents which meant that his money was in the right hands. The other, the Christian hospital, was all right if you only needed medical cure; but for the soul you had to come back to your familiar gods and goddesses. The Christians could make their peace by donating to a saint-something-or-the-other hospital. Not that he had any great animus against the Christians since there were so few of them around anyway. But his father had had a horror of Christians. When somebody had suggested that he send his son to a missionary school, he had reacted like an overheated engine, sputtering and hissing, 'My son is no Kristaan, wagging tail of the Angrez.' That is how they were seen in his day as they went about spreading English education and denouncing some of the existing Punjabi social practices. Even though the only missionary school in town was the most sought after, with a long list of waiting hopefuls, Mr Bakshi's father despised them. In deference to his father's sentiment, Mr Bakshi had diverted all of his charity budget to the greater good of the Ram Tirath Hospital.

He had been much more wary of the Sikhs these days, their anger like a crouched leopard ready to leap at the victim. Look at that Balli, behaving like he had been stung by a swarm of bees, showing me his teeth. Must tell my son not to be overfriendly with him, he thought, despite sitting in captivity, uncertain if he would ever walk out a free man and equally uncertain of being able to dictate a friendship list to his son.

⁂

And now Balli was walking on the floor that may have been paid for by Mr Bakshi and wondering if he had the moral right to be walking here and if the floor would not recognize treachery in a footstep and trip him up for it. The thought made Balli tread even more carefully even though he recognized his fear as superstition.

At his mother's bedside he became a child again, helpless and uncertain about what to do, a set of ten clumsy thumbs when he was called upon to prop up her pillows or propel a spoonful of milk and cornflakes into her unwilling mouth. He would end up depositing most of her food into her lap instead, and would then get into a flurry of cleaning up with those same ten thumbs.

His mother saw him as a little boy too. Not an unusual circumstance, given the fact that most parents continue to see even their grown-up, grey-haired, rickety-in-the-knees offspring as spring chicken.

Balli was standing by her bedside, all of eight years old, his hair tied into a knot on top of his head, a white hanky covering it and held in place by a rubber band, his knickers hoisted almost up to his chest, in perpetual fear of being found at his ankles instead, since his little drum of a stomach would not provide a waisted niche to the belt. There was an expression of extreme concentration on his face as he held a newborn baby in his arms.

'Your sister,' Inder said to him.

'Ma, see how tiny her hands are,' said Balli, measuring his own against the baby's and feeling like a powerful giant.

'Why are you telling him that?' said Inder's mother-in-law. 'He does not need to know. These things must not be spoken about otherwise they become difficult to do.'

'I am sure he will live with these horrible memories anyway.'

'Only if you put labels on things, find words for them. Let them be like swirling mists which he cannot grasp, then they go away.'

Pigeon logic, thought Inder of her mother-in-law. Shut your eyes and danger goes away. Keep quiet about it and it never happened.

'I have been through the same thing,' said her mother-in-law. 'You will thank me for it. I ruled over the household I was married into because I brought them only sons. Nobody need know the rest.'

Balli, in the absence of his father, was filling in for him as the head of the family, but that did not mean he needed to know everything. His father had gone to Manali. They had tried to tell him that it would be very cold there, that temperatures would be running in the minus range, that it was not the tourist season, that it could even be snowing.

'In fact, it is the tourist season,' said Balli's father.

'The tourist season?' said his wife.

'It is to see the snow that I am going and that is what tourists go there for,' he had said.

'Oh, the snow?' said his wife.

'Yes, the snow. Why do you have to repeat everything I say?'

See the snow indeed, thought his wife. No one ever mentioned the mistress in Manali.

He had left in his Gypsy, the sound of the engine rising from a purr to an urgent frenzy as it reversed out of the drive and quickly merged into the roar of the traffic out on the street. Meanwhile, Inder went into her labour pains.

Balli's grandmother was ready with a jug of cold water, which had been kept on the roof through the freezing December night. But now the sun was struggling with the early morning fog, managing to jab the earth with an occasional ray of light, which was promptly blunted by the unyielding vapour. It was important to get this thing over with before the water became tepid.

Balli had felt very important as he participated in the ceremony. It was like sitting at the head of the table and from that vantage, viewing the rest. He thought it might be a story to tell at school the next day.

It wasn't. You can't tell stories in which you are not a hero. And then it makes better sense to tell it like it happened to someone else. But for that you need the guile of an adult or the craft of a storyteller. Balli had neither guile nor craft, so he never told the story at all. And every story that sits festering, undigested in the stomach, has to be expelled as either diarrhea or vomit, otherwise it multiplies into a thousand little monsters that further sprout many heads, until a whole colony has set up camp inside, the pinnacle of their pitched tent stabbing straight into the heart.

He had watched horrified as his grandmother poured the jug of cold water on the baby—his sister. He could mention this to no one. Not even to himself. The baby, red in the face and howling, had suddenly turned silent and blue in his arms, like litmus paper. In later years, Balli had dropped out of studying sciences because he could not handle the litmus test—turning red when immersed in acid and blue in alkali. The searing red and bloodless blue. He would much rather study geography.

Balli, at eight, thought that he had not behaved like a man. Certainly not worthy of the head of the table, he thought. And as it happened, he was to live with manhood as his most pressing problem. But at eight, he had dumped the baby on his mother and run out of the front door. Out into the garden where the plants were still drenched in the juices of the night. And then to the road.

Parsinni was sent to fetch him. Parsinni, with her sari wrapped tightly around her like a winding sheet, was the ultimate caregiver, with a straying husband and many dead children behind her in Bihar, and a fund of maternal sentiments which she had carried with her when she came to Punjab to offer her services as an ayah.

'Come in Baali baba,' she had said.

'I am not coming in,' he had said. So the two of them had walked up and down on the road as though out for a morning walk.

Inder had watched everything from her bed. It had not taken long. Just a quick dousing out of life with a jug of very cold water. But when Balli had left her holding the dead baby, she had gone into paroxysms of sorrow, tear-filled hiccups that echoed loudly in the room with its high ceiling and rafters. Her mother-in-law had tried to comfort her—telling of her own time, of how these things are always done, and done in a certain way, of how there are traditions to uphold, of how society exerts some pressures, of how some who withstand them and others that don't, succumb, and of how she too would have loved it if her own daughter had lived. She had even cradled her in her arms, expressing an empathy which came from her very guts. But Inder lived silently with the horror of it for the rest of her years.

Now, in this sanitized hospital room, she was looking for an equally quick conclusion to her own life but was instead lingering on the fringes of it. In and out she went. Spotting the actors on the television set in front of her and catching the light in the window when she was conscious of her surroundings; grappling with ghosts and blinded by a surreal glow when she was remembering the horrors of the past. When she did finally die, there were beings, the size of little children, armed with iron hooks, who had beckoned to her soul. 'Come out, come out, we will tear you to pieces.'

11

'Don't try that,' said a booming voice, which seemed to have come straight out of a megaphone, like the voice of god in some tacky television serial. 'We will chop you up and feed you to the dogs. We will throw the morsels out of that very window. No one will know where you went.' An elaborate threat, a detailed recipe for annihilation, not the usual unimaginative 'I will kill you.'

Mr Bakshi had been jangling the window latch in a frenzy. He had noticed the window only a few minutes ago, having been completely focused on the door earlier. It had acquired an overwhelming presence, staring back at him with an unblinking evil eye that obliterated all else. The window was sealed and he now remembered that he had been made to climb stairs. A pistol had prodded him on as he stumbled over the blanket that crowded his feet. He had passed out somewhere in the course of this elaborate procedure but he knew that he was on a first floor, so did he really dare to make that leap? In spite of the possibility of splattering himself all over the road below like a casually spewed paan, the window continued to seem like a tempting escape option and he had gone at the latch with the zeal of a fanatic. He had been caught in the act because he made far too much noise.

'Don't try that,' the voice said yet again.

He had not dared to turn around and look.

The voice had gone on to say that if he knew what was good for him he would not try to escape. Mr Bakshi did feel that it would be an excellent idea for him to try and escape, and very good for him too, but there seemed to be no space for argument with booming, faceless voices.

The voice was on the other side of the door and had obviously heard his attempts at the window.

At that moment he made his god all sorts of promises. He would make a pilgrimage to Vaishno Mata in Jammu. Not once but every year for the next five years. A note made to the heavens above in the deepest possible ink. He did not want to be accused of ingratitude. He would make peace with his wife's family, whom he had not quite forgiven for their many acts of what he saw as negligence and slights towards the importance of his person—amongst others, the gift of a shirt and a necktie on his brother-in-law's wedding. Was he expected to remain naked waist below? Why had they not bothered to present him with an accompanying pair of trousers, he had asked his wife.

I will give up eating meat, he thought. Liquor too. He had never smoked so he was in the clear there. He would even forgive Balli for rattling his teeth, and a man could not promise more than that, there being a natural limit to goodness and tolerance.

He might have been heartened had he known that the owner of the voice was just as scared as he was. But then, sometimes there is very little to distinguish between bravery and fear, between the man who shoots because he is bursting with bravado and the other who pulls the trigger because he is terrified. In fact, the world stored in neat little boxes with appropriate labels pasted on them can easily fall into complete disarray, a messy jumble, when the going gets difficult. The bravery in Gurjant Singh's booming voice was quite questionable, though Mr Bakshi froze on the latch on hearing it. Nor was the size of their penises indicative of much else other than physical dimensions. Or maybe there was something to it—Gurjant Singh with his little one being the subject of much speculation and ministration and Mr Bakshi with his being an unsung appendage and a largely unknown entity—large or small, no one, other than his wife, knew.

In any case, Mr Bakshi became an icicle on the latch and Gurjant Singh was afraid of opening the door because that would necessitate action. He would have to go in with the force of a tornado and generate a whirlwind to frighten the man into submission. He would have to threaten and intimidate. He would have to rave and rant and talk in the venomous low tones of a particularly dangerous, hard-heeled gangster. And today he was just not up to it. After all, a man has to have his moods and moments. It is not the prerogative of the artist only. He thought that he might come back another time, and the ferocity of his voice from behind a closed door might suffice for just now. In any case he had had his fill of coercive action for the day. He had thrown the blanket over Mr Bakshi, encircled his waist and hoisted him into the boot of the vehicle like the tailor did his mannequins at Dhakka Colony. Gurjant had been ably assisted by the rest of his gang. He had followed this up with maniacal driving, screeching and swerving at turns, the vehicle tilting dangerously on two wheels as though for action cinema, because he thought that was the appropriate thing to do, though there was no one giving them chase, and a leisurely pace would have reached them to their destination just as well and more innocuously too. But that might have taken away from the enormity of the occasion and he could not afford to slacken just then. After he had metered a decent distance from the scene of the crime, he had brought Mr Bakshi out of the boot and deposited him on the rear seat and driven out of town and onto village roads. He had to wait for the anonymity of darkness to execute the rest. Mr Bakshi's abduction gear was pared down from a blanket to a blindfold, the transition being effected with the precision of a surgeon who transfers his patient to a heart-lung machine before surgery—not a second unaccounted for in between. Mr Bakshi did not manage even a passing glimpse at his surroundings but found himself stumbling blindly through fields, his ears perked up for giveaway sounds—a tubewell tattooing a tuk tuk tuk in the vicinity, the air vibrating with the sound, a road running in the distance, an occasional horn announcing its presence. But he could not fathom where he was.

Once home, Gurjant had decided that the victim must be kept on the first floor. Up the stairs went Mr Bakshi, Gurjant's hand holding a banana, in imitation of a pistol, digging into the other's back. Gurjant did not want to use the real weapon because, as he explained later to his gang members, he was so quick with it that he feared he might do harm even before their purpose had been achieved. Quick on the draw and quick to anger is how he saw himself. He belonged to Bhatinda, which is the Wild West of Punjab, where it was routine practice to shoot to kill over a land dispute and equally routine to fire shots in the air at a wedding out of sheer, undiluted joy. At Bhatinda, venues for marriage parties posted notices disallowing the carrying of firearms. But this only acted as a greater incentive to not only carry them in, but to also discharge them in the course of the festivities. He belonged to Bhatinda, and had to prove his antecedents, if not in letter, then at least in spirit. The banana, therefore, butted into Mr Bakshi's back in keeping with this spirit.

However, they were all quite unclear about this aforesaid 'purpose'. What did they really want? They could not want a Khālistān, a nation of Sikhs. The demand had very nearly gone out of circulation, though it was a suggestion that had surfaced from as far back as the forties, then again in the sixties, the seventies, the eighties—like a well-timed chime. It appeared as a pamphlet in the forties, which saw Khālistān as a buffer state between India and Pakistan; as a political conference in the sixties, which felt that Sikhs had been wronged and were left with no alternative but to ask for self determination; as a resolution in the seventies, which asked for autonomy; and as an agitation in the eighties, which turned to violence. At roadside kiosks posters of the now dead Sant Jarnail Singh Bhindranwale, big daddy of the insurgent movement of the eighties, were displayed carelessly next to those of film stars. Dream girl Hema Malini, her kohled eyes awash with emotion, looking out of one poster while he, his eyes fierce and combative, looked out of another. The demand had since mellowed into a series of jokes—about Khalistani currency, about the national bird of Khālistān, about political parties, all of them playing upon the Punjabi love for good food and bravado, sometimes mindless, sometimes exemplary.

A landlocked nation, some had said, how could it be practical?

'Sardar Sahib, it is not as though we are looking to catch

fish, we are seeking to create a nation,' the enthusiasts had said to these sceptics.

But Gurjant Singh and Co. did not have it that well worked out. They knew they had to have some demand. Any demand. A kidnapping without aim would only be like making wild sword stabs in the air. A demand for money would have made them look like mercenaries, which they were not, they told themselves. They were warriors of the guru. They were his representatives here on earth, bananas and all. Not bandits. The sheen of the Khālistān had to be preserved.

They had discussed it among themselves. In fact, they had discussed it over several rounds of desi liquor. It had made them smell like a freshly dressed wound, that has been cleaned with spirit. They were drinking santri, and though the name suggested an orangey flavour, there was no such subtlety to it. It was a quicky whisky, ready in a jiffy. Molasses from sugar-cane factories fermented into spirit brought to the right proof and distilled, and in two days the whisky was ready. No cellars, no barrels, no bottling dates, no issues of antiquity. It could be called anything from santri to gabru to jugni, from flavours, to youthfulness, to femininity. The names did not really matter to them. The headiness did. It could have been santri or gabru when it came to whisky and Mr Bakshi or Mr Bansal could be their kidnap victims. Names were inconsequential; it was the potency that mattered.

And so they discussed the matter at hand. In the evening they sat in the courtyard of Jagjit Singh Khalsa's house and hoped to draw some inspiration from the man himself. He was no ordinary seventy-six-year-old. A saffron turban clumsily tied, one fold coming unstuck at the back like a tendril shyly peeping out of a lush growth, an array of medals decorating his breast, slung from his neck with satin ribbons. His bushy, white eyebrows hung over his eyes like twin awnings and his white beard cascaded down to his waist. He had retired at the age of fifty-eight as the headmaster of a school, where he had rattled off rules on participles and gerunds and articles at a motorized pace, pausing only occasionally for breath. At sixty he had taken to cycling. He cycled two hundred and fifty kilometres everyday. To Delhi and back, to Bombay and back. Twelve hours to Delhi. Seven days to Bombay. And back. Nothing was a one-way ride. To get a visa for Canada, he had cycled all the way to Delhi and was then told that he would get it much closer home in Jalandhar. He had not baulked, but simply turned his cycle around and cycled back. 'Like a cow,' was how he described himself; 'whichever direction my face is turned, I just go.'

In the old days he had neither beard nor turban, but this new awakening to religion had come, he said, as 'a call from a voice within', though admittedly there were many external voices around saying similar things—things about justice and its travesty and the necessity to adhere to religious practices, with the specific intention of countering a perceived threat to the identity of the Sikhs.

'They don't want Punjab to come forward,' he used to say.

'They? Who?'

If someone asked him, he usually fumbled and thought and said, 'these Madrasis and Bungalis'—those Indians south of the Vindhya Mountains for whom the Punjabis nurtured a healthy contempt. They all came under the broad rubric of 'Madrasis' and 'Bungalis', and it did not matter in the least what Indian state they actually belonged to.

His impressive command over the English language

combined with his physical prowess made him something of an icon. Gurjant Singh and his men always took his words very seriously, particularly when they were spoken in English. Jagjit Singh translated his own verbose English into Punjabi for their benefit.

Now he pumped air into his cycle tyres preparing for his daily odyssey, which would begin at four in the morning, and said in his most floral Punjabi, 'The flower of Punjab's youth, this immense fund of talent is rotting today. And all because of these people.'

That made Gurjant and Co. feel even more persecuted. After all, they were the youth of Punjab and they had to have talent even though they did not quite see themselves as flowers. In any case, Punjabis always think that there is a plot against them. And this sense of grievance gave the kidnapping a lofty purpose.

'I will tell you what we will do,' said Gurjant. He had suddenly become a man with a plan and he was not the gang leader for nothing. Bhola, the innocence of his name inbuilt into his character quite by chance, had suggested that they ask for Chandigarh in lieu of Mr Bakshi.

'Chandigarh should be made a part of Punjab, its capital. After all, they did not give us a Khālistān. At least our state should be given something.'

'Don't be an innocent.' Gurjant had slapped his back in remonstrance. 'You really think they will do that? Give you Chandigarh indeed! They would rather bomb it out of existence than give it to you. And even so, you are not the guy they will give it to, even if you happen to be the last and only man on this earth. You really have an inflated notion of yourself.'

Jawaharlal Nehru had commissioned the building of the city on a flat piece of land, with picturesque hills providing the background. The prime minister had periodically surveyed its progress from a tall tower erected at the heart of the site for this very purpose. The city was an in vitro fertilization, one that sprang out of the lines on a drawing board, an immaculate conception, quite unlike the birth of Ludhiana. Why does everyone have to covet it so much, Gurjant wondered. He had no great love for the city, but when everyone else clamoured for it and listed its denial as one of the many grievances of the Sikh community against the Central Government, he had thought fit to join the chorus. Personally though, he would much rather live in the winding lanes of Ludhiana than in the straight line geometry of Chandigarh. The interstices in Ludhiana allowed for much, for a jhaat, a peek-a-boo, a surprise confrontation, or a secret tucked away, including the stashing away of Mr Bakshi.

And poor Mr Bakshi was feeling like a very well-kept secret indeed. Stashed away, waiting to be transported, he did not know where. Maybe the hereafter, he thought, and that sent a tremor down his spine. He would have been very nervous had he known that he had very nearly become a pawn on the negotiating table to be bartered away for Chandigarh. Men had died before this for staking claim to the city. Darshan Singh Pheruman had fasted in 1969 and died after seventy-four days. He had soon been forgotten. Other leaders, like Sant Fateh Singh, it was rumoured, had pretended to fast, consuming, behind the scenes and in the privacy of night, large dollops of kada parshad, which can be a whole meal in itself—flour, generous quantities of rarified butter and sugar. Certainly an indulgence which would not let anyone die of starvation. The parshad being an offering in a gurdwara also ensured that a sense of virtuousness prevailed over the guilt of having cheated. Neither fasting nor feasting succeeded. No one got Chandigarh. Neither Punjab, nor the neighbouring state of Haryana. The Union Territory came to stand for all that was desirable and yet elusive—wooed by all, giving herself to none.

Bhola had no use for Chandigarh. He had never even been there, but he thought that since his companions were looking around for a cause, this one may just be as good as any other. So, it was in a moment of inspiration that he had suggested Chandigarh. After shooting it down, Gurjant had said, 'I will tell you what we will do. We will let them know that we have done it just to show them what we can do. We will not ask for anything. We will tell them "you bugger us, we will bugger you."'

'Then there is nothing that we want in return for Bakshi? We just return him?' asked one of the gang.

That confused Gurjant a little. But leadership requires decisiveness.

'We keep him,' he said, terse and to the point.

'Keep him?' said the others. 'Forever?'

These questions about eternity are always tricky because they force you to think not just about the immediate in that they project the present into a distant future. Eternity is a long haul. For instance, the query made Gurjant picture Mr Bakshi in that barricaded first floor room in Sunet for the next five years—even the exigency of a forever could not force him to go beyond five. Five was phenomenal enough. There he was, five years later, handing rolled rotis to his prisoner, through a crack in the door, morning and evening. Keeping him alive and yet not quite. Playing hide-and-seek with the police, locking up and leaving the house and then coming back to check if he had forgotten to lock up. Tugging at the locked lock and then feeling foolish. Looking around to see that no one had seen.

'I meant that we keep him and then send him on to eternity,' he said, issuing a clarification with that meaningful look, pretending that that was what he had indicated all along, even though he had only just thought of the amendment.

Mr Bakshi was a fly in his throat he could neither swallow nor spit.

The fly now stepped away from the window and desisted from any further rattling of the latch. Mr Bakshi spent the night working out his opening lines and preparing to pronounce his considered opinion when the door did open, because hunger and fear would not let him sleep.

Gurjant heaved a tired sigh of resignation on the other side of the door early the next morning, and decided that he might as well go in. There was really no point in putting off the moment, after all an artist is also sometimes required to push himself beyond the vagaries of whimsicality. He had tucked a hanky behind his ears to cover his mouth and nose and sharpened the look in his eyes for added effect. He was ready to display his belligerence to his victim, who would by now be considerably disabled with hunger. He pushed open the door, expecting supplication, grovelling, a drool of emotion, a drivel of fear. But he was not prepared for a fusillade of English.

'Today the world is in the phase of ignorance, darkness, greediness, selfishness, theftness, bribeness and moreover the corruption,' said Mr Bakshi in his most studied English, hoping that the weightiness of his words would intimidate and then sink the scales in his favour. It worked quite to the contrary on both counts.

Gurjant was open-mouthed for a moment. Only for a moment though. Then his aggression surged back. Luckily for Mr Bakshi, Gurjant had not understood a word.

But it did give Gurjant an opportunity to make a point. 'Why can't you speak Punjabi?' he said. 'You think your moustache goes up a fraction just because you speak like a yankee?' He was of course talking of a metaphorical moustache since Mr Bakshi did not have any, or only as much as accrues overnight—a tired suggestion of stubble. As it was, it could not have stood in for a symbol of pride.

Gurjant gripped him by the shoulders and shook him into a blur, both for the English that he spoke, which Gurjant would be quite glad to have been able to speak himself, and for the necessity of frightening him into submission. He succeeded in sending Mr Bakshi into a terrified tremble.

'Cold, are you?' said Gurjant, dripping sarcasm while Mr Bakshi was dripping sweat. 'Poor you. Let me wrap you in this blanket and make you cosy.'

It was a red hot day, the blinding white sunlight had made everything hissing hot. Blankets should have been stored away with moth balls for the summer, but this blanket seemed to have become Mr Bakshi's preferred attire.

That English was a mistake, he thought, his brain having been tossed around into a confused jumble of short-circuited wires, which were now melting in the heat.

'I am hungry,' he said, the lines from his stomach to his head still in place.

'Then say that, instead of that long, fancy speech you just gave.'

Gurjant called downstairs for alu paranthas. Bhola quickly scampered across to the dhaba where the 'boys', as Gurjant Singh and Co. were known in the neighbourhood, had a running account, and brought back two wrapped in a newspaper.

Two rolled rotis, thought Gurjant with a sinking sense of dèjá vu, as he handed them over to Mr Bakshi.

12

Sweety was eating with gusto. The night before had been particularly trying. It was difficult to eat a meal with all those drunks on the loose at marriage parties. She had danced till she felt as though she would have dropped dead with fatigue and hunger. The dinner spread had been three hundred dishes. Could have been more, not less. She had only rounded off the figure in her head. She had served herself things with strange names. Kai yakitori and dragon roll, amidst the more familiar alu lajawaab and bhindi kurkuri. She had tried asking the waiters stationed behind the groaning tables. Kai yakitori? But they had only smirked, whether at her or at the yakitori, she did not know. She had decided to be adventurous, to stare down the smirks and yakitori, and to tango with the unknown. But overtures from men who had watched her dance followed her around like a primeval curse that is difficult to shake off. She had opted to give up her plate instead.

In the morning she woke up to the exposition of a raga in her stomach, the notes flowing freely but tending to the single theme of hunger. She got up and made herself a parantha in the makeshift kitchen in the corner of her room.

She was eating when Gurjant came in.

'Be a brother and just scratch my back for me,' she said as she licked her fingers clean.

Gurjant did not feel brotherly at all but obliged nevertheless.

'Just a little to the right,' she said, her eyes closed. 'Lower... no no...that is too low...higher...a little left...yes, just there... go on...keep going...don't stop...hmmmm...hmmmmm...'

The ecstasy of being scratched at just that right spot was an unmatched sensation, thought Sweety. Unmatched yes, but then there were those others. The moment of orgasm, for instance. That was good too, a soaring of senses aboard a jetliner, when issues of sexual morality and survival became but miniatures in the distance down below. But then, it was followed by a feeling of emptiness. Back scratching had no such falling out.

'Hmmmm,' she said again.

'How long?' said Gurjant, his patience wearing thin.

'Already tired? Alright, you can stop.'

Gurjant had come to propose to Sweety, not to scratch her back. It might have been different if she too had scratched his back but then that would have needed a different idiom, the English one, to be applicable. He felt that she might see him in a different light now that he had been man enough to show his muscle. He had Mr Bakshi in custody and was on the verge of making his point to the world at large, even though the point itself was slightly hazy in his head.

His hangers-on had advised him against marriage and particularly to Sweety. You can barely keep yourself going and here you are, thinking about marriage—they had said in varying ways. They had even advised him to place a demand for money as ransom for the release of Mr Bakshi. 'We could set up a chain ransom,' said one of them. 'This cartoon could give us the name of another rich seth whom we could then kidnap. And then, that one in turn could give us the name of yet another one. And we could just build it up like that.' It sounded like a business venture that was bound to grow. 'Two lakh from each and that should keep us going fairly well.' It was a calculation in which imponderables did not exist. No police, no state machinery, no enforcement of law and order, not even an angry, vigilant, retaliatory public. Just a fairy-tale world in which the thief thieves and saunters away with riches.

'And why marry? Why marry someone who has seen it all already? Seen the ups and downs of it all?' They had said it crudely but then that was man to man and he did not mind. What he did mind though, was Sweety addressing him as 'brother'.

'By God,' she said. 'I was really hungry.'

'They did not give you any food last night?' he asked her.

'There was enough food to feed all of Dhakka Colony for one week,' she said indignantly, but wondering all the while why she was taking their part in this exchange. But Gurjant and she were naturally antithetical—two swords in one scabbard. They had to fight. If he had said something about how hot it was, she probably would have contested it, even though the sweat stood in stubborn beads on her forehead.

'Just so, and yet they did not give you any food,' he said, teasing her.

'I chose not to eat,' she said haughtily.

The teasing was not really teasing. It was a mating call.

He did not like her profession even though he was seduced by it in a subterranean sort of way—pornography in his pyjamas, piousness in his pants.

'Why can't you do something else?' he said, invoking the commandment from the insurgents that proscribed dancing.

'Maybe they will employ me as the chief minister,' she said sweetly.

The state was in need of a chief minister just then. The one it had was blown away by a bomb outside the secretariat in Chandigarh. Forensic experts were left picking up the pieces, though in strictly physical terms there was not very much to pick up. A shoe which belonged to the assassin. An assortment of limbs. Mangled metal. Glass shards. The chief minister had disappeared into thin air. There were no remains to make up even a handful for an urn. In later years, the government would try to remedy that by providing a plot of land where a memorial would serve in place of the ashes that had blown away with the pernicious wind. The assassin, a disgruntled policeman in uniform, had worn gelatin sticks under his belt and when he blew himself up, triggered by a nine-volt battery, the sound echoed back into town from the mountains in the background. Insurgency had been quelled a few years ago, but did this announce another beginning, or just a last convulsion, an echo?

'If you marry me you might become important enough for them to consider the option,' he told her, pretending to be facetious but secretly savouring the headlines that he would make.

His predecessors in the insurgent movement had been even more conscious of the headlines and the image. One of them was known to measure the length of exposed forehead with the markings on his forefinger to make sure that his turban sat symmetrically on his head. Gurjant was only keeping up yet another tradition.

'Haan, yes,' she said, playing along with the charade of his pre-eminence, 'maybe they will make you the chief minister and I can be the first lady.' Then she paused and said, 'No, I don't want to marry you.'

'Don't want to marry me?'

'Don't want to marry you.' The repetition gave each some time to mull over the next move.

'I wouldn't marry you even if you were the last man on earth.'

That changed the tone of the exchange from friendly parrying to viciousness. If they were going to trade insults, then he was pretty good at it himself. He could give her as good as he got.

'Are you going to die an old maid then? Who is going to marry you? You don't know a good thing when you see it.'

If Gurjant was the 'good thing' in Sweety's life then there had obviously been some kind of reallocation of the values of good and bad since last she knew of it. They circled each other warily like opponents in a kabbadi match. She wanted to make the home run, and decided to have it out with him.

'Why? Why would I die an old maid? Only a few months ago a man had come with a proposal. Kailla, I think his name was. And he told me that someone in that white kothi of the big sardars had seen me and liked me.'

'Aho, one of those sardars will marry you, will they? They will only make you dance some more in those silly skirts of yours. You look like a fairy doll in a salwaar kameez but in these skirts…you look a karaant.' To Gurjant, a skirt looked like an uncomfortable attempt at being English and Christian.

In the general hierarchy of acceptance, to be English was something to be looked up to but to be Indian Christian was to be looked down upon. The antipathy ran far into the past, from as far back as the nineteenth century when Ludhiana became the centre of Christian missionary activities. The missionaries were seen as the stooges of the British. However, their methods of evangelization were grudgingly admired by the Hindu Arya Samajis and Sikh Singh Sabha. The missionaries had set up the first Punjabi printing press, admittedly for their own ends, but while they churned out publications on Christianity, Punjabi prose developed as a by-product. There was even a Punjabi phonetic reader that lay open under a glass case in the Punjabi Bhawan library. *1914*, by T. Grahame Bailey, MA, BD, Fellow of the Punjab University, University of London Press, London. Punjabi pronunciation made easy by an Englishman! However, 'karaant' was neither literary, nor Punjabi, nor a phonetic feat. It was just the result of an ancient, epileptic anger that had contorted speech. Karaant for Christian. The anger was now forgotten history but the distortion had become part of the vocabulary, not without a value judgement though.

Gurjant's own history was quite illustrious. Not the kind that fetches public accolades, nor merits a photograph in a gallery of heroes, but it was certainly worth a telling. His great-grandfather hadn't died playing at home with his grandchildren. He had died with his boots on, literally. Over a century ago he had marched into Ludhiana on the ninth of June, riding on the wave of the 1857 mutiny against the British. Boots and breeches and bravado. His moustaches pointing fingers at the sky. His spirits pitched even beyond. He had come in with the other mutineers, though they said that most Sikhs were supporting the British, and by that logic, he really was on the wrong side of things. He had made straight for the fort, the same fort that was now like a set of teeth infested with cavities. It was not so then. It was a stronghold from where power emanated. The aspiring nationalists had mounted and manned their guns at the fort and were in a fair way to giving the British a run for their money, the one they had made out of Indian sweat. In that moment of triumph, Gurjant's great-grandfather discovered that he had carried with him blank cartridges instead of balled cartridges, his firepower being reduced to merely the fire that he carried in his head. His looks could then kill but his guns would not. That had briefly taken the shine out of the moment but his natural buoyancy had bobbed him up once again, as he made ready to march on to Delhi along with the others. But an unarmed man is bound to fall to the enemy bullet. And he did. In hindsight, had they stayed on and consolidated their position at the fort, the British would have lost this very important city—which lay on the high road to Delhi—and history might have taken a different course.

Maybe Gurjant's propensity to carry unloaded weaponry, subsequently substituted by bananas, took root way back then, as also the inclination to slip off the high road into the sidings of parody.

He tended to provoke more laughter than tears, even though his intent was otherwise. And whatever the provocation, historical or immediate, Gurjant did not like skirts. Dark hair and dark legs were only karaant. Awkward legs sticking out from under a swirl of material. Legs, which did not know what to do with themselves. Should they be crossed or demure, placed side by side with knees knocking against each other?

'And have you ever seen your mug?' she asked him, raising the pitch yet another notch, of both temperature and volume, as also of physiology, her hand pointing to his face to shift the focus away from her legs and onto his physiognomy.

She, too, was uncomfortable in those skirts but she was not going to admit it and certainly not to Gurjant. She might as well let him have it—above the belt, below the belt, wherever. The argument spiralled its way upwards, like steam from an angrily boiling kettle.

'Why, what is wrong with it?' he asked, thrusting his face at her.

'Uuhah,' she said, simulating a vomit.

That made him ballistic. The neighbours gathered outside. Time for a fight. It had been a long time. And a fight always cleared the air. Everyone went home, spent and satisfied. It worked on the principle of a homeopathic cure. Bring out all the poison, let there be the sudden eruptions of a million sores, festering and weeping, clearing the system and skin after it had all been expended.

Gurjant was rocketing along on a reckless anger, saying and doing things that he would later wish he had not done or said.

'Bitch, whore, bastard woman, fat-arsed buffalo, black witch,' he rattled off. As he ran out of expletives that would be specific to women, he launched into the usual sisterfucker, motherfucker and daughterfucker tirade even though they crossed the gender divide and were employed more as pause and punctuation by vehement Punjabi speakers.

He did not regret the fact that he had gone on from her to the rest of her family, to her father, her mother, her sisters and brothers, abusing them with heartfelt venom even though he did not know any of them. He did not regret having stamped around furiously like a particularly vigorous kathak dancer in an ecstasy of creativity, smoke emanating from all his orifices.

Nor did he regret having flung a few things around, amongst them the little clay animals that he had bought for her, a red-beaked parrot, an open-mouthed bird, a plumaged peacock, a cavorting horse, well-fed bullocks—all of them in the colours of embroidered phulkari—explosive pink, dirty yellow, bright green, since the craftsmen who had fashioned them were not aspiring for verisimilitude. They were trying to capture the vibrancy of spirit. He had bought them at Bhagtu da Mela in Khatkar Kalan, at the fair in memory of Shaheed Bhagat Singh, who had been hanged by the British. This was an annual pilgrimage for him, an hour's bus ride from Ludhiana. Gurjant would visit the martyr's ancestral home, a small unassuming structure, forlorn looking—an indifferent whitewash hiding its original brick construction. There was a visitors book that was a hand down from a snack bar at the Wagah border, with an entry in it that said, 'The family of a martyr should be given due respect, which seems to be still due.' Gurjant would then go to the museum and stare yet again at Bhagat Singh's entry on the second page of the diary issued to him in jail—'lovers, lunatics and poets are made of the same stuff'. He would breathe deeply, inhale the ambience of revolt, of a reckless madness, and a voice in his head would say—'Keep your distance, I am Bhagat Singh'. It made him feel important. He would go out suffused with determination to fight the Indian state even though Bhagat Singh had died fighting for it. That having been done he would loiter about in the grounds and survey the stalls with the air of a dignitary taking a salute from assembled contingents. Ultimately he would buy knick-knacks, eat candy floss that had materialized like a spiderweb in the wheel that was spun by the candy-floss man, and be back on the bus by the evening.

Those keepsakes from Khatkar Kalan now lay around with broken necks and fractured legs. He was also pleased at having broken the only other piece of decoration—the glass paperweight in which colourful specks had danced around and which had sat blinking on the only table in her room.

But he did wish that he had not given her the entire lowdown on his activities in a voice that could be heard down the road. He wished that he had been a little more circumspect. He wished that he had not boasted. In short, he wished that he had not told her of Mr Bakshi going molten in a room upstairs in Sunet. And particularly, that he had not told her in a voice loud enough to be heard by the neighbourhood.

She did not take it very well. In fact, it was her turn to be furious.

13

Two days later, very early in the morning, at one of those hours when it is not quite morning and not really night, when late risers have just begun to get a good night's sleep and early risers were springing out of bed in readiness for the day, the police were standing outside the double-storey structure in Sunet. A truckload of them had descended and fanned out—sultry, khaki lines of surly policemen, the long arm of the law. It was a cordon and search operation. Sources said a man had claimed to have kidnapped the industrialist Bakshi. The news had made headlines in local newspapers: 'Bakshi of Bakshi & Bakshi Enterprises Blindfolded and Bundled away', 'Terror Revisited, Bakshi Abducted'.

'Sources' was an ubiquitous entity that worked both for the police and journalists. 'According to sources…' said the journalists, and that could mean anything, from an actual source of information, to a stray remark by someone at a dinner party or a personal theory pulled out of a fertile brain.

Perhaps it was Sweety. She had been humouring Gurjant all along only because he had seemed harmless—even though he wore jeans a few sizes too tight and moved around with a stiffly starched, deliberate gait that carried him more sideways than forward, was curt when spoken to because it did not behove a *real* man to be soft and pliant, whose repertoire of jokes was limited to the age-old one about the Punjabi athlete Milkha Singh. ('Are you relax-ing? No, I am Milkha Singh.) Gurjant was usually the only one to laugh at this antiquated joke while others wore polite smiles as they heard this one through for the three hundred and fifty-fifth time. His banter included exposing the underside of his shoe, saying 'look into a mirror'. He had grown up in some ways and not in others. But he had also been gentle and responsive to her needs. We all have a dark side, reflected Sweety, but just how dark is dark? It is an internally installed metre that measures umbras and penumbras, the shadows and half shadows. Each metre, a different brand, with different readings.

Maybe she had wrapped herself in an anonymous veil and gone to the police to tell them of the whereabouts of the missing industrialist.

Perhaps it was that man who wore his visor in reverse, always lurking about in the streets, a mukhbir, an informer, a 'cat', as the police liked to call them, because they were expected to be feline and quietly make their way to listening posts. Maybe he had waited for the evening and then cycled to another part of town, to a cigarette kiosk where he pretended to buy cigarettes. 'King of spades,' he had told Roshanlal the vendor, letting drop the code, even as Roshanlal handed him cigarettes from his perch. Or he went to a dhaba where the serving chhotu not only took his order for a tandoori roti and dal but also took the note that he handed to him in such an overtly surreptitious manner that anyone with half an eye would have noticed. Or he asked for fifty kilos of atta to be delivered to his house the next morning from a grocery store.

The verbal messages, or a note, or a sign would be picked up by another man who would then pass it further on, and after a circuitous route devised to hide and jumble its footprints, would arrive at the doorstep of the police. Ultimately someone would contact the man with the visor in reverse and he would tell them all that he saw and heard at Dhakka Colony. A car with darkened windows would take him around town to identify the said man. 'There he is,' he would say, as he spotted Gurjant shading his eyes from the sunlight outside on the road. And then the police would be on Gurjant's tail, following him to the miracle man, perhaps for a second dose of those little globules, to the Subhani building which was threatening to fall on the next visitor's head, to the old clock tower strangulated by a flyover under construction and then finally to Sunet.

In any case, whatever their means of gathering the information, two days after Gurjant proposed to Sweety, the police were there in Sunet.

Gurjant had claimed that he had had a premonition. He had not told his gang that he had lost his cool and spilled all, practically on the street. He had tried to warn his fellow conspirators to make a run for it, citing the instance of his third eye, which not all of them took seriously since this was the first time it had made an appearance.

'A third eye? What is that? Like Lord Shiva's third eye?' they asked him.

He did not want to be seen as alluding to the Hindu pantheon for an analogy and suggested that it was Maharaja Ranjit Singh's eye—the Lion of Punjab, who had consolidated the first Sikh empire in the nineteenth century. Though blind in one eye, the maharaja's one good eye had come to stand for the dispensation of justice.

'But he had only one eye,' said Gurjant's hangers-on, 'and you are talking of a third one.'

'Go fall into a well then, go to hell,' said an irritated Gurjant.

When the police knocked on the door, they had expected to find the ring leader and his entire set of angry young men asleep in their underwear in the summer heat. Not a pretty picture, but very sharply etched in SHO Bachitter Singh's head. Repulsive, he thought, shaking his head, trying to dislodge the image. Hirsute men, unguardedly displaying the remnants of their ancient ancestry. Hairy apes! Why couldn't it be women kidnappers, at least that would make the cat and mouse game a lot more interesting. Imagine discovering an entire contingent of women in nothing but their stringy undergarments. The SHO was momentarily overcome by a surge of fevered fantasy. But then, better to come up against men in a state of undress than to have them sitting all primed and ready with their weapons, waiting for the police to enter. The same police informers could sometimes be informing the other sides. Double agents on a double stipend earning double roti. That kind of thing could put both sides in a fix since both thought they knew what the other was doing.

The police had to break open the lock. Constable Ram Singh was instructed by SHO Bachitter Singh to hammer down the lock with a brick. They had been prepared for a bolt on the inside but not a lock on the outside, which is why they had to resort to slightly archaic methods. The others had stood looking on, their AK-47s ready and pointed. The first brick lying handy on the sidewalk had turned into powder against the door.

'These damn brick kilns and these damn building

contractors,' said Constable Ram Singh as he looked at his hand clutching at red dust. 'Sisterfucker.'

He had been through many such operations and had acquired quite a formidable reputation, which is why he had to be the first one in, though he was no longer very keen on this kind of action. He had won no medals for it. It was mostly brickbats. Not for him personally, but for the police as a whole. Anyone would think that they were remorseless, heartless, flesh-eating vultures. Though, admittedly, that is exactly how he too saw SHO Bachitter Singh, with his peculiar talent for squeezing money out of even the most dehydrated situations—money trickling in from the roadside vendor, the cycle rickshaw man, the garbage collector—the notes browning and limp, soiled with the sweat of their labour. But as SHO Bachitter Singh said, every drop counts. That trickle had built him a house in Model Town, right next to a nascent market. Well-known companies were offering fancy prices to buy him out and build fancy showrooms. But he was proud of his tall house, more vertical than horizontal, and did not want to part with it, even though he was gradually being dwarfed by the giants that were rearing their heads around him.

'Are you going to take all day?' shouted Singh, waking up from his daydream of gun-toting women dressed in underwear, and wanting to blame someone else for it. Constable Ram Singh was a subordinate and available, which made it just so easy.

It was with a sense of peevishness that Constable Ram Singh finally unhinged the lock with a spanner. He makes the dirty money and I have to do the dirty work, he thought.

They went in ready for battle, sticking to the drill on storming a hideout. They tiptoed, took cover, challenged sounds, ran a questioning eye over a room before entering it. But they need not have bothered. There was absolutely no one inside. Not on the ground floor, nor on the second floor. There was only hot air from the flurry of sudden departure.

The kidnappers had also left behind Mr Bakshi tied to his bed. Though he too had once been a lot of hot air, the last two days had beaten all of it out of him. They left him behind because they were all scattering in different directions like a casually thrown handful of marbles. No one wanted Mr Bakshi.

'You take him with you.'

'Why me? He is all yours.'

It had taken them a day to realize the gravity of Gurjant's warning, and that left them only a day to take on other identities, to become one among the many. Lugging Mr Bakshi around as baggage would only have been like wearing an overcoat on a hot summer afternoon and trying to melt into the populace.

They passed the parcel, nobody wanting to be caught with it when the music stopped, or, in this case, started. Finally everyone decided that this hot potato belonged to Gurjant.

'You keep him. You said we had to keep him forever.'

From a cohesive group that spoke in one voice at public forums, they were suddenly many voices at cross purposes. Good times had kept them together, bad times sent them at each other's throat.

'I meant all of us. He is not my uncle. Why would I want to take him along?'

That decided it. Mr Bakshi stayed where he was. All trussed up and nowhere to go.

From Sunet, Gurjant went everywhere. To the UK, the US, Thailand, Nepal, Pakistan. Having evaded arrest once, he subsequently went in and out of jails in different countries. His fate seemed to follow him around like a bad debt. He wondered if someone up there was keeping an account, that too, one that overlooked his serious commitment to religion. It was in the absence of this finer detail in the heavenly account that he was handed out such severe tribulations, he thought.

His travails had begun at Kathmandu, where he had shared a room with four others on the first floor of a guest house. Somebody had sloshed a bucket of water from the balcony. It fell on a guard standing below and the police came and arrested Gurjant. When he got out of that one and reached the US, he was deported very quickly, after doing time in jail there. On the flight back he managed to convince an American woman—his first success at persuasion—in English that was more gesture than speech, that he was likely to be killed the minute he deplaned at Delhi. The woman was suitably horrified and immediately willing to believe the worst of these brown-skinned people with their record of human rights violations. She helped him disembark in Thailand and then on he went to Pakistan. From there he somehow made his way to the UK.

While in Ludhiana his must-carries had included a banana, which he ate before finally leaving on a false passport. He had substituted it with boiled eggs when he was on the run because they offered easy-to-carry sustenance and in any case, his days of threatening people were over, so the banana was quite redundant as a weapon. He had bought the boiled eggs off a street vendor near the railway station, who kept water on the boil and had handed him a dozen of them, along with a generous measure of salt in a pudee—the newspaper scrap cleverly folded many times over to ensure not even a pinch spilled into his pocket.

In all those other lands his pocket also contained a letter from a Khalistani organization certifying him as a member which stated that he was likely to face persecution if he went back to India. He had got the letter and funds from an underground organization. It was underground in more ways than one, since it also operated out of a basement. It employed people who could cook up weepy or gory life stories, depending upon the requirement of the client. Gurjant's letter contained a hair-raising account of his life. From the sound of it, he had been in the forefront of a medieval battle in which his family had been picked up by the police, tortured and raped, he himself subjected to the unheard of, including being pissed upon by a whole police contingent, and then buggered by the same force, and all because he was fighting for the creation of a nation which rightfully belonged to the Sikhs. These stories were not entirely fanciful, they were known to have happened to some and the authors of these stories had merely picked up things from here and there and woven them into a heart-rending narrative.

He thought it sounded better than his own life and that if he had to find asylum in one of these countries, he did need to believe his own story before he could expect others to do so, particularly lawyers and judges. 'My sister was raped before my very eyes and now I have no idea where my entire family is. The police took them away and I have no news of them. I was hung upside down for days together, they pissed and spat on me. I was stretched from both ends till I thought I would break into two halves, like those volunteers at magic shows whom the magician slices into two and puts together again.' This last simile was his own invention and he used it when called upon to narrate his tale. The letter only kept to the sequence of events and did not dabble with things literary. However, his narration was so like a recitation of numerical tables that no one was ever moved. He continued to be an illegal with a letter in his pocket and diminishing hope in his heart.

14

Only mice, thought the policemen. The kind of mice that became emboldened with time spent in human company, sitting on their haunches and staring back with the insolence of a spoilt child, quite at home in the kitchen and drawing room and willing to challenge anyone who might want to evict them. The dull sound of scratching, cutting and sawing came through, breaking silences between whispered words.

The policemen had begun to loosen up after the stress of the past few hours and conversation had gradually risen from nervous whispers to a volume more appropriate for a political rally.

When the grating orchestra of the so-called mice would not be frightened into submissive silence, and in fact, swelled into a deeper layer of resonance, SHO Bachitter Singh said to Constable Ram Singh, 'What is that? Go and see.'

It had to be done through the proper channel because that is how governments function, in a chain of hierarchy that must not be broken. It is a hierarchy behind which the meek and timid can hide and yet hold their heads up high as natural superiors.

'Motherfucker,' said Constable Ram Singh in his head, but went nevertheless, programmed to obey.

And that is how they had found Mr Bakshi, a dead man in his winding sheet. He was not really dead though he looked so. The room was strewn with dead moths' wings, from moths that had winged their way to the single light bulb that burned in the room and singed themselves to death. The light had been a parting kindness, an act of generosity on the part of Gurjant. 'Here, I am leaving this light on so that they will find you.'

There was no response. There could be none since they had stuffed Mr Bakshi's mouth with an underturban. 'Now let me hear you say something in English,' said Gurjant, as his last throwaway line.

'Gggggg' said Mr Bakshi, from the many folds of the underturban. But by then Gurjant had already gone. He was still saying 'ggggg' when they finally found him.

Over the two months of imprisonment before Gurjant had spilled the beans to Sweety, Mr Bakshi had become a lizard on the wall, his ear pressed against it, trying to absorb some of its cool while everything else burned hot. He would listen to sounds and anticipate footsteps, and work out in his mind whether those footsteps meant trouble or food or both. 'Wrong again' or 'right again and that makes twelve rights against eight wrongs, I won, I won'. That is how he kept his sanity, in an insane sort of way. Because when the world is standing on its head, it may just be a good idea to do likewise. He would count cows in his head, go over his life inch by eventful inch, saying and doing the things he had already said and done in a dramatic recreation of the past, and pretend that it was only a question of marking time, of putting it in reverse gear and that the world would right itself in the end, like it had so many times before. Mountains could be moved, he believed. As a four-year-old he could remember going to Murree, and as they circled their way up the hills from Rawalpindi, his insides heaving, he had told his father to remove the mountain. 'The same one keeps coming again and again, just take it away,' he had said in exasperation. As an adult he had continued to believe that mountains could be moved, even if only metaphorically.

But that was before he was tied to the bed, almost becoming one with the weave of the cot, the same tape that made up its warp and weft wrapped around his prone body.

'Gggggggggggggg,' he said, his verbosity severely curtailed by the awkwardness of talking with a full mouth. Constable Ram Singh heard him from the other side of the door, which had been concealed by an ornamental wooden cupboard stationed right there. It was pushed aside to reveal yet another locked door.

'Panna,' said Constable Ram Singh, in the manner of a surgeon demanding his instruments from a compliant nurse.

The requisition was handed down the hierarchy. The bottom of the heap scurried downstairs for the spanner that had been abandoned there and handed it to Constable Ram Singh. He broke into the room. They had missed this locked door earlier. The emptiness of the house had been so deafeningly loud that they had slackened into complacency.

The policemen untied Mr Bakshi, the tape unravelling like Draupadi's legendary sari, the more that was pulled off her, the more there was to pull, keeping her honour intact. The two men detailed for the job squatted on either side of the bed and got into a work rhythm—one threw the tape over the bed, the other hurled it from under. Over and under they went, over and under, until the onlookers were mesmerized into believing in the eternity of the moment. The moment snapped when the tape ran out.

Mr Bakshi stood up uncertainly, like an infant who has just discovered the ability to stand. The blood in his legs was put back into circulation with vigorous rubbing.

⁂

Family and friends had gathered at his house when they learnt that he had been found. They were all going to participate in the happy homecoming. Mrs Bakshi, Harish, Sarita, Tejpal, Harpreet, Balli, Meiyang, and many others who had attended those parties at his house.

Some were now a little scared of being seen in the company of one who was obviously in bad odour with terrorists, but they went nevertheless. 'Doesn't look nice,' said one. 'I have drunk so much of his scotch that we might as well go and see him, though sometimes I do think that these Hindus have brought it upon themselves.'

The drawing room had been cleared of furniture, carpets, statues, lamps, cut glass. In the middle of that uncharacteristic starkness sat a pandit before a fire, surrounded by pots and pans with varying measures of ghee, lentils, rice and shakkar in them, a banana and an out-of-season Chinese apple with a price sticker firmly glued on to it. He was in attendance to perform the rituals of purification and thanksgiving. He started reciting slokas when the time was just right according to the calendar for auspicious and inauspicious moments, lightly touching each of the ingredients before him as he proceeded to make an imaginary, metaphoric meal to propitiate the gods above. There would be fruit and dessert to follow—for the gods and for everybody else.

The police drove Mr Bakshi in. His entry was much more stately than his exit, but he would never live down the ignominy of having been treated like a sack of potatoes. He sat through the ceremony that had been lined up for him but could not be counted amongst the living after that.

'After all, just breathing, sleeping, eating and shitting does not mean that one is alive,' Mrs Bakshi would whisper to all those who subsequently came to ask after him. And then, in a significantly louder voice, she would tell them all about his exemplary courage: 'He had them pinned to the wall,' she would say. That is what he would have said, had he been able.

His movements had acquired a slow viscousness, as though he was moving in a dream. Gone was that aplomb and bluster which was so much the subject of ridicule behind his back and which was sorely missed now that it was gone. It is so much easier to value things and people who are no longer around, than to cope with the daily drudgery of their presence.

'Bauji ganje ho ke aaye hain,' said their cook, noticing Mr Bakshi's suddenly balding pate, which had become more prominent over his captivity.

But at least he had been found.

15

Balli's marriage had been on hold for some time. One reason for this was that his mother had passed away and there had to be a decent interval between death and festivity. Not that Balli felt that marriage was any reason to celebrate. He also had to admit that he felt quite badly about his mother. Hers had been an unhappy life and an unhappy death. Of course, dying can never be edifying but she seemed to be wrestling with something or someone as she left. And he could only stand by and watch helplessly as she flailed her arms in what seemed like self-defence.

The other reason, not quite convincing as reasons go, but Balli insisted on its validity, was that Mr Bakshi had gone missing.

'What has that got to do with you?' his father had asked him. 'He disappeared so he disappeared. It is not like you have put him in your pocket while everyone is looking for him.'

I cursed him, thought Balli, not particularly keen to voice sentiment born of convoluted, emotionally charged reasoning. His father would not have understood. His logic traversed a fairly straight, unsentimental path.

When it came to his son, however, he did betray occasional

traces of that unsavoury stuff called emotion. For the well-being of Balli he had even commissioned twenty-one Akhand Paths, non-stop readings, cover to cover, of the Guru Granth Sahib at the local gurdwara. The bhai who had made the opening was a particulary pious man. He had covered his mouth with a handkerchief all through the performance of his priestly duties to ensure that he did not shower any spittle onto the holy book, though that did mean that his recitation of the verses was an indistinct murmur, especially for those who had chosen to make the effort of sitting there to listen to him. From there on, it was a line-up of Sikh priests who took the baton one by one and completed the relay reading in forty-two hours. One reading of the Granth Sahib took a well documented forty-eight hours. Perhaps someone had measured it with a trip meter at some point of time. But the priests engaged by Balli's father had obviously made short work of it.

In spite of having outsourced it all, the reading and venue, Balli's father had not even a fleeting moment of doubt that the blessings that might accrue thereof would get deposited into the account of the hanky-holding priest instead of working towards getting Balli married.

'Now Mr Bakshi is back,' he said, looking meaningfully at Balli, as they drove back from the homecoming. 'What a lot of smoke!' he remarked. And then, for good measure, resorted to an English idiom, which did not have very much to do with the course of events except in a purely physical sense. 'There can be no smoke without fire,' he said, looking pleased with the aptness of his expression. The tongues of firc in the havan kundli had nearly slurped at the ceiling. The folds of the turban that layered his forehead were drenched in sweat and he had had to suppress frequent bouts of coughing occasioned by the rising smoke that filled the room. It was an act of uncharacteristic politeness and delicacy on his part because, at most other times, he would have let loose without a qualm, giving everyone present the full benefit of infected air.

'Yes, he is back,' said Balli. 'But he does not seem to be quite his normal self. And Kailla is still missing.'

'Sisterfucker. You are now going to give me that as a reason for not getting married?'

Sensing a moment of weakness he quickly increased the pressure, resorting to a small measure of emotional blackmail to gain acquiescence.

'Your mother, if she were alive today—and who knows, she may even now be keeping an eye on things from up there—would be so happy to know that you are getting married.'

And, in fact, he was quite hoping that she was actually looking on since he was no longer visiting his mistress in Manali. The fizz in that one had evaporated. It was stealth that had aerated his extramarital relationship.

Balli buckled to the possibility of his mother's celestial blessings.

It was settled then. Balli would marry Girl Number Two. He would have to stop calling her that and try to get used to her name: Paramjot. Though maybe, he had unknowingly fathered a trend. Sowed a seed. Two years later, film directors in Bombay discovered the formula but with a difference. *Hero No. 1, Khiladi No. 1, Biwi No. 1, Jodi No. 1.* The films were a great success with audiences. And everything and everyone was numero uno. None of this substandard business of being second. But Balli was never encumbered by such aspirations. He had settled for Girl Number Two. And really, the trend was all that he would ever father.

They got married. It was a hurried affair since Balli's father wanted to rush through with it before the onset of second thoughts.

The alliance was doomed from the start. Fissures ran in all directions, including the realm of procreation, though they continued to live together in average matrimonial disharmony.

Paramjot was very keen to have a child. He was not. Paramjot was driven by the instinct to mother. He was wary of fatherhood. This became a growing argument. It quickly grew out of its infancy and was soon on its feet, becoming an ominous presence between them. Balli had managed to shake off the buzz in his head about birds and bees, overcoming his hesitation about matters sexual. But he found it difficult to explain to his wife why he did not want a child.

On his wedding night he came up with the idea of boiling his balls instead of insisting on contraception. As a schoolboy he had digested his textbooks well. The minimal science he had studied had taught him that sperm, born and bred in the testicles, need cool climes to survive. That is why testicles hang outside the heat of the body to provide them an abode. He filled a mug with hot water from the geyser and held his balls in it, hoping to zap to zilch those tiny emissaries of life, before he went to bed.

'Ahhhhhhhhhh,' he said. It was scalding. The wedding night was a success. All the sperm had been incinerated.

16

'But where is Kailla?' said Jassi, as she looked up from her game of solitaire.

Lately, she had taken to regarding the game as a sort of nemesis. Kailla had bought the pack for her on one of his jaunts in the market. His purchases were legendary. A bit surreal, a bit gratuitous, a bit outlandish, and a bit creative—and utterly useless most of the time. A torch that worked as a cigarette lighter though no one smoked, a pair of scissors with an inbuilt bottle opener though no one drank anything aerated, a key chain that said 'here I am' if you clapped loudly though the house was never locked. Everything he bought had to be able to do or display any two disparate things.

'Cards?' she asked him. 'What will I do with them? I am not a gambler.'

She was only voicing a well-entrenched prejudice. Good people did not play cards.

'Move this card, this way and now that way,' he said excitedly, showing her the three-dimensional image on its back. 'See, this baby becomes a full-grown man, depending upon which way you look at it.'

He was totally taken up with his find.

'Keep them,' he said. 'You might need them sometime.'

They were useful now. She would sit cross-legged on her bed in meditation mode, slide the cards out from under her pillow and pat them into position. The cards, laid out in front of her in neat rows in descending order, in alternating colours, kept her occupied and stopped her from thinking about things that she could not bear to think about. She would keep to the rules. No cheating. Not even with herself. But Kailla's disappearance was an unhappiness within, which needed a certain sleight of emotions. There she had to cheat. When she caught herself wondering about the whereabouts of Kailla and agonizing, she would play the cards in her head, moving imaginary sequences up and down. She could even line up people, varying in sex, age, habits—people offered many more colours than the limited four of a pack of cards—and she could shuffle them around. Her father, her mother, Kailla, Harpreet, all those who were a part of her life and all those others who had been in and out of it, and even those she knew of but had never seen. Each move threw up a brilliant explosion of memories and possibilities, of odd combinations and mismatches or reassurances. She placed her husband and that other woman in one of the sequences. If her husband had married that other woman he would have been at the gurdwara every evening, praying, because that is what she did. Or then, alternately, she might have taken to whisky because that is what he did every evening. Or then, they each might have carried on doing what they each did, and scoffed at the other. He was engaged to the other girl before he married Jassi. The engagement broke off and just as well it did, otherwise their home would have resonated with the clanging of swords. Jassi liked speculating gleefully on the sound of the clash. And though she had a name, Jassi still thought of her only as 'that other woman'.

I have saved my husband from the excesses of devotion—of that paradoxical elevation of spirit occasioned by rubbing ones nose in dust. 'The guilty bows double,' she thought, summoning lines from the Asa-di-var, a collection of hymns in the Guru Granth Sahib which added up to a code of conduct for daily life. It was meant to be read in the morning and that is just what she did, enjoying the ordinariness and yet profundity of thought.

This play of people as cards was an absorbing diversion.

'Kailla?' she asked, as Harpreet and Tejpal walked in after their daily round of police stations. If God above had brought back Bakshi, then he should also have conjured up Kailla, she thought. He, at least, should be able to do two things simultaneously, otherwise his being God did not count for very much. Any two divergent things. And Bakshi and Kailla were very different people. He should be able to bring them out of his hat or turban or whatever it was that he wore. Bakshi was back and she expected Kailla to walk in the door next.

⁂

In Tejpal's dreams, the ones in which he had to catch his breath, the old man being tossed up in the air was increasingly beginning to look like Kailla, and he knew that he had to find Kailla or he would be on a nightmare run for the rest of his life.

Harpreet watched Tejpal heaped in front of the television, his neck sinking into his chest, his chest sinking into his stomach, his stomach sinking into his crotch, neither asleep nor awake, neither prone nor upright, with the remote control for the television firmly in his hand. That she felt a heaving of emotion, of caring even for this strange contortionist, meant perhaps that they had a good marriage and had been married long enough to absorb quirks and smelly farts and incipient potbellies. She tried to gently wrest the remote from him. He immediately sprang back to life, into a predatory wakefulness. He was not going to part with it.

'What are you doing?' he said angrily, as though she had transgressed a sacrosanct boundary.

But as soon as he woke up, he was asleep again. His sleeping finger accidentally jabbed at buttons, and channels jumped in and out of the television like fleas on a dog. When surfing stopped momentarily with yet another involuntary jab, they were beaming—the miracle of Lord Ganesha statues drinking milk. They said that a man had woken up early morning that day, dreaming that Lord Ganesha was thirsty and wanted milk. He rushed to the temple to find that the lord was quaffing it down. They said that it was a sign, a very good sign. Hysterical devotees were lining up everywhere.

Ruling party politicians said that it was the far right drumming up yet another god, from Lord Ram to Lord Ganesha, for the Lok Sabha elections.

Opposition party politicians said that a ruling party loyalist had thought the whole thing up to try and divert attention from criminal charges levelled against him.

People in Toronto said that a poor country like India should be feeding the milk to its hungry millions instead of spooning it out to Lord Ganesha.

He was drinking milk at the Mangal Mandir in Montgomery County Maryland, in Southall, in Malyasia, in Thailand, in Nepal, in Bangladesh, in Italy where they were in any case used to Virgin Mary's statue weeping blood.

Officials from the Ministry of Science and Technology cleverly fed the god coloured milk and found that it coated the statue after being sucked up by capillary action. But no one was interested in scientific home truths just then. It was time for an overflow of imagination.

Drains ran milk.

Milk vendors only said 'Balle, balle', performing a joyous bhangra as they sold more and still more milk.

Harpreet looked away from the television but a chiaroscuro continued to dance in her peripheral vision. At the stroke of midnight Lord Ganesha stopped sipping milk, as one of the news anchors had delicately put it, and now the twenty-four-hour news channels were only repeating themselves, letting the same feed run on and on. Perhaps the man at the controls could finally doze, having put the news channel on autopilot.

Tejpal was also dozing. When awake he had wondered why they had not offered the god whisky instead. An ancient god and why, at his age, would he want to drink milk? A few pegs of whisky would have been more appropriate. It might have made for better public relations when they ultimately reported to the heavens above. With that philosophical thought, he had poured himself his daily round of unrestrained whisky and lulled himself into a semi-stupor.

Under the sink in the kitchen, empty bottles stood in a dense grid awaiting the raddi wala. 'Radiiiia, paper walaa, akhbaar, radiiiie,' he would call out in a strange guttural as he cycled past slowly. And still more slowly past their gate. He knew that there was a rapid accumulation of empties in this house and if he hovered around long enough and called out long enough, summoning a voice from the depths of his being, Harpreet would finally emerge. Somebody here sure drank with the appetite of a dehydrated sponge. However, he would not pass judgement. He would only put the whisky, beer and rum bottles in a man-sized gunny sack, their mouths, necks and torsos tossed around carelessly, their protuberances rubbing each other every which way, and carry them away in a cascade of tinkling sounds. He would pay her the appropriate amount for them.

Recycling comes so naturally to us, thought Harpreet, while the West kicks up such a storm about it but only manages to make mountains of discarded cans and cartons. The retreating back of the raddi wala made her philosophical, though she was really thinking about Tejpal and his constant date with the past, the ghosts that danced in his head, the recycling of memories.

Tejpal's head rolled leeward, buffeted by the storm in his mind, his eyelids curtained down, his arm losing its tautness, and he was asleep again.

She hoped that he would get up in time for their appointment with a police official in the ongoing search for Kailla. But she knew that she too would not sleep.

17

'He is a telephone.' That is what people said of the police official whom Harpreet and Tejpal met the next morning. 'There it sits, innocent, passively mute, until someone rings.'

It sounded suspiciously harmless but also ineffectual. That is not how a policeman was expected to be. He was supposed to be ruthless and remorseless and proactive, if not in matters of policing, then at least in matters of amassing wealth. But this one seemed to have been struck dumb, looking at them with large sorrowful eyes. Only later they learnt that he was the strong, silent type—that his silence was only a strategy to intimidate, to pre-empt any ambitious notions of proximity that chattiness might induce and to ensure that his visitors shifted uncomfortably in their chairs. He processed each word deep inside his stomach before he let it see the light of day.

'They say that in his childhood, he used to skin cats alive,' whispered a harried fellow supplicant waiting outside. 'A child prodigy, who knew just what he was going to be doing when he grew up.'

What nobody knew was that in his backyard he had a huge cage of a size which might house a lion. He had enough space for the extravagance of the cage. Government housing was generous to its chosen few. In that cage were hundreds of love birds in myriad colours. Blue and green and yellow, with white crests. Their chirping and flapping filled the atmosphere. He had brought back a pair once and they had multiplied into profusion. Whenever he came back from a bloody encounter with insurgents, the kind that involved cold-blooded killing, he would shut himself in the cage and sit quite still, letting the birds assume that he was only one of the many perches. When he emerged from there he was ready to proceed from where he had left off.

Harpreet and Tejpal had got the appointment through Balli's father's second cousin's daughter, who was married to the official's son.

'You see, it is part of the drill,' he said with an uplifted finger. 'A crime—and—just like that,' he snapped his fingers for a graphic representation of their speed, 'we pick up people—for questioning—those on our files and some others who have been seen loitering about. Nothing personal. You get my point?'

The measured cadences should have had some sinister music playing in the background. Both of them could see the words frosting over.

'Karnail Singh, you said his name was?'

'Yes. We call him Kailla though,' Harpreet said.

He did not think that women should be let loose on the world in this brazen manner. He would have been much more comfortable if Tejpal had come alone.

'You will forgive me,' he said, joining his hands in supplication, 'but you may call him what you like, that is really not my concern. I will check.' The exaggerated politeness only enhanced the sense of affront that he felt on being addressed by a woman.

He made a phone call. Spoke less. Heard more. He said in an ominous undertone with his lips virtually kissing the instrument, 'Karnail Singh. Find out about him.'

And then he went into listening mode. Not an achha, haan or yes or even a soundless hmm escaped his steely lips. The voice on the other side must have known him well enough to presume his continued presence at the end of the line. Tejpal and Harpreet fidgeted. They examined their hands, Harpreet spun her ring around on her finger, Tejpal opened and shut the clasp of his watch, both minutely studied the wall behind the official, hoped for a revelatory sign from the chief minister's portrait hanging on it. They tried to listen intelligently to the meaning of the enveloping silence and wore themselves down to taut yet quivering strings by the time he had finished.

With slow deliberateness, like someone running a forty-eight frames per second recording on twenty-four, his actions played themselves out. His manner invested the whole humdrum business of making a phone call, restoring the handset to its cradle and leaning back in a chair with such heavy import, that when he did finally turn around to them, the moment seemed potent with meaning. As though they were now going to understand eternity, plug into the timeless and feel the heartbeat of the universe.

'He is no longer in our custody. We released him the next day.'

'But where...' began Harpreet.

A finger went up, silencing them. Both of them immediately cowered into compliance.

'Policing these days is difficult business. On some occasions there is no time for niceties. When there are killings and kidnappings we have no time to make polite inquiries over a cup of tea and a pleasant conversation about the weather and then casually ask, "Where do you plan to drop the next bomb, or shoot the next set of innocents?", or then, as in this case, "Where have you hidden the gentleman you picked up from his house?" And mistakes are made which have to be understood as such. Don't quote me on this though. I am telling you all this only because you are…' his voice faded, trying to explain the connection, and ended lamely with, '… you come recommended by known quarters.'

It was uncharacteristic verbosity on his part, but then, as he had said, they had come with a sifarish and that is what had made him open his heart out, the contents of which would be regarded as limited fare in others, but in his case was a clearance sale.

When Tejpal and Harpreet left, they knew even less than when they had come. Kailla was no longer in jail and that closed an inquiry point.

'But where then is Kailla?' said Harpreet, completing her query of a while ago.

18

Kailla never really came back and if he did, he continued to elude everyone. There were many who claimed to have seen him but he had become a rumoured presence, like a whisper in the wind.

'You know my chachaji told me that Kailla was seen near the clock tower…'

Tejpal and Harpreet would jump to it. They would meet the said chachaji who would direct them to a friend he had met at a party, who would then show them to a neighbour's house, where the sighting would be ascribed to a visiting niece who would then be rung up, only to say that she had somehow got this impression when they were all talking about it and someone seemed to have mentioned something to that effect…

Kailla was seen watching a movie, *Beqabu Pyar*, in his favourite Society cinema in Chaura Bazaar. This Bhojpuri film about unrestrained love had so caught his attention that his jaw had dropped a few significant inches. The cleaning woman who came to Harpreet's house told her that her daughter-in-law had seen him.

'Was driving down and saw him, or someone who looked like him, disappearing round the corner, into that little lane that goes to the Masjid-do-manzili. But the traffic was so snarled just then, that I could not stop,' said Balli's father.

'Beeji, he was having himself photographed in that Rajhans Studio in Dhakka Colony,' said the woman who came to give Jassi her weekly oil massage. One of those no-good young men who loiter around street corners as a whole time occupation and do nothing else, had told her.

'Kailla? No, no. Not possible. Must have been someone else. Kailla never even looked at himself in the mirror, why would he want to have himself photographed?' said Jassi. She knew there was some mistake here.

However, she did recall that one spring-cleaning day, she had come upon Kailla critically examining himself in a photo frame. He had taken down a painting from the wall, about to dust it. The painting was of the legendary lovers Sohni and Mahiwal by Sobha Singh, which was a must-have in old houses that had not yet been done over by interior decorators. It had become powder at the base of the frame just as soon as he had unhooked it from its nail. Termites had been working on it and the print was only holding together in a temporary truce. The minute it was moved it had crumbled to dust. And Kailla had found himself looking at his own reflection.

Sweety did not see him again, though she wished she had. What if she had taken up the offer he had come with? And as she pirouetted on the stage, catching her audience in a whirl, she wondered if she could ever stand around holding a glass, looking half bored, half expectant, through a whole evening and half the night. She was too much of a bred-on-the-ground realist to be nurturing any fancies about a fairy-tale transformation in her life. But, no harm done in dreaming. What if Kailla had come to wave a magic wand?

But of course, she had no idea that he had disappeared and that it needed a whoosh of that same wand to bring him back in the first place.

Meiyang wondered if living between identities could make one invisible. He checked in the mirror every morning, pinched himself, as did his mirror image, to make sure that he was still around. He had obviously not become vapour as had Kailla.

It was November once more and the air was beginning to smell of roasted peanuts. The ground was strewn with peanut peels which crackled underfoot on sidewalks, and movie theatres and the atmosphere crackled with the sound of exploding fireworks in anticipation of Diwali.

It was time to take out woollens for yet another approaching winter. The bedding would have to be overturned to open the box bed, naphthalene balls dislodged from the folds of pullovers, the smell of dry-cleaning filling the air as coats were unbuttoned and hung up. And once again Harpreet remembered that she must call in the carpenter to fashion a stay for the lid of the box bed. It was a recurring thought, an annual thought, a November thought, which evaporated every summer. But come November she would ask Tejpal to hold the lid up while she doubled into the cavity to pull out the woollens. And he would complain yet again, about this ridiculous routine in which he was essentially called upon to simulate a car hood support. He would grumble the whole time and she would think about the carpenter while he grumbled. She would call the carpenter tomorrow morning, she would resolve. But by morning there were always many other things to claim her attention and she would forget. The box beds had been made in the November of 1985 to economize on space, because they were already beginning to accumulate the unnecessary baggage of a long stay and were finding it difficult to compact themselves into those two rooms.

Tejpal and Harpreet did not see Kailla even once. Maybe gullibility would help, thought Harpreet. Had Kailla turned into a pestle? But Justice Kailla had decreed that to be a punishment, and why would anyone want to punish Kailla? A butterfly then, one of the many who fluttered around in this season, one of the yellow ones like shooting stars in their green firmament, impossible to pin down with a watching eye? The thought was ridiculous. Even gullibility could not be stretched this far and poetry could not be a substitute for life.

Jassi put the last ace in place and waited.